Studies in Graduate &
Professional Student
Development

Defining the Field

Edited by Laura L.B. Border

NEW
FORUMS
Stillwater, Oklahoma
U.S.A.

NEW FORUMS PRESS INC.

Published in the United States of America
by New Forums Press, Inc.1018 S. Lewis St.
Stillwater, OK 74074
www.newforums.com

Copyright © 2008 by New Forums Press, Inc.

All rights reserved. No part of this publication may be reproduced or transmitted in any form or by any means, electronic or mechanical, including photocopy, or any information storage or retrieval system, without permission in writing from the publisher.

Library of Congress Cataloging-in-Publication Data Pending

This book may be ordered in bulk quantities at discount from New Forums Press, Inc., P.O. Box 876, Stillwater, OK 74076 [Federal I.D. No. 73 1123239]. Printed in the United States of America.

ISSN: 1068-6096   Volume 11, 2008, ISBN: 1-58107-144-2

Contents

Introduction .... *xi*

Section I–Overview: Defining the Field 1
Chapter 1–Graduate Student Professional Development:
    Defining the Field 2
    Laurie Bellows

**Section II–Research on College/University Courses
    & Certification Programs** 21
Chapter 2–An Exploration of the Landscape of Graduate Courses
    on College and University Teaching in Canada and the USA 22
    Dieter J. Schönwetter, Donna Ellis, K. Lynn Taylor, & Valery Koop
Chapter 3–Profiling an Approach to Evaluating the Impact of Two
    Certification in University Teaching Programs
    for Graduate Students 45
    K. Lynn Taylor, Dieter J. Schönwetter, Donna E. Ellis,
        & Martha Roberts

**Section III–Improving Graduate Assistants' Skills
    & Knowledge** 77
Chapter 4–Thinking Beyond the Department: Professional
    Development for Graduate Students of Color 78
    Cathy Schlund-Vials, Karen Cardozo, Mathew L. Ouellett,
        & Kirin Makker
Chapter 5–Beyond Language Skills: International Teaching
    Assistants' Experiences in US-Based ESL Programs 90
    Seonhee Cho
Chapter 6–International Teaching Assistants and Student
    Retention in the Sciences 109
    Mary C. Wright, Joel Purkiss, Christopher O'Neal,
        & Constance E. Cook
Chapter 7–Integrating Teaching & Technology: Facilitating
    Student-Centered Teaching for Graduate Students
    at a Research University 121
    Neeraja Aravamudan, Susanna Calkins, Mary Schuller,
        & Dreana Rubel

Chapter 8–Examining Kinesiology GTAs' Perceptions of a
 Videotape Instructional Analysis and Consultation Process 138
   Jared A. Russell

Section IV–Bridging the Transition to Beginning Faculty Positions 153

Chapter 9–The Background Experiences of Early-Career
 Science Faculty in Research, Teaching, and Service 154
   Kenneth S. Sagendorf

Studies in Graduate & Professional Student Development

Editor

Laura L. B. Border
Director, Graduate Teacher Program
201 ATLAS, 362 UCB
University of Colorado at Boulder
Boulder, CO 80309-0362
Laura.Border@colorado.edu

Associate Editor

Linda von Hoene
Director, GSI Teaching and Resource Center
301 Sproul Hall #5900
University of California, Berkeley
Berkeley, CA 94720-5900
vonhoene@berkeley.edu

Matthew L. Ouellett
Director, Center for Teaching
University of Massachusetts-Amherst

William Rando
Director, McDougal Graduate Teaching Center
Yale University

Dieter J. Schonwetter
Education Specialist, Faculty of Dentistry
The University of Manitoba

Franklin Tuitt
Assistant Professor, College of Education
University of Denver

Editorial Board 2006-2010

Elisabeth O'Conner Chandler
Director, Center for Teaching & Learning
University of Chicago

Alan Kalish
Director, Faculty and TA Development
The Ohio State University

Tom Lehker
Senior Assistant Director
Graduate Student Services
The Career Center
University of Michigan

Karron G. Lewis
Associate Director
Center for Teaching Effectiveness
The University of Texas at Austin

Heather Macdonald
Professor, Geology
College of William and Mary

Virginia Maurer
Associate Director
Derek Bok Center for Teaching
Harvard University
FAS Derek Bok Center

Review Board 2006-2010

Ann E. Austin
Professor, Higher, Adult and Lifelong Learning
Michigan State University

Folahan Ayorinde
Department of Chemistry
Howard University

PJ Bennett
Interim Assistant Director
Graduate Teacher Program
University of Colorado Boulder

Eileen Callahan
Director, Graduate School
University of Wisconsin-Madison

Henry Campa
Department of Fisheries and Wildlife
Michigan State University

Christopher G. Carlson-Dakes
Associate Director, Delta Learning Community
University of Wisconsin-Madison

Tuesday L. Cooper
Associate Dean, School of Education/Prof Studies
Eastern Connecticut State University

Sandra L. Courter
Adjunct Assistant Professor
Engineering Professional Development,
Wisconsin Center for Educational Research
University of Wisconsin-Madison

Daniel Denecke
Director, Best Practice
Council Graduate Schools
Office of Science & Technology

Maureen Dunne
Manager, Instructional Development Office
Memorial University of Newfoundland

Donna Ellis
Associate Director, TRACE
University of Waterloo

Chris M. Golde
Vice Provost for Graduate Education
Stanford University

Linda C. Hodges
Director, McGraw Center for Teaching and Learning
Princeton University

Trevor Holmes
Ed Associate, Teaching Support Services
University of Guelph

Jeff Johnston
Assistant Director, Center for Teaching
Vanderbilt University

Kevin M. Johnston
Director, TA Programs
Michigan State University

Michele Marincovich
Associate Vice Provost of Undergraduate Education,
Director, Center for Teaching and Learning
Stanford University

Jeanette McDonald
Manager, Educational Development
Teaching Support Services
Wilfrid Laurier University

Kathryn M. Plank
Associate Director
Faculty & TA Development
Ohio State University

Brian Rybarczyk
Director, Graduate Student Academic & Professional Development
University of North Carolina at Chapel Hill
The Graduate Student Center

Dieter J. Schonwetter
Faculty of Dentistry
The University of Manitoba

Kathleen Smith
Center for Teaching & Learning
University of Georgia

Rosalind Streichler
Director, Center for Teaching Development
University of California-San Diego

Lillian Tong
Faculty Associate, Center for Biology Education
University of Wisconsin-Madison

Mary C Wright
Coordinator, GSI Initiatives, CRLT
University of Michigan

Nanda Dimitrov
Coordinator, Teaching Assistant Programs
University of Western Ontario
Teaching Support Centre

A peer-reviewed book series on the research, issues, and programs that address the education and development of graduate and professional students.

Publisher: Douglas Dollar
Circulation: Jean McKinney

Studies in Graduate Teaching Assistant Development is published once per year by New Forums Press, Inc., P.O. Box 876, Stillwater, Oklahoma 74076, to highlight those aspects of graduate education and the development of graduate and professional students to prepare them for the multiple roles they play on their campuses and for the professional roles they will fill upon leaving graduate school. The full range of issues involved in the development, programming, research projects, and administration of such programs is address by the series.

SUBSCRIPTIONS: Beginning with volume 11, this publication's content will be broadened and the title will be changed to ***Studies in Graduate and Professional Student Development*** (see page 5 for details). Prices beginning with volume 11 are:
    List ....one year, U.S. $22.95
    .... two year, U.S. $40.95
    .... three year, U.S. $60.95
    Overseas and Canada ....add U.S. $9.00 to above
        rates for each year.
    Call for information about bulk subscription rates.
Please make payment with a check for U.S. funds drawn on a United States Bank in the Federal Reserve System, or with a U.S. Dollar World Money Order, or with a Postal Money Order imprinted in U.S. currency, or through your subscription agency. Send subscription requests to New Forums Press, Inc., P.O. Box 876, Stillwater, OK 74076 U.S.A.

SUBMISSIONS: See "Call for Papers," page *ix*.

ADVERTISING: Requests for classified and display advertising space rates and deadlines should be sent to the publisher.

COPYRIGHT © **2008** by New Forums Press, Inc. All Rights Reserved.

CALL FOR PAPERS
Studies in Graduate and Professional Student Development
Laura L. B. Border, Editor
Linda von Hoene, Associate Editor

Beginning with volume 11, *The Journal of Graduate Teaching Assistant Development* will feature a broader range in content, and the title has been changed to *Studies in Graduate and Professional Student Development*.

Studies in Graduate and Professional Student Development is a peer-reviewed book series designed to provide a platform for the discussion of the research, issues, and programs that address the professional development of graduate and professional students. Areas addressed include:

- Research on teaching, professional development, curricula, assessment and evaluation, training, certification, and career planning and outcomes
- Research on effective disciplinary and interdisciplinary programs and workshop designs, implementation and evaluation for teaching and learning
- Research on the transition from graduate school to full-time faculty positions
- Basic research on teaching and learning

The intended audience for this journal comprises:

- Disciplinary societies and their subcommittees on teaching and learning
- Personnel in the Office of the Graduate Dean
- Administrators, chairs, graduate faculty, and graduate directors
- Administrators, chairs, graduate faculty, and professional advisors in the professional schools
- Research faculty, research associates, and postdocs at research institutions
- Faculty who teach departmental, discipline-specific teaching methodology courses
- Faculty who serve as teaching assistant coordinators or supervisors
- TA development personnel at research institutions
- Preparing future faculty personnel at research institutions

(Continued on page viii.)

- Graduate student professional development personnel at research institutions
- Faculty development personnel at research, four-year, and two-year institutions
- Centers for Teaching and Learning
- Career development personnel who focus on nonacademic careers for master's and doctoral graduates
- Administrators and faculty at two-year and four-year institutions who hire candidates into faculty positions
- Graduate and professional students in all fields
- The Council of Graduate Schools
- The National Association of Graduate-Professional Students

To view authors' guidelines and subscription procedures, please visit the New Forums Press website at http://www.newforums.com/

If you would like to submit your name to become a reviewer, please contact: Laura L. B. Border, Editor, at laura.border@colorado.edu

Introduction

Defining the Field of Graduate and Professional Student Development

The field of graduate and professional student development has grown gradually over the last 25 years and is currently being recognized as an important aspect of the graduate school experience. Milestones along the pathway include the First National Conference on the Training and Employment of Graduate Teaching Assistants, held at the Ohio State University in 1986, which was followed by four other national conferences (Seattle, 1989; Austin, 1991; Chicago, 1993; Denver, 1995; Minneapolis, 1997). Participation of graduate school personnel, faculty and TA developers, and educational researchers in these Pew Charitable Trusts-funded conferences led to the development of programs in most major research institutions to improve in-service support for graduate student instructors. This in-service focus was soon expanded to include a "future faculty" perspective, reflecting concerns that two and four-year institutions had about the preparation of "research graduate students" to teach on their heavily undergraduate-focused campuses. The American Association of Colleges & Universities and the Council of Graduate Schools embraced this concern and through the support of the Pew Charitable Trusts, the National Science Foundation, and the Atlantic Philanthropies funded a series of "Preparing Future Faculty" grants that prompted the development of professional development activities to prepare graduate students not only for grading, office hours, and recitation duties during their graduate studies, but for the full-fledged role of faculty on campuses around the nation (Gaff & Pruitt-Logan, 2000). In the US and in Canada, parallel development efforts and interests have launched the beginnings of a solid research base on graduate and professional student development. The reconfiguration and renaming of this journal reflects the growth of the field which now includes in-service activities to prepare graduate students to teach on their campuses, course development around graduate student professional development issues, disciplinary and interdisciplinary concerns, preparing future faculty for their roles, expanding the job horizons of graduating master's level students and doctoral students beyond the academy, and mounting interest in creating a solid research foundation on which to base graduate and professional student development on university campuses.

The mission of the *Studies in Graduate and Professional Student Development* series is to serve as a peer-reviewed journal designed to provide a platform for the discussion of the research, issues, and programs that address the professional development of graduate and professional students.

The call for manuscripts for the initial issue focused on defining the field, thus this issue reflects the themes and concerns prevalent in the articles submitted as well as the interests of the Editorial Board in defining the field.

Section I: Defining the Field

Because the field of teaching assistant development has grown and expanded well beyond the original confines of graduate student preparation for their immediate responsibilities of teaching laboratory and discussion sections, this reformulation of the *Studies in Graduate and Professional Student Development* series presents a unique opportunity. The *Studies in Graduate and Professional Student Development* series was so named because at most research intensive institutions, the advanced student population falls either into the category of "graduate student," for example in colleges of arts and sciences, or into the category "professional student," for example, in schools of business or law. The name of the series reflects this diversity. Laurie Bellows' article which follows uses the term "graduate student professional development," however, her use of the term is not meant to exclude graduate students in the professional schools who are preparing for careers as future academics. Rather Bellow's emphasis is on the need for departments, programs, and universities to prepare graduate students more broadly and for more diverse environments.

In Chapter 1: "Graduate Student Professional Development: Defining the Field," Laurie Bellows presents a thoughtful analysis of how the traditional "socialization" model of graduate education has expanded to include a focus on nonacademic careers and progressed over the last several decades through explicit and intentional activities to improve support for graduate students. Bellows emphasizes that graduate student professional development supplements discipline-specific training through "value-added" experiences that go beyond the traditional TA training program offered by departments for first-year teaching assistants to focus on helping graduate students develop a professional/career identity either within or beyond academe. Dr. Bellows calls attention to the reality that "graduate student professional development" has indeed become "a distinct field of practice." Areas of interest are academic development, instructional development, career development, and leadership development: all providing a rich field for collaboration within and across institutions and fertile ground for evidence-based research to take hold and flourish.

Section II: Research on College/University Courses & Certification Programs

On many large research campuses across the United States and in Canada, the education and preparation of graduate students for academic careers has come to include either a departmental methodology course on teaching in the discipline or, in some cases, a series of centralized courses offered by the graduate school. As courses have proliferated, some due to the impact of the Preparing Future Faculty Program, they have incorporated varying kinds of content, different foci, and variations in depth and breadth. In Chapter 2: "An Exploration of the Landscape of Graduate Courses on College and University Teaching in Canada and the USA," Dieter J. Schönwetter, Lynn Taylor, Donna Ellis, and Valery Koop compare 155 Canadian and American college and university teaching courses taught during 2002-04 using qualitative and quantitative data. Their review of the literature supports a definition of such courses as informative, theoretical, if rarely evidence-based, while their research identifies four types of courses: teaching centered, generic, intentional, and focused on issues in higher education. Based on a website analysis of courses, the authors identified 57 variables which they then reduced to seven clusters of criteria: location, enrollment procedures and eligibility requirements, course scheduling demographics, sponsors, course credit, general course information, and specific course information. Their research expands the current literature on college/university courses and suggests that a diversity of teaching and learning features now characterizes such courses, for example, shadowing faculty to learn about their roles, creating resource portfolios, and using current readings on teaching and learning in place of textbooks. The authors encourage further research and analysis of such courses to provide administrators and faculty with reasonable criteria to create, refine, and evaluate the effectiveness of courses on university and college teaching.

On a growing number of campuses, the development of teaching methodology courses has paralleled the development of certificates in university teaching. Requirements for university teaching certificates vary, as do the rationales for the certificates. There are enough in place at different institutions to warrant study and comparative research projects. In Chapter 3: "An Approach to Evaluating the Impact of Two Certification in University Teaching Programs," K. Lynn Taylor, Martha Roberts, Donna E. Ellis, and Dieter J. Schönwetter discuss their research on two university teaching certificates in Canada. Certificate programs for university teaching began in the late 1980s— the first were at the University of Colorado at Boulder (1989), the University of California at UC Davis, and Syracuse University (1991) (Border, 1993), but existing literature on the topic was limited to descriptive articles or to "satisfaction" surveys and did not address the effectiveness of the programs over time. The Canadian research team was able to address the need for rigorous research on the topic by grounding their research methodology on approaches identified in existing research literature regarding curricular components for graduate student development, research on early career faculty, and a conceptual framework based on control theory. The authors were able to demonstrate the value of a theory-embedded evaluation approach and identified three teaching related factors: the candidates' preparedness to teach, the importance of teaching issues and perceived control, and the provision of a framework for organizing and interpreting evaluation results.

Section III: Improving Graduate Assistants' Skills and Knowledge

As teaching centers, graduate schools, schools and colleges, and departments have moved to better prepare their graduate students to teach in the 21st century, various programs and scholars have attempted to catalogue the skills and knowledge necessary to a well prepared graduate. Some programs are based on local needs assessment instruments, others are derivative of various models. While much more research needs to be done on this particular topic, a comparison of most programs is likely to reveal that many attempt to address the topics of diversity, international teaching assistants, technology, consultation on teaching, and disciplinary aspects of teaching in some manner. A brief review of such topics reflects the impact that cultural, demographic, technological, practical, and disciplinary issues have on program development.

In Chapter 4: "Thinking Beyond the Department: Professional Development for Graduate Students of Color," Cathy Schlund Vials, Mathew Ouellett, Karen Cardozo, and Kirin Makker discuss a program at the University of Massachusetts, Amherst designed to integrate minority students more rapidly into the culture of academe. While many graduate students are confused by the unspoken norms of graduate departments and graduate programs, the authors' work highlights the disproportionate difficulties experienced by graduate students of color. They emphasize that campuses need to offer supplementary support to students to help graduate students of color succeed in challenging environments and that the value of such centralized support may be based on its ability to distinguish the particular from the general, thus helping students to better understand the forces at work in academe. They describe a center-sponsored learning community for graduate students of color from different disciplines that produced a mentoring program pairing graduate students of color with faculty. The cross-disciplinary nature of the programs allowed participants to reframe perceptions based on individual experiences and better understand their personal experiences within the framework of the institution as a whole.

In Chapter 5: "Beyond Language Skills: A Perspective of International Teaching Assistants in US-Based ESL Academic Disciplines," Seonhee Cho, studied a small group of internationals and identified areas of concern. While many programs for international graduate student instructors focus on the improvement of their oral English skills or on the acquisition of the culture of the American classroom, Cho's study emphasizes the fact that many international instructors are simply inexperienced teachers in the classroom. While their language skills may compound the issue, international instructors may need more assistance in adapting to, negotiating, and strategizing appropriate instructional strategies in the classroom.

In Chapter 6: "International Teaching Assistants and Student Retention in the Sciences," Mary C. Wright, Joel Purkiss, Christopher O'Neal, and Constance E. Cook from the University of Michigan address concerns about potential effects on undergraduate students in courses taught by international teaching assistants in the STEM disciplines. The authors contrasted student satisfaction data with student retention statistics in order to better define the challenges faced in classrooms taught by international graduate students and to suggest potential program modifications for existing international teaching assistant programs. Their project showed that undergraduates might perceive that international instructors have a greater impact on student learning than they actually do. Their results also point to the need to improve teaching assistant training for both domestic and international teaching assistants, as both groups need improved communication skills.

In Chapter 7: "Integrating Teaching and Technology: Facilitating Student-Centered Teaching for Graduate Students at a Research University," Neerja Aravamudan, Susan Calkins, Mary Schuller, and Dreana Rubel's research addresses what they call the "critical nexus" between teaching, learning, and technology. Their work reflects an expanding interest in the need to prepare current graduate student instructors and future faculty for a classroom environment that is technology dependent yet focused on student learning. Their study shows that graduate students feel poorly prepared to teach in general and that the addition of technologies with which they are unfamiliar is particularly challenging. Participant feedback from an earlier iteration of their project led them to focus on participants' awareness of tools with a clear sense of when to use a variety of technologies to achieve certain course goals in a learner-centered environment. Their conclusions focus on the implications of faculty attitudes toward teaching and technology and the need to further examine how to prepare future faculty to understand and initiate the effective use of technology to enhance teaching and learning in college and university classrooms.

In Chapter 8: "Examining Kinesiology GTAs' Perceptions of a Videotape Instructional Analysis Process," Jared A. Russell addresses the lack of research on and the paucity of instructional development for graduate teaching assistants in typical kinesiology graduate programs. Because videotape instructional analysis has been identified as a productive intervention in preparing beginning instructors to teach, Russell studied a videotape instructional analysis and consultation process based on planning, implementation, and reflection. His data show that graduate instructors reported increased confidence, preparedness and motivation, and experienced a sense of appreciation and professionalism because of their videotape consultation experience: results that inform graduate students' future career aspirations as faculty in their field.

Section IV: Bridging the Transition to Beginning Faculty Positions

Robert Boice has attempted to chart the needs and talents of beginning faculty members (Boice, 2000). His research demonstrates the need to connect the preparation of future faculty more directly to the roles of beginning faculty in different types of postsecondary institutions. As programming for and research on graduate preparation for future academics develops, we should be better able to tailor graduate programs to assure smoother transitions in faculty roles. An examination of graduate programs and new faculty work is likely to reveal major lacunae, though the number may be decreasing given the growth of preparing future faculty programs.

In Chapter 9: "The Background Experiences of Early-Career Science Faculty in Research, Teaching and Service," Ken Sagendorf's research based on early career science faculty shows that recent developments in graduate education may have had an effect on the preparation of graduate students to teach. However, the common experience shared by this group included only teaching lectures and laboratory classes indicating a continued need to broaden teaching preparation at the graduate program level. His data suggest a need to continue the development and refinement of preparing future faculty-type programs.

The articles selected for this volume provide a starting point for defining the field of graduate and professional student development. Future volumes will move this project forward by focusing on specific disciplines and expanding upon and probing topics addressed in earlier volumes. Because much of the programming for graduate student professional development is relatively recent, research on these programs and their impact on graduate and professional student development is only now beginning to emerge. It is our hope that this journal will encourage additional research in this growing field and provide a forum for making that research available to a wider audience.

Laura L. B. Border, Editor

References

Boice, R. (2000). *Advice for new faculty members: Nihil Nimus*, Needham Heights, MA: Allyn & Bacon.

Border, L. L. B. (1993). The graduate teacher certification program: Description and assessment after two years, In K. G. Lewis (Ed.), *The TA experience: Preparing for multiple roles: Selected readings from the 3rd National Conference on the Training and Employ-*

ment of Graduate Teaching Assistants, November 6–7, 1991, Austin, Texas. Stillwater, OK: New Forums Press.

Gaff, J. G., Pruitt-Logan, A. S., & Weibl, R. A. (2000). *Building the faculty we need: Colleges and universities working together.* Washington, DC: Association of American Colleges and Universities and Council of Graduate Schools.

In Memory of

Donald H. Wulff

Editorial Board 2006-2008

Section I
Overview: Defining the Field

Copyright © 2008, New Forums Press, Inc., P.O. Box 876, Stillwater, OK 74076. All Rights Reserved.

Chapter 1
Graduate Student Professional Development: Defining the Field

Laurie Bellows
University of Nebraska-Lincoln

This article defines graduate student professional development as a field. It includes a brief overview of the field's origins, presents a framework for conceptualizing the profession, and describes the knowledge, skills, and attitudes necessary for practitioners in the field. Implications and future directions are discussed.

Graduate student development has been characterized as an enculturation process or apprenticeship experience through which the student is socialized into the discipline or into a professional career, such as the professoriate, that requires advanced knowledge and skills (Austin, 2002a; Boyle & Boice, 1998; Weidman, Twale & Stein, 2001). In this model, graduate faculty members are the primary socializing agents responsible for assimilating graduate students into the discipline, while the department serves as the vehicle through which graduate students are socialized.

Recent research on the graduate student experience suggests that graduate student socialization is not as organized or systematic as it should be (Austin, 2002a). That is, graduate students learn about faculty work through "careful observation . . . how faculty members spend their time, what they say about engaging in research and working with students, how they comment casually on tasks they must do, and how they organize their time" (Austin, 2002b, p. 129). Graduate students are expected to attach themselves to research mentors with the assumption that what they need to learn about the profession can be gained through interacting with their mentors and observing how things work. Unfortunately, this model results in uneven exposure to critical topics that might not be explicitly addressed through the mentoring experience or in the graduate curriculum; such topics include—but are not limited to—the responsible conduct of research, grant writing, advising/mentoring undergraduate students, interviewing, teamwork, and curriculum vitae preparation (Fischer & Zigmond, 1998). As a result, graduate students are not only under-prepared for faculty work but are similarly ill prepared for positions outside academia (Austin, 2002a; Nyquist, Manning, et al., 1999; Smith, Pedersen-Gallegos, & Riegle-Crumb, 2002).

In contrast to the traditional socialization model, graduate student professional development is a more explicit and intentional approach comprising both informal and formal activities designed to enhance the graduate student experience. Assessments of graduate students' needs confirm what the national reports recommend: Graduate students recognize that professional development opportunities are required to better prepare them for a variety of career options (Bellows & Weissinger, 2005; Coulter, Goin, & Gerard, 2004; Poock, 2001). Graduate students want opportunities to develop their teaching skills, to participate in interdisciplinary study, to be exposed to a wider array of career opportunities, and to obtain more effective career guidance (Austin, 2002a; Nerad & Cerny, 1999). Further, the fact that only about half of doctoral degree recipients will find work as tenure-track faculty members in a college or university, while the other half will seek non-academic careers, has prompted this qualitatively different approach to preparing graduate students for their future roles and responsibilities (Austin & Wulff, 2004; Gaff, 2002; Golde & Dore, 2001; LaPidus, 1998; O'Meara, Kaufman & Kuntz, 2003).

Graduate student professional development provides *value-added* experiences that supplement discipline-specific training. The field covers a variety of activities, such as conducting orientations to help graduate students connect to their campus, department, faculty, and to one another; sponsoring workshops and colloquia on research, teaching, and service; fostering positive faculty-student mentoring relationships; offering postsecondary teaching and professional development certificates; and providing both academic and non-academic job search skills. Graduate student professional development therefore involves more than training for first-year teaching assistants, career counseling, or job placement services. Instead, it includes a wide range of programs that focus primarily on helping graduate students develop a professional identity (Darwin, 2000). In this respect, the field of graduate student professional development is distinctly different from the field of graduate student services, whose mission is to provide essential non-academic services to graduate students including housing, wellness and counseling, child care, and financial aid.

During the 2004 Professional and Organizational Development (POD) Network's annual conference in Montreal, the TA Development Committee was renamed the Graduate Student Professional Development Committee to reflect the expanding view of graduate student professional development. In the process of renaming the committee and refining its focus, members of the original TA Development Committee cited national reports on graduate education calling for a more accurate and comprehensive definition of graduate student professional development, prompting those of us in graduate education to rethink our roles in preparing graduate students for future careers. The committee's mission is now more comprehensive, including academic and non-academic career development in addition to the instructional development issues related to international and domestic teaching assistants. A major task of this Committee is to assume a national leadership role in contributing to and further defining the field of graduate student professional development.

Recognizing the importance of these recent developments, this article examines graduate student professional development as a distinct field of practice and provides an overview of its expanding roles and responsibilities. The following discussion pertains to graduate students pursuing research doctoral degrees that prepare them for careers in academe, business, industry, or government service, although portions arguably may apply as well to students enrolled in professional master's programs at some institutions. After briefly presenting graduate student professional development in its historical context, this article provides an expanded framework for conceptualizing graduate student professional development and summarizes the knowledge, skills, and attitudes considered necessary for practitioners in the field. Finally, conclusions, implications, and future directions are discussed.

Our Professional Heritage: Origins of Graduate Student Professional Development

If graduate student development has a "professional heritage" (Chickering & Reisser, 1993), it emerged from the early teaching assistant training and preparation programs of the late '70s and early '80s (Lewis, 1997). TA training programs initially focused on how to teach a particular discipline and included pre-service orientations offered by specific academic departments. Centralized, campus-wide TA programs followed and offered year-round support services, including instructional consultations, credit-based seminars on teaching and learning, and certification programs. From designing orientations, to supplementing departmental training programs, to developing resources and services, departmental and centralized TA development programs prepared graduate students primarily for their classroom teaching responsibilities (Lewis, 1997; Mintz, 1998; Ronkowski, 1998).

As TA development programs emerged on campuses across the country, there began a corresponding national conversation surrounding efforts to prepare graduate students to teach (Chism, 1998). The first national conference on teaching assistants was convened in 1986 at The Ohio State University; other similar conferences throughout the United States followed. While these early conferences focused chiefly on the selection and assignment of graduate teaching assistants, subsequent national conferences addressed the preparation of TAs (Chism, 1998). A broader notion of professional development emerged during the 1995 TA conference in Colorado when the first reports of the Preparing Future Faculty (PFF) Program initiative were shared with conference participants.

Established in 1993 as a partnership between the Council of Graduate Schools and the Association of American Colleges and Universities (AAC&U),

PFF introduces doctoral students to the full scope of faculty roles and responsibilities in the areas of teaching, research, and service. Through professional development seminars and structured mentoring experiences with faculty at partner institutions, PFF participants observe and experience faculty responsibilities at a variety of academic institutions with varying missions, diverse student bodies, and differing expectations for faculty. The PFF initiative emerged primarily in response to national recognition that doctoral education was largely incomplete and traditional teaching assistant programs far too narrow in their approach to graduate student training. At the same time, several national reports emphasized the need for graduate preparation to extend beyond teaching and research to include preparation for jobs outside academia (COSEPUP, 1995; Golde & Dore, 2001; Nerad, Aanerud, & Cerny, 2004; Nyquist & Woodford, 2000). In response, Preparing Future Professionals programs were launched on several campuses to help doctoral students explore and plan career paths outside the academy.

Perhaps the most significant shift in the field of graduate student professional development, however, has been efforts by the National Science Foundation (NSF), National Institutes of Health (NIH), the Department of Education (DOE), and other national funding agencies to include professional development components in training grant proposals. For example, the Integrative Graduate Education and Research Traineeship (IGERT) is a NSF program that provides interdisciplinary training for graduate students who wish to pursue careers in the sciences, mathematics, engineering or technology. Every IGERT program must include a professional development component to help students develop the technical, professional and personal skills required for the varied career demands of the future. Requests for Proposals—especially those in the sciences—now call for the inclusion of leadership and teambuilding skills to help students develop collaborative team skills necessary to establishing and maintaining an integrated research program. A recent RFP requires "documentation of specific activities related to professional development activities," indicating how such activities contribute to the development of "independent professionals" (Office of Research Integrity, 2006). Highlighted professional development activities include attending lectures on the responsible conduct of research, completing a course on plagiarism, and supervised teaching experiences.

Elements of Graduate Student Professional Development Programs

Over the past ten years, graduate education has expanded and become even more complex. Similarly, graduate student professional development programs have evolved and become more varied. Table 1 illustrates the many elements that form graduate student professional development programs at selected institutions.

As noted previously, *TA instructional development* provides support for teaching and may include one-on-one consultative services and teaching-related workshops, seminars, or methodology courses to help TAs develop instructional skills. With increased attention being paid to the scholarship of teaching and learning, many TA instructional programs have structured their development efforts to include a teaching-as-research model. The DELTA Program at the University of Wisconsin in Madison, Wisconsin, incorporates the use of research methods to develop reflective teaching practices. The research approach to teaching and learning also is central to the instructional development program at the University of Washington and the University of Colorado at Boulder's Teaching Institute for Graduate Education Research (TIGER).

Preparing Future Faculty (PFF) programs encourage advanced doctoral students to examine the multiple roles faculty play on various campuses through seminars and mentoring internship experiences at partner institutions. *Teaching certificate programs*, like Michigan State's Certification in College

Table 1. Graduate Student Professional Development Program Elements for Selected Institutions

Institution	TA Development Services	Preparing Future Faculty Program	Teaching Certificate Program	Teaching Documentation Program	Additional Professional Development Programs for Graduate Students
Arizona State Univ.		•			•
Duke University		•			•
Florida State Univ.	•	•			
Marquette University		•	•		
Miami University		•		•	
Michigan State Univ.	•		•		•
Northwestern Univ.		•	•		•
Ohio State University	•	•			
Purdue University	•	•	•		•
Univ. of Texas-Austin	•	•			•
Univ. of Washington	•	•			
Northwestern Univ.	•	•			•
Syracuse University	•	•			•
Univ. of California-Berkeley	•	•			•
Univ. of Colorado-Boulder	•	•	•		•
University of Illinois at Urbana-Champaign	•		•		•
Univ. of Massachusetts-Amherst	•			•	
Univ. of Missouri-Columbia	•	•	•		•
Univ. of Nebraska-Lincoln	•	•		•	•
Univ. of North Carolina Chapel Hill	•	•			•
Univ. of Wisconsin-Madison			•		•
Univ. of New Hampshire		•	•		
University of Washington	•	•			•
Vanderbilt University	•	•	•		•

Teaching or the Graduate Teacher Certificate at the University of Colorado at Boulder, go beyond traditional TA training by providing a more systematic approach to preparing graduate students for an academic career while simultaneously creating a formalized structure for documenting their teaching experiences. Depending on the institution, certificate programs may include graduate coursework, a series of workshops or seminars related to teaching, a supervised teaching experience, videotape consultation, and the development of a comprehensive teaching portfolio (Border, 1993; Border, 2002). Similarly, *teaching documentation programs* that rely on student feedback, goal setting, individualized consultation, and self-evaluation offer additional opportunities for graduate students to trace teaching development and record accomplishments.

Several institutions such as Purdue University, Syracuse University, the University of Nebraska-Lincoln, the University of North Carolina-Chapel Hill, the University of Texas at Austin and the University of Wisconsin-Madison have centralized graduate student professional development offices—housed in the respective graduate colleges—that provide a full range of professional development opportunities for graduate students preparing for positions as future faculty in academia or for leadership or research positions in business, industry, or government service. Alternatively, graduate student development programs, such as the Graduate Teacher Program at the University of Colorado at Boulder, may be offered in partnership with teaching and learning centers, academic departments, the graduate school, or sometimes with career services staff whose strength lies in dealing with graduate students seeking jobs outside of academe in business, government or industry.

The primary goal of graduate student professional development is to help departments and disciplinary societies prepare and train future professionals. To better understand and conceptualize graduate student professional development as a field, it is useful to think developmentally about the skills and abilities needed to make the transition from graduate student to professor or from graduate student to employee (Nyquist & Sprague, 1998).

Conceptualizing Graduate Student Professional Development

The literature regarding graduate students and new faculty highlights the skills needed to be successful in academia (Adams, 2002; Austin, 2002b; Fischer & Zigmond, 1998). New faculty must be able to (a) conduct discipline-specific research and connect their work across disciplines; (b) understand the teaching and learning processes; (c) use technology in their teaching; (d) engage in public service and link their work to issues beyond campus; (e) communicate with a range of audiences; (f) work collaboratively with diverse groups; (g) understand their roles as institutional and global citizens; and (h) appreciate the essential purposes and core values of higher education. Departments, schools, and colleges may benefit from reviewing and discussing potential content, formats, resources, and outcomes of programs and activities that would best serve their graduate students.

A corresponding set of skills is needed in industry. Those who hold the doctorate must have a solid understanding of their field and also be prepared to work on interdisciplinary teams; they must be able to communicate with a diverse group of colleagues and constituencies, resolve conflicts, have well-developed analytical thought processes, and be able to manage projects (LaPidus, 1998; Smith, Pedersen-Gallegos, & Riegle-Crumb, 2002). Through discussions and interviews with doctoral students and those who prepare, fund, and hire individuals who hold the doctorate, Nyquist (2002) identified "core competencies" of successful doctoral graduates, which include the skills listed above, as well as an understanding of ethical responsibilities as professionals and the development of a global perspective. Similarly, Border's *Inventories on Graduate Student Development* (2006) is useful as a guide to developing programs, resources, and services to meet graduate students' professional development needs.

Graduate student development may be described in terms of progress toward degree completion (Baird, 1995; Girves & Wemmerus, 1988; Nettles & Millett, 2006; Nerad & Cerny, 1991; Stewart, 1995) or changes in skill sets or competencies. For example, Nyquist and Sprague (1998) note that graduate teaching assistants and graduate research assistants experience developmental changes in competence, from senior learners to colleagues-in-training, until they finally achieve status as junior colleagues (Nyquist & Sprague, 1998). From a developmental perspective, then, there are specific milestones or achievements that a graduate student must master if he or she is to progress through graduate studies, including choosing an advisor; developing a plan of study; mastering the subject matter; understanding disciplinary norms and departmental structures; and developing advanced professional skills in such areas as mentoring undergraduate students and acquiring grant-writing skills (Baird, 1995; Fischer & Zigmond, 1998; Golde, 1998).

Table 2 presents a framework for conceptualizing graduate student professional development. The model is organized around three developmental stages—early, middle, and advanced—that reflect the experiences of graduate students as they move in, move through, and move out of graduate school. This model is similar to those suggested by Baird (1995) and Stewart (1995) and collapses the various levels identified by Nerad and Cerny (1991), Girves and Wemmerus (1988) and Nettles and Millet (2006), recognizing that different milestones may exist depending on fields or disciplines. Additionally, the model is directed more specifically to doctoral students, although the developmental stages and corresponding tasks also may be relevant to master's students.

Table 2. Framework for Conceptualizing Graduate Student Professional Development

Stage	Graduate Student Developmental Tasks	Professional Development Categories				
		Academic Development	Instructional Development	Career Development	Leadership Development	Engagement
Early						
Goal: Learn what it takes to be successful in graduate school	•Become acclimated
•Understand program/ university requirements
•Find a group of peers
•Find a faculty mentor
•Understand the language and structure of the discipline/field
•Identify fellowship opportunities	•Provide mentoring handbooks for students and mentors
•Provide guide to graduate student's professional development
•Mentoring workshop for grad students and grad faculty
•Offer a campus-wide or department orientation
•Establish peer mentor program
•Electronic newsletter for all grad students
•Begin research ethics training	•Campus-wide workshops for teaching assistants
•Offer individual teaching consultations
•Provide a TA Instructional Guide
•Departmental courses in college teaching	•Explore academic & non-academic career options
•Co-sponsor department colloquia & seminars
•Schedule workshops on alternative careers
•Web site of career resources	•Provide students list of campus organization or department graduate student organization
•Provide list of co-curricular opportunities to build leadership skills
•Offer a leadership course for graduate students	•Help students connect to broader community
•Sponsor monthly interdisciplinary colloquiums where students can share/discuss research

| Stage | Graduate Student Developmental Tasks | Professional Development Categories ||||||
		Academic Development	Instructional Development	Career Development	Leadership Development	Engagement
Middle						
Goal: Develop and demonstrate competence	•Identify intellectual and professional interests •Prepare for comprehensive exams •Explore career options •Develop professional competencies (teaching and research) •Document teaching •Write dissertation proposal	•Provide opportunities for interdisciplinary research •Offer workshops in: making conference presentations; writing for publication; developing poster sessions •Provide fellowship information and/or assistance •Connect graduate students to undergraduate research opportunities •Sponsor thesis/ dissertation support groups	•Offer teaching portfolio workshops •Help students document teaching	•Offer professional development seminar •Provide job search preparation and support •Sponsor internships	•Organize a leadership retreat •Create opportunities to assume leadership of new graduate students (peer mentoring program)	•Offer credit course on the scholarship of engagement •Connect problem-based research projects to community
Advanced						
Goal: Prepare for transition to academic or non-academic professional role	•Prepare for and complete thesis or dissertation •Prepare for the job market	•Offer grant writing workshops •Support dissertation/ thesis writing groups •Provide post-doc scholars handbook and/or resources	•Develop and promote teaching as research (Scholarship of Teaching and Learning)	•Preparing Future Faculty and/or Professionals •Mock interviews •Practice job talks with feedback	•Organize a LeaderShape Conference with undergraduates	•Organize community-based internships

In this model, each stage relates to specific developmental tasks that must be negotiated during the graduate experience. In the early stage, students must learn what it takes to succeed in graduate school; in the middle stage, they focus on developing and demonstrating competence; in the third and final stage, they prepare for transition to their professional roles. Developmental tasks are then linked to five general categories: academic, instructional, career, leadership, and engagement. These categories are not all-inclusive but do reflect those general skills needed for graduate students to be "quick starters" (Boice, 1992). For each professional development domain, interventions or programs that can be offered to help graduate students prepare for their future are listed.

Briefly, *academic development* refers to those skills that graduate students need to be successful as new professionals. Preparation for academic and professional writing, ethics and professional responsibility, and developing effective oral communication skills help graduate students make a successful transition into a new position as assistant professor. The transition from graduate student to professor will also be smoother if graduate students have some experience publishing, presenting at professional conferences, and writing and applying for grants.

Instructional development emphasizes general as well as content-specific pedagogical training designed to develop reflective teaching practices. Instructional development programs include campus-wide orientations or programs on teaching, workshops highlighting specific teaching issues, individual consultation services for teaching assistants, methodology courses in the students' home departments, and the use of teaching portfolios.

The *career development* component encourages masters and doctoral students to explore various academic and nonacademic career paths for which their degrees prepare them. The Preparing Future Faculty Program, supported by the Council of Graduate Schools and the AAC&U, and its related programs at many institutions, emphasizes preparing graduate students for job interviews at and careers in two-year and four-year postsecondary institutions as well as in research extensive and intensive environments. The Graduate College Career Services Office at the University of Illinois, Champaign-Urbana, serves as a centralized resource for all graduate students to provide advising, workshops, web resources, and referrals to help students with career choices and with their independent job search. The Graduate Teacher Program at the University of Colorado at Boulder offers, in collaboration with their career services office, a Professional Development Certificate for Business, Government and Industry.

Leadership development centers on developing graduate students as future academic leaders in their departments, schools and colleges, national associations, and disciplines. Leadership skills address managing change and working with others on projects. The Graduate Student Leadership Development Program at the University of Wisconsin-Madison promotes the leadership development of graduate students through a variety of opportunities such as leadership retreats, leadership groups, and the LeaderShape Institute. The Lead Graduate Teacher Network at the University of Colorado at Boulder prepares advanced graduate students to identify departmental issues, improve undergraduate teaching through graduate student development, generate solutions, and leave a legacy of change in their departments. This program is identified as a "best practice" by the Woodrow Wilson Foundation and received the Theodore M. Hesburgh Award for Exceptional Faculty Development Programs in 2006.

Engagement refers to community-based research and service learning; however, it goes beyond the traditional notions of outreach and service, emphasizing instead, collaboration with the community. The University of Texas at Austin's Professional Development and Community Engagement program provides graduate courses, workshops, and internships, as well as structured opportunities for students to bring their expertise to bear on important community issues. Additionally, a course in *Academic and Professional Consulting* is designed to "show students the ways in which their expertise and experience are valuable in a number of realms, both academic and non-academic" (University of Texas at Austin Graduate School, http://www.utexas.edu/ogs/pdce/grs/descriptions.html). Through their participation in community engagement projects, students learn to articulate their expertise and develop a portfolio of consulting skills.

In summary, this developmental model provides an excellent guideline for both students and graduate student development practitioners, but is not so linear that it doesn't allow for flexibility dictated by a student's particular needs. For example, a student may easily move through the early stage of academic development, but may require more time to master tasks in other areas, such as instructional or leadership development.

Thinking developmentally about the field supplies a necessary *philosophical* foundation – echoing the more general field of student development that emphasizes the development of the whole student – suggests a field of *research* that has yet to be fully tapped, and guides the *practice* of developing meaningful programs to facilitate graduate students' learning and development (Rodgers, 1990). For practitioners, a developmental structure provides a common knowledge base and implies a mission that ultimately connects process to practice. Thinking developmentally about graduate students' professional development needs and the developmental processes of graduate education can help educational developers guide the design of programs, services, and resources. Additionally, a developmental structure like the framework proposed here provides students a "cognitive map" to help them learn how to move through their graduate career with success (Lovitts, 2004). Thinking developmentally about the field of graduate student professional development helps faculty, educational developers, and, most important, graduate students make sense of their experience.

Graduate Student Professional Development as a Field: Required Knowledge, Skills, and Attitudes of a Practitioner

In their synthesis of recent research on graduate education and the challenges and concerns related to graduate student preparation, Wulff and Austin (2004) offer five general recommendations for supporting graduate student professional development:

- Help students get started in graduate school in ways that promote success.
- Help students connect with the people and cultures of their department.
- Prepare students for a broader conception of the faculty role, including systematic preparation for teaching, research, and service/engagement.
- Help students understand the academic labor market and employment options outside of academe, and prepare students for the job-search process.
- Help departments/students incorporate good mentoring practices.

While these five recommendations are well founded, they neglect an important aspect of academic life: Faculty work within a department, the department works within an institution, and the institution works within a culture. Graduate student development programs housed in Graduate Schools—and staffed by doctoral-level experts— can provide appropriate structural support needed to serve graduate student's professional development needs.

Although the backgrounds of those who practice in the field are likely to be as broad and diverse as the programs and services provided, there are specific attributes necessary for successful performance. The following section briefly describes core competencies needed to practice in the field. It is not intended to be a comprehensive inventory of the required abilities but rather an overview of the knowledge, skills, and attitudes considered necessary for practitioners in the field.

Knowledge

Knowledge relates to the information, models, and theories needed to practice effectively in a given discipline or field; that is, a practical grounding in the research, teaching, service, and scholarship of teaching and learning of the discipline. In the field of graduate student professional development specifically, practitioners must be doctoral level experts in an academic discipline, but their preparation must also include six critical areas: (a) the complex and integrated nature of graduate education and the institutions and communities it serves; (b) relevant theories and models related to adult student development and learning; (c) postsecondary pedagogical methods; (d) the scholarship of teaching and learning; (e) the graduate mission of the university and its educational processes; and (f) the job market.

Because the underlying structure of the field is essentially developmental, knowledge of learning, teaching, and adult student development theories (i.e., cognitive, academic, social, career, leadership) is central to effective practice. A general knowledge of theories and models underlying the structure of the field should serve as the basis for the programs and accompanying resources designed to enhance graduate students' professional development. Knowledge of relevant theories also can help the profession build its research base, thus contributing to both the theory and the practice of graduate student professional development. Knowledge of the graduate mission of the university, educational processes, and, to some degree, the job market can help practitioners shape campus policies and practices that will lead to a more connected and intentional educational experience for graduate students.

Knowledge alone, however, is not sufficient for practicing in the field of graduate student development. Effective practitioners also must develop the skills needed to apply their knowledge and expertise.

Skills

In such a multidisciplinary field, perhaps the most important skill needed by practitioners is the ability to collaborate and make connections with other programs on campus. Each of us has an area of expertise that we have developed, but the ability to rely on others—either on campus or at other institutions—to help design and develop graduate student development initiatives is paramount. To accomplish the task, academic departments, graduate schools, programs for teaching assistant development and preparing future faculty, centers for teaching and learning and, in the case of careers in business, government and industry, career services staff with doctorates who specialize in graduate education resources, must engage in a "dramatically improved alliance" (The Woodrow Wilson National Fellowship Foundation, 2005).

Research skills are needed to gather and interpret information about graduate students and the impact of the programs and services provided. And as the field of graduate student professional development continues to mature, we will see a corresponding increase in the need for knowledge related to the developmental pathways of graduate students.

Graduate student professional developers also must practice excellent organizational, planning, evaluation, and communication skills. Being able to communicate the value of the field to others is equally critical. Administrators as well as faculty members may not clearly understand the field of graduate student professional development, especially if their own experiences as graduate students were based on the traditional apprenticeship model. Fortunately, five national conferences on graduate education, as well as initiatives like the Council of Graduate School's Preparing Future Faculty Program, the Woodrow Wilson Foundation's Responsive PhD Project, the Re-envisioning the PhD project, and the Carnegie Initiative on the Doctorate, have highlighted an agenda for change. Still, practitioners will need to be spirited advocates for the development and support of programs and services on their individual campuses if these changes are to be realized.

A broad base of knowledge combined with the appropriate skill set is key to the successful practice of graduate student professional development. The third, and possibly most essential, element for effective practice is the practitioner's mind-set or approach to the field and to the students and faculty members being served.

Attitudes

Practitioners in the field of graduate student professional development should have supportive, service-oriented, and collaborative attitudes aimed at enhancing and supplementing the programs and services offered by departmental units. However, personal communication with other professionals who work in the field makes it clearly evident that their collective mind-set goes beyond support and service. Practitioners in the field of graduate student professional development share a deep and abiding passion for the work they do. While many may have initially entered the field because they saw a gap that needed to be filled in graduate students' disciplinary training, they now view graduate student professional development as a mission—an *intentional* obligation—that includes an ethical responsibility to help graduate students better prepare for their future professional roles and responsibilities. Thus, it is a philosophical conviction shaped by experience that guides their practice.

Conclusions, Implications, and Future Directions

Graduate student professional development comprises the informal and formal activities designed to support and enhance graduate students' skills, knowledge, and ability to practice as professionals. As a field, it is broad-based, multidisciplinary in many respects, marked both by its various components and by the people who practice in the field. It shares interests with those who practice in career development, discipline-based pedagogy, student development, and the scholarship of teaching, discovery, learning, and engagement. At its center is the development of graduate students as future professionals and the desire to help them develop their own vision of how to "assume the stage as engaged public intellectuals with their research and teaching" (Applegate, 2002, p. 5).

Graduate student professional development can play an important role in facilitating the retention of graduate students. Research indicates that approximately 50% of doctoral students fail to obtain a doctoral degree (Lovitts, 2004). However, attrition is less a function of what students bring with them to graduate school than of what happens to them after they enroll (Lovitts, 2004; Lovitts & Nelson, 2000). Students who develop networks, bond with their departments, and understand expectations associated with graduate education are more likely to become integrated into the system, persist, and be successful (Lovitts, 2004). Graduate student professional development programs enhance the quality of graduate student life, and, as a result, contribute significantly to the graduate mission of their institutions.

As an emerging field, graduate student professional development harbors rich potential for research. Despite the common notion that student development is complete once an undergraduate degree is obtained, we know from experience that there is much to learn about how students develop intellectually, socially, and professionally during their graduate careers. In comparison to undergraduate education and undergraduate student life, graduate student development is under-researched. To develop the field, we need to continue identifying graduate students' needs, assess the impact of our programs, provide evidence, and share our work through a scholarship of research and practice.

The field also must expand its network for collaboration, recognizing that there is a blend of skilled professionals—in graduate offices, teaching assistant development and preparing future faculty programs, departments, teaching and learning centers, career services and student affairs—who serve the academic and professional needs of graduate students. Coordinating resources and information with professional and disciplinary organizations as well as with those stakeholders who fund and hire graduate students can help strengthen the field by widening support systems, generating advocates, and, possibly, establishing appropriate funding.

This article is an initial step to define the field of graduate student development as an area of specialized practice, grounded in the research on student learning, teaching, and adult development, and carried out by practitioners with specialized knowledge, skills, and attitudes. Like any worthy endeavor, the definition of graduate student professional development will benefit greatly from ongoing dialogue. The conversation has begun, but it certainly does not end here. Who we are—and what we do—as graduate student professional developers depends on our individual and collective efforts to refine the definition of the field and its importance to graduate education.

References

Adams, K. A. (2002). *What colleges and universities want in new faculty* (Preparing Future Faculty Occasional Paper, Number 7). Washington, DC: Council of Graduate Schools.

Applegate, J. L. (2002). *Engaged graduate education: Seeing with new eyes* (Preparing Future Faculty Occasional Paper, (pp. 1-20). Washington, DC: Council of Graduate Schools.

Austin, A. E. (2002a). Preparing the next generation of faculty: Graduate school as socialization to the academic career. *The Journal of Higher Education, 73*(1), 94-122.

Austin, A. E. (2002b). Creating a bridge to the future: Preparing new faculty to face changing expectations in a shifting context. *The Review of Higher Education, 26*(2), 119-144.

Austin, A. E. & Wulff, D. H. (2004). The challenge to prepare the next generation of faculty. In D. H. Wulff & A. E. Austin (Eds.), *Paths to the professoriate: Strategies for enriching the preparation of future faculty* (pp. 3-16). San Francisco: Jossey-Bass.

Baird, L. (1995). Helping graduate students: A graduate adviser's view. In A. S. Pruitt-Logan & P. D. Isaac (Eds.), *New directions for student services: No. 72. Student services for the changing graduate student population* (pp. 25-32). San Francisco: Jossey-Bass.

Bellows, L. & Weissinger, E. (2005). Assessing the academic and professional development needs of graduate students. In S. Chadwick-Blossey & D. Reimondo Robertson (Eds.), *To improve the academy: Vol. 23. Resources for faculty, instructional, and organizational development* (pp. 267-283). Bolton, MA: Anker.

Boice, B. (1992). *The new faculty member.* San Francisco: Jossey-Bass.

Border, L. L. B. (1993) The Graduate teacher certification program: Description and assessment after two years. In K. G. Lewis (Ed.) *The TA experience: Preparing for multiple roles* (pp. 113-121). Stillwater, OK: New Forums Press.

Border, L. L. B. (2002). The Socratic portfolio: A guide for future faculty. *PSOnline, XXV*(4), 739-742.

Border, L. L. B. (2006). Two inventories for best practice in graduate student development, *Journal on Excellence in College Teaching, 17*(1, 2), 277-310.

Boyle, P. & Boice, B. (1998). Best practices for enculturation: Collegiality, mentoring and structure. In M. S. Anderson (Ed.), *New directions for higher education: No. 26. The experience of being in graduate school: An exploration* (pp. 87-94). San Francisco: Jossey-Bass.

Chickering, A.W. & Reisser, L. (1993). *Education and identity* (2nd ed.). San Francisco: Jossey-Bass.

Chism, N. (1998). Evaluating TA programs. In M. Marincovich, J. Prostko, & F. Stout (Eds.), *The professional development of graduate teaching assistants* (pp. 249-262). Bolton, MA: Anker.

Committee on Science, Engineering, and Public Policy (COSEPUP) of the National Academy of Sciences, The National Academy of Engineering, and the Institute of Medicine. (1995). *Reshaping the graduate education of scientists and engineers.* Washington, DC: National Academy Press.

Coulter, F.W., Goin, R.P., & Gerard, J.M. (2004). Assessing the needs of graduate students: The role of graduate student organizations. *Educational Research Quarterly, 28*(1), 15-26.

Darwin, T. J. (2000, November 12). *Professional development as intellectual opportunity.* Paper presented at the National Communication Association Conference in Seattle, WA. Retrieved November 5, 2003, from http://www.utexas.edu/ogs/rc/td.html

Fischer, B. & Zigmond, M. (1998). Survival skills for graduate school and beyond. In M. S. Anderson (Ed.), *New directions for higher education: Vol. 26. The experience of being in graduate school: An exploration* (pp. 29-41). San Francisco: Jossey-Bass.

Gaff, J. G. (2002). Preparing future faculty and doctoral education. *Change, 34*(6), 63-66.

Girves, J. E. & Wemmerus, V. (1988). Developing models of graduate student degree progress. *Journal of Higher Education, 59*(2), 163-189.

Golde, C.M. & Dore, T.M. (2001). *At cross purposes: What the experiences of today's doctoral students reveal about doctoral education.* Retrieved March 15, 2008, from http://www.phd-survey.org/

Golde, C. (1998). Beginning graduate school: Explaining first-year doctoral attrition. In M. S. Anderson (Ed.), *New Directions for higher education: Vol. 101. The experience of being in graduate school: An exploration* (pp. 55-64). San Francisco: Jossey-Bass.

LaPidus, J. B. (1998). If we want things to stay as they are, then things will have to change. In Anderson, M. S. (Ed.), *New Directions for higher education: Vol. 101. The experience of being in graduate school: An exploration* (pp. 95-102). San Francisco: Jossey-Bass.

Lewis, K. G. (1997). Training focused on postgraduate teaching assistants: the North American model. *The National Teaching and Learning Forum, 7*(1). Retrieved March 15, 2008, from http://www.ntlf.com/html/pi/9712/toc.htm

Lovitts, B. (2004). Research on the structure and process of graduate education: retaining students. In D. H. Wulff & A. E. Austin (Eds.), *Paths to the professoriate: Strategies for enriching the preparation of future faculty* (pp. 115-136). San Francisco: Jossey-Bass.

Lovitts, B. E. & Nelson, C. (2000). The hidden crisis in graduate education: Attrition from PhD programs. *Academe, 86*(6), 44-50.

Mintz, J. (1998). The role of centralized programs in preparing graduate students to teach. In M. Marincovich, J. Prostko, & F. Stout (Eds.), *The professional development of graduate teaching assistants (*pp. 19-40). Bolton, MA: Anker.

National Association of Graduate-Professional Students. (2001). *The 2000 national doctoral program survey.* Retrieved March 15, 2008, from http://survey.nagps.org/

Nettles, M. T. &. Millet, C. M. (2006). *Three magic letters: Getting to the PhD.* Baltimore, MD: The John Hopkins University Press.

Nerad, M., Aanerud, R., & Cerny, J. (2004). So you want to become a professor: Lessons from PhDs—ten years later study. In D. H. Wulff & A. E. Austin (Eds.), *Paths to the professoriate: Strategies for enriching the preparation of future faculty* (pp. 137-158). San Francisco, CA: Jossey-Bass.

Nerad, M. & Cerny, J. (1991, May). From facts to action: Expanding the educational role of the graduate division. *CGS Communicator,* 1-12.

Nerad, M. & Cerny, J. (1999). From rumors to facts: Career outcomes of English PhDs. Results from the PhD's—ten-years later study. *CGS Communicator, 32*(7), 1-12.

Nyquist, J. (2002, November/December). The PhD: A tapestry of change for the 21st century. *Change,* 12-20.

Nyquist, J. N., Manning, L., Wulff, D.H., Austin, A.E., Sprague, J., Fraser, P.K., Calcagno, C., & Woodford, B. (1999, May/June). On the road to becoming a professor: The graduate student experience. *Change,* 18-27.

Nyquist, J.D. & Sprague, J. (1998). Thinking developmentally about TAs. In J.P.M. Marincovich, & F. Stout (Eds.), *The professional development of graduate teaching assistants* (pp. 61-87). Bolton, MA: Anker.

Nyquist, J. D. & Woodford, B. J. (2000). *Re-envisioning the PhD: What concerns do we have?* Retrieved March 20, 2008, from Center for Instructional Development and Research and University of Washington Web site: http://www.grad.washington.edu/envision/project_resources/concerns.html

Department of Health & Human Services. (2006, December). NSF Geoscienced directorate urges mentoring for postdocs and grad students. *Office of Research Integrity Newsletter, 15*(1), 5. Retrieved January 5, 2008, from http://ori.hhs.gov/documents/newsletters/vol15_no1.pdf

O'Meara, K., Kaufman, R.R. & Kuntz, A.M. (2003). Faculty work in challenging times: Trends, consequences and implications. *Liberal Education, 89*(4), 17-23.

Poock, M. C. (2001). A model for integrating professional development in graduate education. *College Student Journal*, 35, 345–352.

The Woodrow Wilson National Fellowship Foundation. (2005, September). *The responsive PhD: Innovations in U.S. doctoral education.* Retrieved April 10, 2006 from http://www.woodrow.org/newsroom/otherpublications.php

Rodgers, R. F. (1990). Recent theories and research underlying student development. In D.G. Creamer (Ed.). *College student development: Theory and practice for the 1990s* (pp. 27-80). Alexandria, VA: American College Personnel Association.

Ronkowski, S.A. (1998). The disciplinary/departmental context of TA training. In M. Marincovich, J. Prostko, & F. Stout (Eds.). *The professional development of graduate teaching assistants (*pp. 41-60). Bolton, MA: Anker.

Smith, S. J., Pedersen-Gallegos, L., & Riegle-Crumb, C. (2002). The training, careers, and work of PhD physical scientists: Not simply academic. [Electronic version]. *American Journal of Physics, 70*(11), 1081-1092.

Stewart, D. (1995). Developmental considerations in counseling graduating students. *Guidance and Counseling, 10*(3), 21-23.

Weidman, J., Twale, D. J. & Stein, E.L. (2001). *The socialization of graduate & professional students in higher education.* San Francisco: Jossey-Bass.

Wulff, D. H. & Austin, A. E. (2004). *Paths to the professoriate: Strategies for enriching the preparation of future faculty.* San Francisco: Jossey-Bass.

Dr. Laurie Bellows is Professor of Practice and Director of Graduate Student Development in the Office of Graduate Studies at the University of Nebraska-Lincoln. In her work supporting graduate students at the University of Nebraska-Lincoln, she co-directs the Preparing Future Faculty program, administers the Institute for International Teaching Assistants, organizes the campus-wide TA orientation, conducts professional development workshops, and consults with departments and individual graduate students on professional development issues. Dr. Bellows earned her PhD in Psychological and Cultural Studies at the University of Nebraska in 1994. She has served on the executive board for the Professional and Organizational Development (POD) Network in Higher Education and is a current member of the Graduate Student Professional Development subcommittee.

Section II
Research on College/University Courses & Certification Programs

Copyright © 2008, New Forums Press, Inc., P.O. Box 876, Stillwater, OK 74076. All Rights Reserved.

Chapter 2

An Exploration of the Landscape of Graduate Courses on College and University Teaching in Canada and the USA

Dieter J. Schönwetter
The University of Manitoba

Donna Ellis
University of Waterloo

K. Lynn Taylor
Dalhousie University

Valery Koop
The University of Manitoba

Graduate courses on college/university teaching have existed since the early 1970's. However, the extent to which these courses share similar goals, objectives, assignments, resources, and teaching and learning strategies is largely unknown. Moreover, are the patterns represented by the components of these courses likely to meet the goal of preparing our future faculty as outlined by theories and models of teaching this type of course? To support the critical assessment of such courses, this paper presents the results of qualitative and quantitative data of 155 Canadian and US graduate courses designed to prepare graduate students for teaching in higher education and taught during 2002-2004. This study reveals trends in current course objectives, course content, recommended texts, expected assignments, promoted bibliographies, and teaching and learning strategies. A synthesis of these findings, in conjunction with current literature on preparing graduate students for future careers, guides a discussion on how these courses can be developed, improved, and refined.

Professional development programs for graduate students as teach-ing academics are developing rapidly across academe (Gaff, 2002; Marincovich *et al.*, 1998). North American universities are beginning to recognize that the paradigm of graduate education adopted by many universities is so strongly research oriented that it fails to prepare graduate students for contemporary faculty roles (Adams, 2002; Austin, 2002; Rice, 1996; Wulff & Austin, 2004), especially in teaching. Many graduate students aspire to careers as faculty in institutions of higher education but receive little formal training for the task of teaching. Historically, graduate programs produced effective teachers by "happenstance rather than design" (Boyer, 1990). More recently, the obligation of graduate schools is to provide an environment where teaching is valued and graduate students are well prepared to teach successfully in their new roles as faculty (Adams, 2002; Austin, 2002; Wulff & Austin, 2004). In response, a number of institutions of higher education have taken this challenge seriously and have developed programs to prepare future research scholars to teach (Burk, 2001), integrating these two dimensions of academic careers.

One of the most significant elements of many of these programs is a course on college or university teaching. Despite their widespread use, there is a paucity of research on common course elements and the extent to which these teaching and learning courses subscribe to similar course objectives, course content, recommended texts, expected assignments, promoted bibliographies, and teaching and learning strategies. Moreover, do the common course elements align with current principles and theories on preparing our future faculty? The present study focuses on current trends by examining 155 courses on college/university teaching taught during 2002-2004 in Canada and the USA. The findings are valuable for the novice instructor planning to teach such a course for the first time, for the veteran looking for new ideas to incorporate into an existing course, and for the experts attempting to capture the current landscape of courses against the backdrop of their theoretical frameworks of the teaching of courses on college and university teaching.

Literature Review on College/University Teaching Courses

Literature that supports the importance of pedagogy courses on postsecondary teaching can be defined as informative, theoretical, and in rare cases, as evidence-based. Informative, literature comprises historical background information and identifies types of courses. Theoretically, the literature highlights the importance of these courses and provides explanations as to what is most desired in such courses, often based on the national and collaborative efforts of leading experts. Evidence-based literature can be best classified as focusing directly on the study of actual courses. However, such studies are limited in number. Most of the literature tends to focus indirectly on thematic analyses of graduate teaching assistant (GTA) training programs.

Articles with an historical focus discuss the importance, the beginnings, and the types of both courses and programs offered to the future professoriate (Boyer, 1990; Chism, 1998; Richlin, 1995). Numerous articles identify themes viewed as significant in the training of the future professoriate (Lewis, 1992), relying on national and international discussions at conferences such as POD or AAHE (Chism, 1998), and on the dissemination of information through journals such as *The Journal of Graduate Teaching Assistant Development*.[1] Courses on teaching at the college or university level are just one of many facets of effective programming for the preparation of future faculty, identified in studies on graduate teaching assistant programs (Parrett, 1987) or evident as trends in conference themes on graduate teaching assistant issues (Ronkowski, 1995).

The literature includes articles with a visionary focus on futuristic programs geared at preparing our future college and university teachers (Chism, 1998; Cox & Richlin, 1993; Smith & Waller, 1997). Initiatives such as Boyer's Scholarship Reconsidered (Boyer, 1990) and the Carnegie Commission, as well as national programs such as the Carnegie Foundation, formerly part of the American Association for Higher Education's "Scholarship of Teaching," provide the direction for further development of the future professoriate. Given the broad efforts to prepare the future professoriate, the literature provides ample information on what important elements in providing such courses are, how to set them up, and even descriptions of how these courses work.

However, with the exception of a small number of studies this literature lacks empirical comparisons of the various courses offered to prepare the future professoriate to teach. In one such study, Marincovich (1998) provides a useful overview of the types of courses available. As seen in Table 1, four types of courses exist. Each type can be influential in helping graduate students prepare for their roles as teachers.

The first type, as represented by the first row in Table 1, provides graduate students with information to enhance immediate teaching roles in a given department. The generic course, as represented by row two in Table 1, provides some content on general teaching in the discipline and focuses on preparing graduate students for long-term teaching in a given discipline. The intentional course, as represented by row three in Table 1, on preparing a university citizen provides more general teaching information, usually across the disciplines, and is a more common type of course currently offered by teaching and learning centers. The fourth type, as represented by the fourth row in Table 1, is one that explores specific issues in higher education and might provide graduate students with skills in curriculum development and assessment, ethics surrounding teaching and learning, and so on. Although it is important to classify the types of courses that exist, of further significance would be a study that focuses on current trends that can be observed in these types of courses, specifically those that represent Marincovich's third type of course – the intentional course on teaching.

Guidelines for developing and implementing such courses have been provided in leading publications such as Lewis's (1992) *TA Handbook* and Marincovich's (1998) essay as well as in other articles (Diamond & Wilbur,

---

[1] The *Journal of Teaching Assistant Development* has been replaced by the *Studies in Graduate and Professional Student Development* book series.

Table 1. Types of Courses on Teaching (adapted from Marincovich, 1998)

Type	Offered by	Purpose	Taught by	Focus
Course on teaching	An academic department	Prepare graduate students to TA or teach a particular course	Content specialist	TAs' immediate teaching roles
Generic course on teaching	An academic department	Exposing graduate students to instruction in the discipline	Content specialists, tenured faculty, guest speakers, etc.	Teaching role in the discipline and as university citizens
Intentional course on university citizen preparation	School of Education, a graduate division, or a teaching and learning center	Prepare graduate students as university citizens	Educational specialist, member of a teaching and learning center or faculty member	Faculty roles in higher education
Higher education	Postsecondary program on teaching and learning at a more high-level approach	Cover a broad range of aspects of higher education including teaching and learning	Taught by experts in higher education	Contribute to graduate students' knowledge of important facets of higher education

1990; Vattano & Avens, 1987; Wright, 1987). Such articles tend to specify the various criteria deemed significant in developing and implementing pedagogy courses for future academics on college/university teaching, including course goals, objectives, course content, assignments, potential textbooks, and the "instructional thrust" of the course (Marincovich, 1998). These criteria have been instrumental in guiding the development of courses on college teaching. However, the extent to which such courses actually subscribe to these criteria remains somewhat of a mystery.

Paulsen's case study is an exception, focusing on the criteria used in a course taught over a period of twelve years (Paulsen, 2001). Paulsen reflects on the various distinct features of the course that have proved to make it very effective. These include the interaction of theory and practice, a solid grounding in learning theory and research, an environment that allows students to take risks while feeling safe, and the teaching-learning clinic (Paulsen, 2001). Although insightful in providing instructors guidance on how to teach a course on college/university teaching, the case study provides a view of only one course.

Another study provides a survey of courses on teaching and explores the various course criteria used. In the early 1990's, Piccinin and Picard (1994) conducted a survey of all known courses on teaching and learning at the college/university level in Canadian universities ($N = 6$). Variables included target population, sponsorship, course format, instructor, stated objectives, topics, and assessment and grading. All of these courses were available to graduate students; however, the class sizes were limited due to restricted resources. Half of these courses were sponsored directly by the faculties (schools or colleges) of graduate studies. Although representing a small sample size, the findings are foundational in comparing a number of different courses on college/university teaching and provide information on the important variables to include in such a study.

Other research that indirectly provides helpful information on conducting a study on courses on college/university teaching includes the content analyses of training manuals for graduate teaching assistants that demonstrate an emphasis on both intellectual and interpersonal material (Lowman & Mathie, 1993). A second study provides a taxonomy derived from a systematic program content analysis of TA training programs which includes research and theory, skill building, professional attitude and philosophy of teaching and learning in higher education, and general orientation activities (Bort & Buerkel-Rothfuss, 1991). Each of these studies provides guidance in the current study.

Present Study

The training of GTAs has been categorized as either intensive or protracted (Hiiemae *et al.*, 1991). Intensive training involves pre- or early-semester teaching assistant training workshops, usually offered over a short period of time. Protracted refers to more long-term training that usually occurs over a full semester. In our study, we were mainly interested in the protracted training of graduate teaching assistants that occurs in a credit course on college/university teaching. Thus in order to be included in our study, the course had to be viewed as protracted. As an exploratory study, many courses were expected to demonstrate similar course objectives, course content, recommended texts, assignments, bibliographies, and course delivery modes. However, what is common among these courses is just as much of interest as that which is unique. Common elements may demonstrate a trend in following a certain school of thought when it comes to teaching a course on college/university teaching whereas courses utilizing elements that differ from the status quo may represent new ways of teaching the course. Also critical is the extent to which common trends in college/university teaching courses parallel what is recommended by experts as critical and significant for the training of our future college and university teachers. Perhaps a comprehensive review of 155 course outlines on college/university teaching could reveal valuable information for the teacher planning to teach a course on postsecondary teaching for the first time and also for the veteran who has taught this type of course numerous times. Of significance to the study is mounting evidence that course trends are either ascribing or not ascribing to the theoretical frameworks emerging in the teaching of courses on college and university teaching.

Method

Lists of higher education institutions were consulted and data collected from 873 North American universities, of which 98 were Canadian institutions. Three websites were explored: www.mit.edu:8001/people/cdemello/ca.html (Canadian Colleges and Universities), www.tss.uoguelph.ca/stlhe/links.html (Instructional Development Sites in Canada), and www.sic.hr/eng/canada.htm (List of Canadian Universities by Province). For the 775 institutions in the USA, the following websites provided important links: www.clas.ufl.edu/CLAS/american-universities.html (American Colleges and Universities listed alphabetically), and for doctoral institutions www.carnegiefoundation.org/Classification/CIHE2000/PartIfiles/partI.htm. A search was conducted for each institution providing graduate programming. The search began with the institution's homepage and followed links—usually through the graduate studies program, education or higher education departments or degrees offered (i.e., Ed.D. or PhD). A dead search resulted in a new but general search of the institution's homepage with keyword descriptors (i.e., "college teaching", "university teaching", "higher education teaching", or "center teaching"). Once an institutional website identifying a course on college/university teaching for graduate students was located, specific information was recorded. In cases where information was not available, a contact person was identified (i.e., course instructor, graduate assistant, administrative assistant, or a director for the center for teaching), and an email requesting information on the course was sent. In some cases where institutions listed no courses on college/university teaching for graduate students but had a center for teaching, an email was sent to the director inquiring about the existence of such a course.

In order to be included, each course had to be offered between September 2002 and August 2004. The rationale for including two years is that some courses are offered only every second year. To fit the criteria for the present study, the course had to provide graduate students with theoretical and/or practical training in college or university teaching.

The first stage of data collection involved selecting courses that met these requirements and entering them in a database for analysis. At this point, course descriptions were sorted by institution and carefully screened to ensure that duplications were removed. Once entered, the data were analyzed for content, identifying variables characterizing information in the course descriptions. These variables, in turn, were clustered to create larger categories that framed the data analysis. Because some requirements logically fell under multiple categories, a low level of inference was maintained in entering data. For instance, course resources could include text(s), readings, references/bibliography, and other tools and/or resources. Only explicit references to each of these components were recognized in the data analysis.

Results and Discussion

Data collected from September 2002 through August 2004 included 155-course outlines. Based on the content analysis, a total of 57 variables were identified in the various course descriptions, each of which was further categorized into one of seven clusters. Each of these seven clusters is identified and a specific criterion for each is provided in brackets. These include: *location* (i.e., institution, city, province or state and country), *enrollment procedures and eligibility requirements* (i.e., application processes and/or instructor's permission, student population), *course scheduling demographics* (i.e., year of course inception, year of course offering, number of hours/meeting, number of weeks, time of day, and semester or term), *sponsors* (i.e., number of partners, supporting center(s), department, faculty or school of graduate studies, name and type of program), *course credit* (i.e., number of credit hours and assessment outcome), *general course information* (i.e., name of course, related course(s)), and *specific course information*. Specific course information was further delineated by the *stated rationale/purpose, goals, course objectives, method of teaching, resources* (i.e., text(s), readings, references or bibliography and other tools and/or resources), *content area*, and *course requirements/assignments*. Below, details for each cluster and accompanying variables of interest are explained in more detail.

Location

Of the 155 course outlines analyzed, 21 were from Canadian institutions and 134 from institutions in the USA. For the Canadian sample, only doctoral universities offered these types of courses, and the present sample identified 21 (21.43%) of the 98 Canadian higher education institutions offering graduate training as having such courses. This is an encouraging finding, and a substantial increase (350%) since. Piccinin and Picard (1994) found only six such courses in Canadian institutions. For the US sample, three institutions represented colleges or technical schools offering such courses. The remaining 131 courses represented 17.29% of the 775 higher education institutions consulted in the USA. Unfortunately, no earlier studies exist to provide an historical comparison in the USA.

Enrollment Procedures and Eligibility Requirements

Course outlines identified two methods of enrolling in the courses studied. Predominantly a formal application process was required, usually through the graduate department. Eligibility criteria included an interest in teaching ($N = 14$ required), current teaching experience ($N = 12$ required and $N = 2$ preferred), instructor's permission ($N = 12$ required), prior teaching experience ($N = 2$ required and $N = 7$ preferred), and at least one year of work completed at the graduate level ($N = 2$ required). Populations invited to attend included graduate students in general ($N = 44$), only doctoral students ($N = 26$), only master's students ($N = 12$), faculty ($N = 12$), postdoctoral fellows ($N = 6$), and in one case, bachelor-level students who met certain criteria could register. A number of the course outlines did not specify enrollment information, so our results are not conclusive on this point.

Course Scheduling Demographics

Course scheduling demographics included variables such as the year of course inception and course offering; the number of hours/meetings and weeks; and the time of day and semester or term. Only five outlines reported the year of course inception, ranging from 1989 to 2004. The number of hours scheduled for each course meeting ranged from one hour to a full day, with 51 courses holding 2.25 hour to three-hour classes, 21 courses holding 1.25 to two-hour classes, five courses holding classes of 1 hour or less, four courses holding 3.25 to four-hour classes, and four courses holding classes of more than 4 hours. Course durations ranged anywhere from one day to one year, representing a variety of times for classes. The most popular time of day for such courses was in the evening after 6:00 p.m. ($N = 40$), followed by afternoon classes occurring between noon and 6:00 p.m. ($N = 36$), morning before noon ($N = 12$), and six over the period of an entire day. (Note: some courses had two time offerings and are reported in the two appropriate categories.) Spring ($N = 43$) and fall ($N = 41$) are the most common times when these courses are offered (summer $N = 14$ and winter $N = 9$). A few courses ran over two semesters (fall and winter, $N = 6$). It appears that these courses were held at times of the day and year when they would least interfere or overlap with participants' regular discipline-based studies, perhaps indicating that course instructors or administrators may have difficulties competing with students' regular degree programs. Also of potential significance are research projects that many graduate students may be completing during the regular office hours from 9:00 a.m. to 5:00 p.m., and thus, classes scheduled later are less likely to compete with research time.

Course Sponsors

Courses sponsored jointly with other departments included anywhere from one ($N = 57$), two ($N = 58$), or three ($N = 12$) different partners. The most common single course sponsor included Graduate Studies ($N = 10$), followed by Education ($N = 8$) and Leadership/Educational Leadership ($N = 8$). As seen in Table 2, a wide range of partners is connected with supporting college teaching courses, the most common partners being teaching centers and Faculties or Schools or Colleges of Education. Note that the numbers in the table include all combinations of partners and thus are different than above.

Courses also tended to be related to various teaching programs such as certification in university teaching programs ($N = 19$), doctoral programs ($N =$

Table 2. Sponsors Supporting Courses on Teaching College and University Courses

Sponsors	≥ Frequencies
Teaching Centers	46
Faculties (Schools or Colleges) of Education	46
Graduate Studies	40
Leadership or Educational Leadership Centers	25
Centers of Higher Education	15
Departments of Psychology	7
Departments of Educational Administration	5

18), preparing future faculty programs ($N = 16$), master's programs ($N = 13$), graduate programs or degrees ($N = 10$)[2], or graduate teaching assistant programs ($N = 5$), and other ($N = 5$).

The range of sponsors indicates that there is no clear sponsor or departmental home that gives these courses their legitimacy and our data seem to concur with Marincovich's findings (1998) that a variety of faculties (schools or colleges) and/or departments may offer these courses.

Course Credit

Regarding course credit, courses ranged from non-credit to six credit hours, the most common being three credit hours ($N = 70$), followed by two credit hours ($N = 11$), one credit hour ($N = 8$), non-credit ($N = 8$), four credit hours ($N = 1$), and six credit hours ($N = 1$). The course assessment involved grades ($N = 67$), pass/fail ($N = 29$), optional grades ($N = 5$), or no assessment ($N = 1$). The credit hour data are difficult to analyze without knowing each institution's standard credit hour system. However, it is encouraging that 91 courses (58.7%) offer some type of credit, helping to give the courses some legitimacy within the institution. Yet, one third of the courses implemented a pass/fail process, which could either detract from the value of the course or may contribute to collaborative learning. At this point, our data do not show whether the courses were counted as degree credit or are taken as extra credit. Even though many of these courses are part of a master's or doctoral program, we were unable to determine if the courses replace another discipline-based course or are an add-on to the general program.

General Course Information

Various descriptors were used in the course name. The most popular course names included College Teaching ($N = 70$), Teaching and/or Learning in Higher Education ($N = 30$), Seminar ($N = 25$), University Teaching ($N = 14$), other titles with Teaching ($N = 14$) or Instruction ($N = 14$), Graduate Student/Teaching Assistant ($N = 8$), Preparing Future Faculty ($N = 6$), Practicum and/or Supervised ($N = 4$), and Academic Career/Profession ($N = 3$). In the "other" category, course titles included "Advanced Methods in College Teaching", "Principles or Issues in College Teaching", "Academic Programs and Instruction in Higher Education", "Becoming a More Effective College Teacher", "Classroom Teaching Techniques for Graduate Assistants", "Professional Skills for Academics", and "Understanding, Assessing, and Improving College Teaching". Clearly, the focus of these courses is on teaching.

---

[2] Given that information was gathered from course outlines that sometimes provided very general descriptions (i.e., "part of a graduate program") it is unclear how these differ from masters or doctoral programs.

Specific Course Information

Specific course information was further delineated by the stated rationale or purpose, goals, course objectives, methods of teaching, resources, content area, course requirements and assignments, and grading policies.

Stated Rationale/Purpose

The stated rationale or purpose of the courses studied can be divided into nine subcategories, including "to provide background knowledge or information on teaching and learning" ($N = 24$), "to develop or improve practical skills in teaching" ($N = 16$), "to train graduate students in teaching" ($N = 15$), "to enhance professional development" ($N = 7$), "to enhance the opportunity of teachers and learners to learn from each other" ($N = 7$), "to enhance teaching in the institution" ($N = 3$), "to increase self-reflection in one's teaching" ($N = 3$), "to keep up with the changes in students and higher education" ($N = 3$), and other ($N = 2$). Surprisingly, 106 of the course outlines did not include any explicit purpose or rationale, although course instructors may have felt that the goals or objectives sections presented similar information, so only chose to put this type of information in one place.

Goals

In a previous study, Piccinin and Picard (1994) identified three categories into which the term *course goals* falls:
- theory and research on learning and teaching,
- applied teaching skills, covering professional, ethical, and
- philosophical issues in higher education.

In the present study, these goal categories were present as well as a few others. Course goal themes included applied teaching skills ($N = 77$), knowledge and understanding of teaching and learning ($N = 63$), professional/philosophical/ethical issues ($N = 62$), theory on teaching and learning ($N = 36$), research on teaching and learning ($N = 28$), and principles of teaching/learning/design ($N = 20$). Again, we were surprised that 47 of the course outlines failed to detail goals for the course.

Course Objectives

Course objectives were further divided into Skills-Based and Knowledge-Based. As seen in Table 3, the top five Skills-Based course objectives included learning assessment, course design, applied teaching, reflective teaching practice, and teaching philosophy. The course design objectives may encompass other objectives, so the coverage may be more thorough than it first appears. Follow-up with course instructors could help to clarify this point. It is also interesting to note the courses that include more professional development objectives, such as teaching philosophies, teaching portfolios, job hunts, and curriculum vitae, would suggest that at least some course instructors are not only interested in helping students develop teaching skills but also in helping them to secure teaching positions.

Table 3. Theme Types of Skill-Based Course Objectives in Courses on Teaching

Number of Courses	Skills-Based Course Objectives
57	Learning assessment
51	Course design
44	Applied teaching
42	Reflective teaching practice
42	Teaching philosophy
27	Syllabus development
25	Teaching assessment
23	Lecture/presentations
21	Teaching portfolio
21	Technology
15	Critical thinking/problem solving
15	Learning objectives
12	Professional collegiality
11	Leading discussions
10	Accessing teaching and learning resources
9	Organizational skills
8	Lesson plans
7	Job hunt
6	Classroom management/conduct
5	Curriculum vitae
3	Teaching observation

As seen in Table 4, the most frequent Knowledge-Based course objectives included teaching strategies/methods, professional issues/development, theories of learning and teaching, teaching/learning styles, research on teaching, and diversity issues. Perhaps some instructors used more learner-centered approaches to teaching and had students set goals/objectives in conjunction with the instructor, but this was not explicitly stated.

Table 4. Theme Types of Knowledge-Based Course Objectives in Courses on Teaching

Number of Courses	Knowledge-Based Course Objectives
70	Teaching strategies/methods
35	Professional issues/development
32	Theory on learning
30	Theory on teaching
30	Teaching/learning styles
30	Research on teaching
28	Diversity issues
16	Roles/responsibilities of faculty
15	Research on learning
15	Higher education structure/history/trends
14	Life-long learning
14	Ethical issues
11	Student motivation
11	Current issues in teaching and learning
6	Student development

Methods of Teaching

Various methods of teaching are identified through the outlines. As seen in Table 5, the variety of methods presented is encouraging, particularly if students are encouraged to reflect on how they could use such variety in their own teaching. Exposure to various methods is an important first step in having the variety transfer to one's own classroom.

Resources

Most resources included texts, although readings and references or additional resources were also identified from the course outlines. As seen

Table 5. Methods of Teaching Used in Courses on College/University Teaching

Number of Courses	Teaching Method
110	Readings
73	Discussions
59	Written Assignments
48	Student presentations
44	Reflective writing
35	Lecture
34	Group work
33	Guest lectures/panels
28	Micro teaching
27	E-mail/online dialogue
20	Active learning activities
20	Seminar format
19	Videos/media/technology
18	Collaboration
17	Case studies
16	Peer review/critique
14	Self-assessment/reflection
13	Web CT
11	Interviews
11	Student-led session
11	Distance education format
9	Experiential learning
7	Problem-based learning
6	Exercises
5	Demonstrations
5	Workshops
5	Team teaching
5	Role playing
4	Modeling
2	Simulations
34	Missing data

in Table 6, McKeachie's *Teaching Tips* led the list of texts.

Some courses had a special course pack of readings ($N = 17$), used the university handbook for teaching assistants ($N = 7$), and/or included the style manual used by the discipline ($N = 2$; i.e., APA Style Manual). In addition to texts, a wide variety of journals offer articles on teaching. Table 7 ranks these in order of frequency of courses listing these as readings. Based on the comparison between Tables 6 and 7, there is a larger grouping of courses that are pro-textbooks as compared to current journal articles. A closer look at the type of books selected indicates a strong reliance on applied resources (i.e., McKeachie & Davis), whereas the more theoretical texts (i.e., Feldman & Paulson, Weimer & Neff) are less popular. This finding is surprising considering that many of these courses represent graduate courses, which typically rely on more theoretically-based and evidence-based resources.

Table 6. Texts Used in Courses on College/University Teaching

Number of Courses Using Text	Author	Title	Date
40	McKeachie, W.J.	Teaching tips: Strategies, research and theory for college and university teachers	1999 and 2002
20	Davis, B.G.	Tools for teaching	2001
11	Feldman, K.A., & Paulsen, M.B.	Teaching and learning in the college classroom	1998
7	Palmer, P.J.	The courage to teach: Exploring the inner landscape of a teacher's life	1998
6	Angelo, T., & Cross, P.	Classroom assessment techniques	1993
5	Lowman, J.	Mastering the techniques of teaching	1995
3	Nilson, L.B.	Teaching at its best: A research-based resource for college instructors	1998
3	Weimer, M., & Neff, R.A. (Eds.)	Teaching college: Collected readings for the new instructor	1998
3	Huba, M.E., & Freed, J.E.	Learner-centered assessment on college campuses: Shifting the focus from teaching to learning	2000
2	Pregent, R.	Charting your course: How to prepare to teach more effectively	2000
2	Fink, L.D.	Creating significant learning experiences: An integrated approach to designing college courses	2003
2	McGlynn, A.P.	Successful beginnings for college teaching	2001
2	Newton, J., Ginsburg, J. et al.	Voices from the classroom: Reflections on teaching and learning in higher education	2001
2	Pratt, D.D.	Five perspectives on teaching adults in higher education	1998
2	Brookfield, S.	The skillful teacher	1990
1	Schoenfeld, A. C., & Magnan, R.	Mentor in a manual: Climbing the academic ladder to tenure	1992

Table 7. References Cited as Part of the Reading for the Courses on College/University Teaching

Number of Courses Using Reference	Citation
9	Barr, R.B., & Tagg, J. (1995, November/December). From teaching to learning - a new paradigm for undergraduate education. *Change*, 27(6), 12-25.
8	Chickering, A.W., & Gamson, Z. F. (March 1987). Seven principles for good practice in undergraduate education. *AAHE Bulletin*, 39(7), 3-7.
8	Brookfield, S. (1995). What it means to be a critically reflective teacher. In *Becoming a Critically Reflective Teacher* (pp. 1-27). San Francisco: Jossey-Bass.
7	Chism, N.V.N. (1997-1998). Developing a philosophy of teaching statement. *Essays on Teaching Excellence: Towards the Best in the Academy.* 9 (3).
5	Davidson, C.I., & Ambrose, S. (1994) "Characteristics of student learning." Ch. 1. In Davidson, C.I. & Ambrose, S. *The New Professor's Handbook*. Bolton, MA: Anker.
4	Reis, R. (1997). *Tomorrow's professor: Preparing for academic careers in science and engineering.* New York: IEEE Press.
4	Forsyth, D. & McMillan, J.H. (1991). Practical proposals for motivating students. *New Directions for Teaching and Learning* (Spring), 53-65
4	Fuhrmann, B. S. & Grasha, A. (1998). The past, present, and future in college teaching: Where does your teaching fit? In Feldman, K. A., & Paulsen, M. B. (Eds.) *Teaching and learning in the college classroom* (2nd ed.) (pp. 5-17). Needham Heights MA: Simon and Schuster.
3	Boyer, E. L. (1990). *Scholarship reconsidered: Priorities of the professoriate*. Princeton, NJ: Carnegie Foundation for the Advancement of Teaching.
3	Hardiman, R. & Jackson, B. W. (1992). Racial identity development: Understanding radical development in college classrooms and on campus. *ASHE Reader*
3	Davis, B.G. (1993) Learning styles and preferences. In Davis, B.G, *Tools for Teaching*. (pp. 185-192). San Francisco: Jossey-Bass.
3	Kurfiss, J. (1983, May). *Intellectual, psychosocial, and moral development in college: Four major theories*. Unpublished manuscript. (ERIC Document Reproduction Service No. ED 295 534).
3	Tatum, B. (1992). Talking about race, learning about racism: The application of racial identity theory in the classroom. *Harvard Educational Review, 62(1)*, 1-24.

Content Areas

Content areas, from the most common to the least common themes, are listed in Table 8. Again, the breadth of coverage is promising. It is interesting how assessment is separated from course design when it may be viewed as a course design activity. It is also noteworthy to see topics such as technology

Table 8. Content Areas Used in Courses on College/University Teaching

N	Content Area	N	Content Area
121	Curriculum and/or course design and/or planning	15	Job search or hiring or interview
105	Assessment and/or evaluation of learning	14	Distance learning
102	Teaching strategies, methods, and/or models	14	Effective teaching
72	Technology in teaching	14	Feedback
60	Diversity	14	Reflective practice or self assessment
59	Learner variables and/or styles	14	Student-centered teaching
52	Course and/or teaching assessment or evaluation	13	Gender issues
47	Lectures – presentation and communication	13	Teaching resources
44	Learning theories (not styles)	12	Learning process
39	Discussions	11	Faculty and/or professional development
37	Ethics and/or academic integrity	11	Questioning
37	Teaching dossiers or portfolios	10	Simulation
36	Student motivation	9	Philosophy of education or higher education
35	Syllabus design	9	Tenure and promotion
32	Course goals and objectives	8	First-day activities
32	Philosophy of teaching	7	Laboratory teaching
31	Collaborative learning/strategies	7	Academic integrity
27	Faculty issues	7	Role play
27	Scholarship of teaching or learning	6	Online course delivery systems
24	Classroom climate, culture or environment	6	Disability issues
23	Active learning	6	Lesson plans
22	Research	5	Context
21	Case study	5	Racial issues
21	Problem-based learning	5	Time management
21	Writing	5	University governance
20	Experiential learning	4	Curriculum vitae development
18	Group work	4	Equity
18	Teaching roles or responsibilities	4	Field work
17	Adult learning	4	Games
17	Assignment development	4	Microteaching
17	Classroom management	3	Demonstration
17	Teacher variables and/or styles	3	Ethnicity
16	Cooperative learning	3	History
16	Critical thinking	3	Interactive lectures
16	Mentoring students or academic advising	3	Multiple intelligences
16	Service learning	2	Stories and/or narratives
15	Class size	2	Team teaching

and diversity figuring so prominently in these courses and being separated out from other categories where they could logically fit (e.g., technology could fit under teaching strategy, and diversity could go under learner variables and/or teacher variables).

Assessment

As seen in Table 9, there was an average of 6.16 course assignments across 124 courses that provided complete assignment lists. Requirements/assignments as found in Table 10, ranged from readings to creating rubrics.

For many of the courses, attendance was required ($N = 76$) and active participation encouraged ($N = 66$). Given the content focus on course design and assessment, it is interesting to note that the majority of courses did not require proof of mastery of these components. Additionally, because reading is a relatively passive activity it does not enable an instructor to understand how well a student can put ideas into action.

Overall Discussion

A number of common elements within each course (i.e., course objectives, course content, etc.) have been identified, demonstrating an encouraging consistency across a number of courses on college and university teaching in Canada and the US. What is even more heartening is the alignment across the various elements across the course criteria. A number of the course elements appear across the Knowledge-Based and Skills-Based objectives, course content, and assignments. For instance, teaching strategies/theory (knowledge objective) is consistent with the applied teaching (a skills objective) and the teaching strategies and technology in teaching (course content) and the presentations or microteaching (class assignments). Next, course design (a skills objective) is supported by the course design (course content) and the syllabi/outline development (assignments). Critical to the success of students in any type of course is the correspondence of course elements according to each of the three course criteria (course objectives, course content, and course assignments), but the frequency counts to support such correspondence indicate that even more consistency should be sought. Students need to have solid course design skills modeled for them, and a course on college/university teaching would seem to be one of the very best places to do this.

Also of significance is that many of the common course elements align with the criteria and theories recommended for teaching these courses. For instance, the various criteria deemed as significant in developing and implementing pedagogy courses for future academics on college/university teaching, including course goals, objectives, course content, assignments, potential textbooks, and the "instructional thrust" of the course according to leading experts

Table 9. Number of Assignments Required

Number of Courses	Number of Assignments Required in a Course
1	13
2	12
2	11
7	10
9	9
14	8
18	7
24	6
12	5
15	4
14	3
4	2
2	1
Total: 124 courses	Average: 6.16 assignments/course

Table 10. Course Assignments in the College and University Teaching Courses

Readings	106
Written reflection	69
In-class presentation or teaching	61
Attendance and/or participation mark	60
Teaching philosophy	51
Course syllabus and/or outline	44
Teaching dossier or portfolio	41
Research paper or report	38
Micro teaching	32
Teaching observation	32
Critical essay or review	22
Peer review or assessment	22
Videotaped teaching or presentation	22
Learning assessment strategies or materials	21
Exam	17
Self-teaching assessment	17
Lesson plan	16
Interview a faculty member	15
Annotated bibliography or resources for teaching	14
Course or curriculum design	10
Course portfolio	10
Being mentored	8
Case study	7
Curriculum vitae	7
Designing an assessment tool	5
Workshop and/or seminar participation	5
Web page design	4
Grading key or rubric	4

(Diamond & Wilbur, 1990; Lewis, 1992; Marincovich, 1998; Vattano & Avens, 1987; Wright, 1987) are being demonstrated by the courses in the present study. Moreover, a better sense of the extent to which such courses actually subscribe to these criteria is less of a mystery.

Future Considerations

Elements identified in courses on teaching at the college or university level provide an overview of the commonalities as well as the extent to which these commonalities align with the specific criteria recommended by experts for such courses. However, the innovative approaches used to teach this type of course are equally important. Basing our views on the criteria set out by leading experts, we found a small group of courses demonstrating a diversity of approaches. This includes things such as assignments that require students to create teaching resource portfolios (i.e., annotated resource lists on teaching and learning issues), shadowing faculty or observing excellent teaching and providing reflections on these observations, interviewing current teaching academics, and using current readings on teaching and learning issues rather than specific textbooks. Instructors and course designers developing such a course for the first time as well as instructors who have experience teaching this type of course are invited to use the present findings to find new ways to build on the current strengths of their courses. From course goals to course objectives, from course content to course resources, and from course requirements to course assignments, the findings in this study provide a framework from which to refine and redevelop existing courses. Moreover, administrators and faculty developers interested in creating courses on college or university teaching can use these findings to support future planning.

Researchers also have an important continuing role to play. This study is not conclusive. Readers are cautioned that the present findings are based only on course outlines gathered from the web or kindly volunteered by the instructors or program directors of such courses. The next step would be to contact the instructors teaching these courses and to request specific information in the form of a standardized questionnaire. It is quite possible that the information gleaned from course outlines may not necessarily reflect what transpires in these classes. More detailed information may also be helpful in analyzing the degree of alignment of elements within a course, such as objectives, content, and assessment, because one would hope the alignment is greater than the frequency counts in this study would suggest. Gathering the specific details of the assignments would also provide more utility for others teaching these courses. Also of value would be a study on students who have taken these courses to provide insight into the impact their learning experiences on their current academic teaching roles and the gaps that need to be addressed and/or areas that need to be improved upon. Another research question worth pursuing is the disciplines that these courses represent and the extent to which such courses are either more prevalent in certain disciplines, such as education and/or psychology, or the extent to which they are relevant across disciplines.

Awareness of current course trends is critical for GTA developers and educational developers concerned with providing the faculty of the future with effective resources and support in their development as teachers. Moreover, such trends provide administrators and education developers with the criteria necessary for creating or refining pedagogy courses on their campuses as well as suggestions for GTA developers and education developers who are teaching these pedagogy courses.

Author Notes

Parts of this paper were presented at the Educational Developers Caucus Winter Meetings, Queens University, Kingston, Ontario, Canada (February 25, 2005); International Consortium of Educational Developers, Ottawa, Ontario, Canada (June 21, 2004); and the Professional and Organizational Development Network in Higher Education, Denver, Colorado, USA (October 2003). This article was supported by a University of Manitoba Social Sciences and Humanities Research Council of Canada Small Research Grant (431-4501-60), and a Social Sciences and Humanities Research Council of Canada Standard Grant (332-2501-01). Further inquiries or requests for reprints should be sent to Dieter J. Schönwetter, PhD, Education Specialist, Faculty of Dentistry, The University of Manitoba, Winnipeg, Manitoba, Canada, R3E 0W2, telephone: (204) 480-1302; fax (204) 789-3912; email: schonwet@cc.umanitoba.ca.

References

Adams, K. A. (2002). What colleges and universities want in new faculty. Retrieved February 3, 2003, from http://www.aacu-edu.org/pff/PFFpublications/what_colleges_want/index.cfm

The Association of Graduate Schools in the American Association of Universities. (1990). *Institutional policies to improve doctoral education: A policy statement.* (available from the Author at www.aau.ed).

Austin, A. E. (2002). Preparing the next generation of faculty. *Journal of Higher Education, 73*(1), 94-122.

Bort, M., & Buerkel-Rothfuss, N. L. (1991). A content analysis of TA training materials. In J. D. Nyquist, R. D. Abbott, D. A. Wulff & J. Sprague (Eds.), *Preparing the professoriate of tomorrow to teach* (pp. 29-39). Dubuque, IA: Kendall/Hunt.

Boyer, E. L. (1990). *Scholarship reconsidered: Priorities of the professoriate.* Princeton, NJ: Carnegie Foundation for the Advancement of Teaching.

Burk, J. E. (2001). Preparing the professoriate: Instructional design training for GTAs. *Journal of Graduate Teaching Assistant Development, 8*(1), 21-26.

Chism, N.V.N. (1998). Preparing graduate students to teach: Past, present, and future. In M. Marincovich, J. Prostko, and F. Stout (Eds.), *The professional development of graduate teaching assistants* (pp. 1-17). Bolton, MA: Anker.

Cox, M. D., & Richlin, L. (1993). Emerging trends in college teaching for the 21st century. *Journal on Excellence in College Teaching, 4*, 1-7.

Diamond, R. M., & Wilbur, F. P. (1990). Developing teaching skills during graduate education. In R. Boice, N. Diamond, L. Gardiner, D.E. Morrison, & M.D. Sorcinelli (Eds.), *To improve the academy: Vol. 9. Resources for student, faculty, and institutional development* (pp. 199-216). Stillwater, OK: New Forums Press.

Gaff, J. G. (2002). The disconnect: Graduate education and faculty realities: A review of recent research. *Liberal Education, 88*(3), 6-13.

Hiiemae, K., Lambert, L. M., & Hayes, D. (1991). How to establish and run a comprehensive teaching assistant training program. In J.D. Nyquist, R.D. Abbott, D.A. Wulff & J. Sprague (Eds.), *Preparing the professoriate of tomorrow to teach* (pp. 123-134). Dubuque, IA: Kendall/Hunt.

Lewis, K. G. (1992). *Teaching pedagogy to teaching assistants: A handbook for 398t instructors*. Austin: University of Texas Center for Teaching Effectiveness.

Lowman, J., & Mathie, V.A. (1993). What should graduate teaching assistants know about teaching? *Teaching of Psychology, 20*(2), 84-88.

Marincovich, M. (1998). Teaching teaching: The importance of courses on teaching in TA training programs. In M. Marincovich, J. Prostko, and F. Stout (Eds.), *The professional development of graduate teaching assistants* (pp. 145-162). Bolton, MA: Anker.

Marincovich, M., Prostko, J., & Stout, F. (Eds.). (1998). *The professional development of graduate teaching assistants*. Bolton, MA: Anker.

Parrett, J. (1987). A ten-year review of TA training programs. In N.V.N. Chism (Ed.), *Institutional responses and responsibilities in the employment and education of teaching assistants* (pp. 67-79). Columbus: The Ohio State University Center for Teaching Excellence.

Paulsen, M. B. (2001). After twelve years of teaching the college-teaching course. In D. Lieberman & C.M. Wehlburg (Eds.), *To improve the academy: Vol. 19. Resources for student, faculty, and institutional development* (pp. 169-192). Bolton, MA: Anker.

Piccinin, S., & Picard, M. (1994). Credit courses on university teaching for graduate students in Canadian universities. *The Canadian Journal of Higher Education, 24*(3), 58-70.

Rice, R. E. (1996). *Making a place for the new American scholar*. Washington, DC: Association for Higher Education.

Richlin, L. (1995). Preparing the faculty of the future to teach. In W.A. Wright (Ed.), *Teaching improvement practices* (pp. 255-282). Bolton, MA: Anker.

Ronkowski, S. A. (1995). Trends in TA training: An analysis of national conferences on TA-ing from 1986 to 1993. In T. A. Heenan & K. F. Jerich (Eds.), *Teaching graduate students to teach: Engaging the disciplines* (pp. 169-178). Chicago: University of Illinois.

Smith, K.A., & Waller, A.A. (1997). Afterwards: New paradigms for college teaching. In W. E. Campbell & K.A. Smith (Eds.), *New paradigms for college teaching* (pp. 269-281). Edina, MN: Interaction Book.

Vattano, F. J., & Avens, J. S. (1987). Courses on college teaching. In N.V.N. Chism (Ed.), *Institutional responsibilities and responses in the employment and education of teaching assistants* (pp. 180-186). Columbus: The Ohio State University.

Wright, A. (1987). A seminar on college teaching. In N.V.N. Chism (Ed.), *Institutional responsibilities and responses in the employment and education of teaching assistants* (pp. 177-179). Columbus: The Ohio State University.

Wulff, D. H., & Austin, A. E. (2004). Future directions: Strategies to enhance paths the professoriate. In D. H. Wulff & A. E. Austin (Eds.), *Paths to the professoriate* (pp. 267-292). San Francisco: Jossey Bass.

Dieter Schonwetter is the Director of Educational Resources and Faculty Development in the Faculty of Dentistry at the University of Manitoba. As an educational specialist, he is responsible for the management of the dental and dental hygiene curriculum as well as promoting the scholarship of teaching and learning in the oral health profession.

Lynn Taylor is an educational development specialist and the Director of the Centre for Learning and Teaching (CLT) at Dalhousie University. CLT houses a graduate course in university teaching and coordinates a Certificate in University Teaching and Learning for graduate students. Lynn's areas of practice and scholarship include teaching and learning in higher education, education development, the scholarship of teaching and learning, and academic leadership.

Donna Ellis is the Associate Director of the Centre for Teaching Excellence at the University of Waterloo, Ontario, Canada. As one of many managerial responsibilities, she provides oversight on Waterloo's Certificate in University Teaching, a program designed primarily for doctoral students who plan to enter the professoriate. Donna's research interests include new faculty enculturation experiences and student's perceptions of instructional innovations.

Valerie Koop, at the time of the data collection, was an active research assistant and was working on completing her Bachelors in Social Work.

Chapter 3
Profiling an Approach to Evaluating the Impact of Two *Certification in University Teaching* Programs for Graduate Students

K. Lynn Taylor
Dalhousie University

Dieter J. Schönwetter
The University of Manitoba

Donna E. Ellis
University of Waterloo

Martha Roberts
Carleton University

Recent literature bemoans the lack of rigorous research efforts to evaluate the effectiveness of graduate student professional development programs. This article describes an approach to program evaluation that may come to serve as a model for such research efforts. The authors describe the methodology they followed in a longitudinal study evaluating the impact of two similar but different Canadian programs designed to prepare graduate students for their teaching roles. They provide the instrument used to capture changes in graduate student affective, behavioral, and cognitive perceptions. They also use some of their findings to illustrate the kinds of program evaluation information that can be generated using such an approach.

Universities worldwide are beginning to recognize that the dominant paradigm of graduate education is so strongly research oriented that it fails to prepare graduate students for contemporary faculty roles, including teaching (Austin, 2002; Gaff, 2002; LaPidus, 1997). Early-career faculty themselves report gaps in their graduate preparation with respect to their teaching roles, but also with respect to other facets of academic careers, including job search strategies, providing feedback to colleagues, organizational and managerial skills,

---

The research reported in this paper was supported by a Standard Research Grant (#410-2002-1584) from the Social Sciences and Humanities Research Council of Canada to the second author (PI) and the first and third authors (Co-applicants). Parts of this paper were presented at the Annual Meeting of the American Educational Research Association Montreal, Quebec, Canada, April 2005; the Society for Teaching and Learning in Higher Education, Ottawa, Ontario, Canada, June 2005; and Professional and Organizational Development Network in Higher Education, Denver, CO, October 2003.

institutional governance, and managing research budgets (Austin, 2002; Gaff, 2002; Golde & Dore, 2004; Nerad, Aanerud & Cerny, 2004). In response, professional development programs for graduate students are developing rapidly across academe (Marincovich, Prostko, & Stout, 1998; Wulff & Austin, 2004a).

Until recently, there was limited research on the extent to which these programs help graduate students enhance their teaching skills or make successful transitions to academic careers (Chism, 1998). Where there was empirical evidence, the most common measure used was the satisfaction ratings of participants (Chism, 1998). Weimer and Lenze (1997) called for more comprehensive program evaluations on teaching programs for graduate students, given that most instructional interventions are based on "virtually no empirical justification as to their effectiveness" (p. 234). This empirical approach is illustrated in the recent research on the graduate learning experience and on the transition from graduate school to academic careers (e.g., Austin, 2002; Gaff, 2002; Golde & Dore, 2004; Nerad, Aanerud & Cerny, 2004) but the need for more robust, longitudinal studies is still pressing (Wulff, Austin, Nyquist & Sprague, 2004). In response, the purpose of this paper is to model one approach that addresses some of these concerns about the lack of rigorous evaluation of professional development programs for graduate students. The paper describes the methodology followed in a longitudinal study evaluating the impact of two different Canadian programs designed to prepare graduate students for their teaching roles and uses some of the findings to illustrate the kinds of program evaluation information that can be generated using such an approach.

Conceptual Perspective

The conceptual framework underlying the design of these two programs and the design of the evaluation methodology itself is based, first, on instructional interventions identified in reviews of Weimer and Lenze (1997) and Chism (1998), Marincovich, Prostko and Stout's (1998) collection of professional development resources, and McKeachie's (1997) 50-year perspective on efforts to improve teaching. These studies indicate that early-career faculty require basic knowledge and skills with respect to teaching techniques (e.g., lecturing, discussion, and group work), assessment and feedback (e.g., constructing tests, marking, and grading), use of technology, classroom management, and course and curriculum planning. The ongoing development of these two programs is further informed by the proliferation of recent work in the field (e. g., Austin, 2002; Golde & Dore, 2001; Nyquist, Austin, Sprague & Wulff, 2001; Wulff & Austin, 2004a) and by our own research designed to support program development (Ellis, Schönwetter, Roberts, & Taylor, 2004; Schönwetter & Taylor, 2003). These sources emphasize the need for a broader perspective on the communication and interpersonal skills that characterize effective teaching and for a more holistic stance on providing a broader spectrum of professional development opportunities that position graduate students for success in academic and professional careers (Austin, 2002; Wulff & Austin, 2004a).

Second, the study was also informed by literature describing both formative and/or summative evaluations of graduate teaching assistant (GTA) programs (Chism, 1998) and descriptive overviews of GTA programs and resources available for program evaluation (Chism & Szabo, 1996). While earlier studies relied more on measures of participants' satisfaction than on formal experimental designs focused on outcomes (Weimer & Lenze, 1997), more recent studies provide valuable insights with respect to program curriculum components, research methodologies and potential research questions (Nyquist, Austin, Sprague & Wulff, 2001; Smith & Kalivoda, 1998).

Third, to further elaborate the conceptual framework, the research on newly hired faculty was also reviewed to identify factors that influence the transition into successful academic careers, and with respect to teaching-related factors, in particular (Austin, 2002; Menges, & Associates 1999). This well-established literature demonstrates that when faculty members assume their first tenure-track position, they are frequently under-prepared for teaching or service roles (Boice, 1992; Tierney & Bensimon, 1996), to publish articles (Boice, 1995), or to manage the multiple tasks that compete for faculty time (Rice, Sorcinelli & Austin, 2000; Rosch & Reich, 1996). These observed gaps provide additional evidence on which to base programs designed to prepare graduate students for diverse careers.

The gaps identified in these studies are further illuminated by the research of Perry and his colleagues (Perry, Menec & Struthers, 1999; Perry et al., 1997) on the role of perceived control in early-faculty career transition. Control theory is a conceptual tool that can be applied to explain the importance to human performance of people's beliefs about the abilities they possess and how well they can use those abilities to deal with particular situations (Bandura, 1986). Beliefs about competency mediate cognitive, affective, and behavioural aspects of how people experience complex tasks such as teaching or career development (Perry et al., 1997; 1999; Weary, Gleicher, & Marsh, 1993). Perry et al. (1997, 1999) demonstrated that on the whole, higher-control faculty are more satisfied, experience less stress, produce more scholarship, and are less likely to quit than their low-control colleagues. Based on these findings, one of the goals of the two programs studied was to increase both participants' teaching competencies (a form of perceived control), and their confidence in their abilities to use those competencies. Situating the evaluation of the two programs in this theoretical framework created links to a larger body of research on early-career faculty and enriched the collection and interpretation of the data beyond their descriptive value.

Added to this mix of research is Smith's work on teaching competencies thought to be critical for faculty members in higher education (Smith & Simpson, 1995). Smith identified 33 critical teaching competencies that were validated by expert faculty developers. However, studies have has used this research to guide a pre- versus post- comparison of graduate students taking certificate programs to see if any changes have occurred in their perceptions of competency in teaching, perceived control in these teaching competencies, or their perceived importance in these competencies.

These complementary areas of the literature formed, in large part, the conceptual framework for the evaluation of these two programs. To test the utility of this conceptual framework, pilot studies were conducted to identify key variables for a longitudinal study and to test the variables and the research instruments. The results of these pilot studies, in turn, contributed the final component of the conceptual framework in that they were used to refine the survey instrument used in the study. Based on Smith's (Smith & Simpson, 1995) teaching competencies, Perry's perceptions of control, and the current authors' desire to better understand graduate students' perceptions of importance on each of these teaching competencies, the present study focuses on a pre-certificate program training versus post-certificate program training comparisons. The comparisons dealt specifically with the perceived importance of, perceived control over, and level of competence for each of these teaching competencies.

The Programs

As seen in Table 1, the two certificate in university teaching programs evaluated in this study are designed to foster the development of graduate students' teaching expertise and to help graduates secure academic positions by increasing their confidence, perceptions of control, and effectiveness with respect to teaching. As seen in the rationale section of Table 1, each program is also intended to prepare participants for other careers where presentation and communication skills are an asset. The programs contain similar content, but are organized in different ways.

The specific objectives of Program M (Manitoba) include: understanding the theory and practice of teaching and learning in higher education; developing teaching and presentation skills; learning to balance the research, teaching, and service components of an academic career; and providing formal recognition for preparing for the teaching role. Program M provides theory, practice, and professional development components that address these goals. The theory component of Program M utilizes a three-credit hour course or an alternative research paper option to explore selected theoretical teaching and learning frameworks, and relevant empirical research, and to engage in critical analysis of teaching beliefs and strategies. The practice component develops teaching effectiveness by actively engaging graduate students in planning, implementing,

Table 1. Comparison Between Two Program Descriptions and Elements

	University of Manitoba	University of Waterloo
	University Teaching Services	University Teaching Program Centre for Teaching Excellence
Name of Certificate	Certification in Higher Education	Certificate in University Teaching
Created	1998	1998
Noted on Transcript	Yes	Yes
Program Rationale	• Help departments prepare PhD students • Introduce graduate students to theory, experience and knowledge of higher education • Develop participants' teaching and presentation skills under supervision • Prepare graduate students for demands of academic and nonacademic work environments • Provide certified recognition of grad student preparation	• Motivate development of effective & reflective teachers • Motivate graduate students to prepare as future faculty • Provide forum in which to discuss teaching issues with others • Help graduate students develop skills to compete in today's job market • Provide certified recognition of graduate student preparation
Required Activities of Program	• 3 Credit Graduate course: Teaching & Learning in Postsecondary Instruction • Extended workshops and papers • TA work • Mentor supervised teaching • 20 hour workshop requirement • Teaching Dossier • Curriculum vitae (CV) • Exit interview	• Attend 6 workshops on teaching and learning issues: 2 required: "Understanding the Learner" and "Course Design" — GS 901 • Write 4 application-based 2-page response papers for 4 of the 6 workshops, including the 2 required ones — GS 901 • Attend two preparatory workshops: one on teaching dossiers and another on doing library research in education — GS 902 • Write a teaching dossier (maximum of 20 pages) — GS 902 • Prepare and deliver a research project (3 options: 20-minute research presentation and 20-page paper; 45-minute mini-workshop & supporting documentation; or research poster and supporting documentation — GS 903) • 3 Observations of authentic class setting—one large class (pre-meeting, post-observation feedback report, and response paper to feedback received) • Note: students with oral or written language problems may be required to withdraw and take language courses • Exit interview

and evaluating their own teaching and by providing formative and summative feedback from experienced faculty. Constructive feedback on teaching practice is considered a critical element of the practice component and is generated through self-assessment, mentor observation and feedback, videotape analysis, and feedback from students. The professional development component is designed to help candidates in Program M develop the habit of continuing professional development by assessing their own learning needs and by participating in professional development workshops and seminars chosen from a wide array of options. Finally, the development of a teaching dossier is used as a tool to synthesize each candidate's knowledge of teaching and learning and to prepare for the job market. Together, the components of Program M are designed as vehicles to increase teaching confidence and effectiveness.

In Program W (Waterloo), the goals of the curriculum are to help participants become more effective and reflective teachers and communicators; increase their knowledge of teaching and learning; provide a forum in which to discuss teaching issues with others; and develop presentation and writing skills for the job market. Program W is organized into three courses that can be completed in any order or simultaneously. Each course is recognized on the transcript as an academic credit towards the Certificate, but not toward the primary degree program. In the first course, candidates participate in a teaching dossier workshop and five other workshops on teaching and learning topics of their choice, and write a series of short, reflective response papers indicating how they might apply ideas from each workshop. Each candidate receives feedback on each paper submitted to support the development of the ideas expressed. In the second course, candidates complete two additional workshops and reflective papers, write a major research paper and make a presentation based on this paper. The final requirement in this course is the development of a teaching dossier. The third course is a teaching practicum in which the candidate's plan, a trained observer's feedback, and the candidate's response to that feedback are documented for at least three episodes of teaching.

Although structured differently, the two programs share many common content and process elements. The content for both programs is centered on the development of teaching skills, teaching and learning theories, reflective skills (i.e., teaching dossier and teaching philosophy), and communication and presentation skills. The procedures that engage participants in this content include workshops, paper writing, and teaching. The evaluation for the two programs includes formative assessment for most process elements (e.g., reflective papers, presentation and communication elements, teaching dossier and teaching philosophy paper). The completion of the certificate is noted on the academic transcript, as is successful completion of the credit course components. The only stark difference is that Program W has a two-year completion requirement whereas Program M is not bound by deadlines, other than completion prior to graduation. This has resulted in a range of completion dates from six weeks to six years. Thus, the two programs for the most part share similar content and process elements, yielding very similar results in graduate teaching assistant training.

Methods

Based on the shared conceptual framework that guided the design of each program and the evaluation study, a three-phase survey methodology was developed to facilitate a systematic and detailed evaluation of the impact of these learning experiences. Phase 1 involved a 115-item entry survey (Appendix A) that provided baseline measures of teaching attitudes, perceptions of teaching competence, and emotions experienced with respect to the teaching role taken prior to participants enrolling in two different certificate programs. Apart from demographic data, responses were based on five-point Likert scales. Of specific interest were the independent variables viewed as critical to career development in teaching (Menges 1996; Perry et al., 1997; Perry, Menec & Struthers, 1999; Smith & Simpson, 1995; Smith & Kalivoda, 1998): general perceptions of control, gender, and teaching experience. Dependent variables of interest are teaching outcomes as defined by teaching expectations; motivation to teach and learn more about effective teaching; perceived competence in various teaching behaviours; perceived stress related to teaching; perceived control and success in teaching situations; and teaching optimism. Open-ended questions such as ""How will your experience in the certificate program contribute to your professional development?" allowed respondents to provide information not anticipated in other survey items. When structured by a conceptual framework, rather than a description of the learning experience alone, the survey instrument produced data of more complexity and set the stage for more detailed analysis.

Phase 2 was designed to determine post-program outcomes. On completion of the program, candidates were invited to complete an exit survey that is very similar to the entry survey in order to provide repeated measures on all variables (see Appendix B). Phase 3 was a similar follow-up survey conducted 18 months into the certificate participants' first appointments. Because this was a longitudinal study, new data files will continue to be added to the analysis as they are received, and the sample size will continue to grow in all categories. The present paper focuses on the analysis of entry and exit survey data.

As part of the registration process for this program at both institutions, participants were asked to complete a research consent form that invited them to partake in a longitudinal study. Participants then volunteered to complete the pre-program survey, upon completion of their program, a post-program survey, and then 18 months into an academic position, the follow-up survey. Each of these three phases received ethical approval. The length of the pre-, post-, and follow-up survey were each 60-75 minutes. However, given the value of the certificate programs, almost all participants were more than willing to contribute to each phase of this longitudinal study. Given that participants met with the program directors on a one-on-one basis both at program registration and at program graduation, the importance of the longitudinal research project could be explained and described and as a result, there was a high response rate.

In this longitudinal study, the survey instrument was structured so that affective, behavioural, and cognitive changes in regard to teaching could be analyzed using factor analysis, correlation, regression, and ANOVA techniques, comparing the teaching development outcomes on entry to the program and on completion. Note that a variety of statistical methods are carefully pre-selected in order to provide valuable information for this kind of longitudinal study. Based on the types of research questions being addressed, the appropriate types of statistical procedures were selected and used to guide the type of questions being asked. For instance, given the limited studies supporting evaluations of GTA programs, the current study represented an explorative perspective.

To test whether key theoretical perspectives found in literature on new hires would fit GTA training, factor analysis was selected and used to identify the common factors that predicted GTAs' perceptions with regard to teaching and teaching preparation and confidence.

Correlational tools were also of interest to identify relationships among demographic variables and the dependent variables in the study. Regression tests were used to tease out the diverse levels of previous teaching experiences of each graduate student who entered the program to see if experience had any bearing on specific perceptions of teaching and confidence about teaching. Finally, ANOVA tests were used to identify specific differences between pre- and post-program data with specific comparisons in mind (i.e., gender, MA vs. PhD levels, discipline, etc.).

Selected results are presented to demonstrate not the technical aspects of these statistical tools but the kinds of results that can be obtained using these tools when data are collected using such an instrument. Qualitative analysis was also conducted on the open-ended responses provided by participants to identify key themes, and quotes from these data are used to illustrate another dimension of the data collected. Each of these approaches to testing the data pre-planned and used to help identify key patterns related to change in participants' affect, behaviour, and/or cognition as a result of the program. The strengths and challenges of the current program were revealed and used to provide guidance for mid-program corrections and strategic planning in refining these types of programs.

The results presented are based on an analysis of data provided by 234 participants who have completed the entry survey and 62 participants who have completed the exit survey (see Table 2). Participants represent a range of different disciplines. Responses to all 115 quantitative items on the survey were entered into an SPSS database for analysis. In this study, the primary quantitative analyses were primary, but illustrated by quotes from the open-end questions.

Results

At a "meta" level, a factor analysis revealed important patterns in the data set through the statistical identification of three main factors: preparedness to teach, importance of teaching, and perceived control with respect to teaching. A fourth factor was of interest: the concomitant positive change in perceptions about research abilities. This factor points to questions about the general influence of the graduate experience on variables of interest in the present research. Control group data, currently being collected in an institution that does not have a certificate program, has the potential to strengthen the interpretation of the data collected to date and to address this issue specifically.

Factor analyses also revealed that specific factors had different weightings in different programs in terms of the amount of variance explained by each factor and that, within programs, the weightings changed between entry into the certificate program and program completion (see Table 3). In a complex set of data such as this one, it was valuable to use a data collection instrument

Table 2. The Participants

Program	Entry survey	Exit survey	Matched samples
W	172	37	16
M	62	25	3
Total	234	62	19

Note: "Matched samples" indicate that of the 234 entry participants and 62 exit participants, a total of 19 completed the exit and the entry survey and thus are matched across the pre- and post-program.

Table 3. Factor Analyses for Each Program

Program	Entry Survey Factor Order	Exit Survey Factor Order
Program W	• Preparedness to teach • Importance of teaching • Research • General negative feelings	• Importance of teaching • General positive feelings about teaching • Preparedness to teach • Research
Program M	• Preparedness to teach • Importance of teaching • General negative feelings • Research	• Importance of teaching • General positive feelings about teaching • Preparedness to teach • Research

that first, permitted the identification of large themes in the data, and second, demonstrated how the contributions of individual factors that contributed to the participants' development with respect to teaching varied between when candidates entered and completed the programs.

Pre-post Comparisons

Although the meta-structure of the results is an important framing device for interpreting the results, it is the specific patterns of change that are of most interest in an evaluation study. Results were obtained for each of the three main factors related to teaching: perceptions of preparation, importance of teaching, and perceived control.

Preparation

With respect to preparation, participants demonstrated an increase in the mean rating of preparedness from 2.90 to 3.87 in Program W and from 2.92 to 4.17 for Program M. As one participant from Program W commented,

> The certificate program contributed immensely to my professional development. The workshops detailing course design and preparing for academic interviews provided valuable insight into preparing for academic and teaching activities that I would otherwise not have been exposed to during my graduate program.

Factor analysis of items pertaining to preparation, as seen in Table 4, revealed that both groups had made a shift from feeling prepared for teaching duties that reflected their teaching assistant roles (e.g., specific teaching techniques such as asking/answering questions) to duties more related to being a professor (e.g., preparing a teaching dossier, understanding teaching theory, course preparation, and self-evaluation). Certificate graduates demonstrated a shift not only in what teaching factors they were now thinking about, but also in

Table 4. Factors Contributing to Perceptions of Preparation to Teach

Program	Entry Survey Factor Order	Exit Survey Factor Order
Program W	• Classroom performance • Research – presenting and discussing • Teaching techniques – specific to TA duties, reflection	• Teaching techniques – self evaluation, teaching dossier, theory • Research – presenting and discussing • Teaching techniques – classroom performance
Program M	• Teaching techniques – specific to TA duties, preparing a class session • Research – presenting and discussing	• Teaching techniques – understanding theory, self monitoring, philosophy • Job market preparation

the level of sophistication with which they conceptualized teaching and learning. As one participant observed, "I learned that behind teaching there are theories. It is not just the talent of the teacher."

Importance of Teaching

The mean of responses with respect to the importance of teaching issues was high on entry to both programs (Program W = 4.16 and Program M = 4.31 on a five point scale). This is not surprising, since all candidates had committed to a substantial investment in developing their teaching expertise. The exit survey results showed only a slight increase in mean perceptions of importance, indicating that candidates' valuing of teaching as an important role was maintained throughout the program. However, a factor analysis revealed more subtle shifts in the importance of specific aspects of teaching over time (see Table 5).

Following the trends established in other aspects of the data, there was a developmental shift from the importance of more pragmatic concerns such as specific skills and preparation for the job market to the importance of more complex and sophisticated conceptualizations of teaching and learning including reflective teaching and the development of a teaching philosophy. A participant in Program M illustrated this trend when she observed at the end of the program, "I can now express myself as a teacher. I am more able to evaluate myself as a teacher."

Perceived Control

The results with respect to perceived control illuminate an interesting conundrum. Candidates entered these programs with a healthy degree of perceived control, as demonstrated by mean ratings on a five-point scale of 3.79 and 3.90 in Programs W and M, respectively. At the end of the programs, the mean rating of overall control was down slightly in Program W (3.70) and up slightly in Program M (4.08), but still fairly robust. As one respondent reported, "[Program M] helped me to discover my strengths. It built my self-confidence

Table 5. Factors Contributing to Perceptions of Importance of Teaching

Program	Entry Survey Factor Order	Exit Survey Factor Order
Program W	• Teaching effectiveness and understanding career demands • Research • Writing and communication in the classroom • Time management	• Techniques – classroom performance in context, theory, philosophy, self reflection in teaching • Research – presentation, discussion, writing
Program M	• What it means to be an academic • Research • Preparation for job market	• Personal reflection on teaching, teaching techniques in context • Teaching theory and philosophy • General academic issues

and has helped me become an enthusiastic presenter." References to increased confidence were the most commonly expressed theme in the responses to an open-ended question about how the program contributed to personal growth.

The pre-post means do not tell the whole story, however, and deeper analysis suggests that candidates may apply different standards with respect to perceived control of teaching as a result of participation in the programs. The strongest aspects of the factor analysis with respect to perceived control show shifts in factor weightings in Program W, depending on the context. In "boring" courses, a greater portion of the variance was accounted for by negative feelings of control whereas positive control with respect to course preparation and to teaching, more broadly, was weighted second. In Program M, there was a general shift in factor weightings from positive to negative feelings of control. One explanation is that, as candidates gain knowledge about teaching in Program M, they become aware of what they do not know and their sense of control is eroded. This is not to say that the reported levels of control were detrimental, just that it was observed that overall perceived control was not reported to have increased as a result of the program. As data files are added, and particularly as control group data is added to the study, it may be possible to address this question more definitively.

Specific Knowledge and Skills

The design of the surveys also permitted the measurement of the development of specific aspects of teaching expertise. In Program W, where there were 16 matched samples available to date, the comparison of entry and exit measures in these cases can be direct. Table 6 summarizes the items on which the strongest mean growth was reported (all differences were significantly different, $p < .01$), and highlights a number of areas in which growth was not statistically significant.

Table 6. Differences in Selected Entry and Exit Measures in Program W

Specific ability	Mean rating on entry	Mean rating on exit	Difference
Preparing a teaching dossier	1.7	3.9	2.2*
Presenting research	2.7	4.2	1.5*
Discussing teaching with employers	2.8	4.2	1.4*
Presenting a teaching philosophy	2.5	3.9	1.4*
Developing a course	1.8	3.2	1.4*
Reflecting on teaching techniques used	2.9	4.2	1.3*
Awareness of current literature on teaching	2.0	3.3	1.3*
Preparing an individual class session	3.3	4.3	1.0*
Responding to students' questions in class	3.4	3.8	0.4
Developing rapport with students	3.5	3.9	0.4
Limiting disruptions in class	3.3	3.1	0.2
Using computers in class	3.2	2.9	-0.3

*Denotes significance, $p > 0.01$

Another type of analysis is illustrated using data from Program M. Because there are only three matched samples to date, a group analysis was done comparing mean ratings for entry survey respondents ($n = 62$) and exit survey respondents ($n = 25$) on a similar set of items (Table 7). These results demonstrate that both of these programs are effective in helping candidates develop sophisticated abilities such as preparing teaching dossiers and philosophies, discussing their teaching, and developing a course. There are also some differences with respect to some of the other abilities developed. Program W participants indicated stronger development of reflection and awareness of literature on teaching and learning, whereas Program M graduates indicated stronger development of more practical aspects of teaching such as assessing student learning, adapting teaching to improve learning, and understanding practical teaching issues. These differences may be explained due to the fact that more doctoral students are enrolled in Program M and the latter would also have more teaching assistant opportunities, reflecting higher scores in the more practical elements of teaching.

A topic that stood out as not being well developed in either program was the use of computers in class. This is a finding of some concern in that the use of technology is frequently identified in academic job postings as an asset (Schönwetter, Taylor & Ellis, 2006).

Table 7. Differences in Selected Entry and Exit Measures in Program M

Specific ability	Mean rating on entry	Mean rating on exit	Difference
Preparing a teaching dossier	2.3	4.3	2.0*
Presenting a teaching philosophy	2.5	4.3	1.8*
Selecting appropriate teaching techniques	2.5	4.3	1.8*
Adjusting techniques to improve learning	2.6	4.3	1.7*
Developing a course	2.5	4.3	1.8*
Discussing teaching with employers	2.7	4.4	1.7*
Preparing an individual class session	2.9	4.5	1.6*
Assessing student learning	2.8	4.4	1.6*
Understanding practical teaching issues	2.8	4.3	1.5*
Responding to students' questions in class	3.2	4.2	1.0*
Developing rapport with students	3.2	4.2	1.0*
Limiting disruptions in class	2.8	3.7	0.9*
Using computers in class	3.2	3.5	0.3

*Denotes significance, $p > 0.01$

Discussion

The purpose of this paper was to demonstrate the value of a systematic, theory-embedded approach to the evaluation of certificate programs in teaching for graduate students. The study was motivated by a pragmatic need to support the development of two new programs by collecting data to evaluate the strengths and weaknesses of each program. The design of the particular methodology was informed by criticisms in the literature that such studies in the past had been descriptive, atheoretical, and tended to focus on satisfaction, rather than learning measures (Chism, 1998; Weimer & Lenze, 1997), and that more comprehensive, empirical studies would strengthen both the programs studied and the scholarship supporting professional development programs for graduate students (Weimer & Lenze, 1997). The approach described in this paper is one of a diverse set of qualitative and quantitative methodologies that have been applied in responding to calls for rigorous evaluation of such programs and the graduate learning experience more generally.

The design of the study addressed several gaps in the historical literature. First, data were collected on measures related to participant learning, development, and perceived control, rather than overall satisfaction alone (Chism, 1998; Weimer & Lenze, 1997). Second, as the data set grows, data collection methods are designed to facilitate differentiated analysis across levels of graduate study (MA versus PhD programs) and across disciplines to determine program impact and needs for different groups of participants (Weimer & Lenze, 1997). Third, this approach was designed to evaluate the outcomes of similar programs in two different university environments, addressing the paucity of studies that cross institutions (Weimer & Lenze, 1997) and as a result, contribute to broader understandings of the professional development needs of graduate students that may constitute the core curriculum of such programs.

The types of results illustrated in this paper illustrate the value of a more comprehensive, theory-embedded evaluation approach. A factor analysis of the entry-exit survey data revealed three teaching-related factors: preparedness to teach, importance of teaching issues and perceived control relative to teaching roles, and provided a framework for organizing and interpreting the evaluation results. With respect to preparedness, participants reported significant growth in a range of aspects of teaching, with major patterns in shifts from technical to conceptual understandings of the teaching task. Participants also reported positive pre-post shifts in the overall importance of teaching and emphasis on conceptual aspects of teaching and, intriguingly, negative shifts in perceived control in some cases.

Having a meta framework for this study also allowed the researchers to collect detailed data about specific aspects of teaching knowledge, the relative importance of that knowledge, and emotions experienced with respect to the teaching role. These data provide valuable feedback to each program on specific outcomes and on how each program can be strengthened. The data presented illustrate the richness of this information, but also identify how two programs with different structures and learning experiences compare in their outcomes. On major components such as the development of teaching dossiers and course planning, different approaches can clearly achieve the same aims. However, there were differences between the two programs in the extent to which reflective dispositions toward teaching and practical skills were developed, suggesting that, there are differences that provide valuable insights as to how to achieve different goals. There were also aspects of teaching, such as the use of technology in class that both programs may wish to strengthen.

Based on a sampling of the results, it is also possible to observe how an explicit use of a theoretical framework, through the use of common language and constructs, helps to relate the results of an evaluation study to other studies and contributes to scholarship in related fields. In this study, previous research and scholarship in the domain of graduate student development was intentionally applied. Consequently the results of this study, primarily intended to inform the development of two specific programs, also map on to previous work with transparency. Similarly, the explicit application of control theory created a more comprehensive approach to studying the experiences of candidates in these programs, but also created a bridge to connect the findings of this work to established research on early-career faculty (Perry et al., 1999). This connection enhances the value of bridging these two related literatures that can clearly inform each other in reciprocal ways.

Procedurally, key elements in evaluating certificate program effectiveness are also highlighted. First, it is critical to maintain a strong theoretical approach in conducting research. In the current study, a research framework was developed and based on models of new hires (Menges, 1999). This allowed for careful exploration of the affective, behavioral, and cognitive domains critical to developing future academic teachers. Second, the selection of appropriate statistical tools to address the research questions at hand was crucial. Careful pre-planning in the current study yielded a number of critical research questions, statistical tools, and the survey questions that would help to address these questions. Third, full ethical support to conduct the research over the three phases was critical in the collection of the data and assured credibility of the study to the research participants. Fourth, the logistics of running a full research program alongside an already time-intensive certificate in university program were clarified. In order to ensure the success of the research program, timing of both the pre- and the post-survey collection was incorporated into existing meetings with participants, both at registration time into the program and at graduation. In both cases, given the small group sizes of graduate programs, the program director reserved time to meet with them on a one-to-one basis. This further strengthened the perceived value of the pre- and post-program data collection to the participants. Finally, critical to the success of the research program was the financial support through research grants to hire research assistants to enter the data, analyze the data, and provide preliminary reports at the end of each semester. Due to the efforts of the research assistants hired throughout this research program, the evaluation of the two programs was successful, allowed for mid-program refinements, and guided strategic planning for future certificate development.

Although data collection is ongoing, the approach taken in this study validates the calls of researchers such as Chism, (1998) and Weimer and Lenze, (1997) for more systematic, theory-based approaches to evaluating professional development programs for graduate students. Such research will not only improve our collective efforts in this domain, but, by satisfying the characteristics of scholarship in all domains — clear goals, adequate preparation, appropriate methods, significant results, effective presentation, and reflective critique (Glassick, Maeroff & Huber, 2000) — will also contribute to the development of the scholarship of graduate student development.

References

Austin, A. E. (2002). Creating a bridge to the future: Preparing new faculty to face changing expectations in a shifting context. *The Review of Higher Education, 26*, 199–144.

Bandura, A. (1986). *Social foundations of thought and action.* Englewood Cliffs, NJ: Prentice-Hall.

Boice, R. (1992). *The new faculty member: Supporting and fostering professional development.* San Francisco: Jossey-Bass.

Boice, R. (1995). Developing writing, then teaching amongst new faculty. *Research in Higher Education 36*, 415-456.

Chism, N. V. N. (1998). Evaluating TA programs. In M. Marincovich, Prostko, J., & Stout, F. (Eds.). *The professional development of graduate teaching assistants* (pp. 249-262). Bolton: Anker.

Chism, N. V. N. & Szabo, B. L. (1996). *Research report: A study of how faculty development programs document their usage and evaluate their services.* Columbus, OH: The Ohio State University, Office of Faculty and TA Development.

Dunn, D., Rouse, L., & Seff, M. A. (1994). New faculty socialization in the academic workplace. In J.C. Smart (Ed.), *Higher education: Handbook of theory and research* (Vol. X, pp. 374-416). New York: Agathon Press.

Ellis, D. E., Schönwetter, D. J., Roberts, M., & Taylor, K. L. (2004, June 22). *Evaluating Certificate in University Teaching Programs: Focusing on How Participants Develop.* Presentation at the International Consortium for Educational Development in Ottawa, Ontario, Canada.

Gaff, J. G. (2002). The disconnect between graduate education and faculty realities. *Liberal Education, 88*, 3, 6-13.

Glassick, C.E., Huber, M.T., & Maeroff, G.I. (1997). *Scholarship assessed: Evaluation of the professoriate*. San Francisco: Jossey-Bass.

Golde, C. M., & Dore, T. M. (2004). The survey of doctoral education and career preparation: The importance of disciplinary contexts. In D. H. Wulff & A. E. Austin (Eds.), *Paths to the professoriate* (pp. 19-45). San Francisco: Jossey Bass.

Marincovich, M., Prostko, J., & Stout, F. (Eds.). (1998). *The professional development of graduate teaching assistants*. Bolton: Anker.

McKeachie, W. J. (1997). Critical elements in training university teachers. *The International Journal for Academic Development, 2*, 67-74.

Menges, R. J. (1999). Dilemmas of newly hired faculty. In R. Menges & Associates (Eds.), *Faculty in new jobs* (pp. 19-38). San Francisco: Jossey-Bass.

Nerad, M., Aanerud, R., & Cerny, J. (2004). "So you want to become a professor!" Lessons from the PhDs — Ten years later. In D. H. Wulff & A. E. Austin (Eds.), *Paths to the professoriate* (pp. 137-158). San Francisco: Jossey Bass.

Perry, R. P., Menec, V. H., & Struthers, C. W. (1999). Feeling in control. In R. Menges & Associates (Eds.), *Faculty in new jobs* (pp. 186-215). San Francisco: Jossey-Bass.

Perry, R. P., Menec, V. H., Struthers, C. W., Hechter, F. J., Schönwetter, D. J., & Menges, R. J. (1997). Faculty in transition: A longitudinal analysis of the role of perceived control and type of institution in adjustment to postsecondary institutions. *Research in Higher Education, 38*, 519-556.

Rice, R. E., Sorcinelli, M.D., & Austin, A.E. (2000). *Heeding new voices: Academic careers for a new generation*. Washington DC: American Association for Higher Education.

Rosch, T., & Reich, J. N. (1996). The enculturation of new faculty in higher education: A comparative investigation on three academic departments. *Research in Higher Education, 37*, 115-131.

Schönwetter, D. J. & Taylor, K. L. (2003). Preparing future professors for their teaching roles: Success strategies from a Canadian program. *Journal of Teaching Assistant Development. 9*, 101-110.

Schönwetter, D. J., Taylor, K. L., & Ellis, D. E. (2006). Reading the want ads: How can current job descriptions inform professional development programs for graduate students? *Journal on Excellence in College Teaching, 17*(1/2), 159-188.

Smith, K. S., & Kalivoda, P. L. (1998). Academic morphing: Teaching assistant to faculty member. In M. Kaplan (Ed.), *To Improve the Academy: Vol. 17. Resources for faculty, instructional, and organizational development*, (pp. 85-101). Bolton, MA: Anker.

Smith, K. S., & Simpson, R.D. (1995). Validating teaching competencies for faculty members in higher education: A national study using the delphi method. *Innovative Higher Education 19*, 223-233.

Tierney, W. G., & Bensimon, E. M. (1996). *Promotion and tenure: Community and socialization in academe*. Albany, NY: State University of New York Press.

Weary, G., Gleicher, F., & Marsh, K. L. (1993). *Control motivation and social cognition*. New York: Springer-Verlag.

Weimer, M., & Lenze, L. F. (1997). Instructional interventions: A review of the literature on efforts to improve instruction. In R. P. Perry, & J. C. Smart (Eds.), *Effective teaching in higher education: Research and practice* (pp. 205-240). New York: Agathon Press.

Wulff, D. H., & Austin, A. E., (Eds.). (2004a). *Paths to the professoriate*. San Francisco: Jossey-Bass.

Wulff, D. H., & Austin A. E., (2004b). Future directions: Strategies to enhance paths to the professoriate. In D. H. Wulff & A. E. Austin (Eds.), *Paths to the professoriate* (pp. 267-292). San Francisco: Jossey-Bass.

Wulff, D. H., Austin A. E., Nyquist, J., D., & Sprague, J. (2004). The development of graduate students as teaching scholars: A four-year longitudinal study. In D. H. Wulff & A. E. Austin (Eds.), *Paths to the professoriate* (pp. 46-73). San Francisco: Jossey-Bass.

K. Lynn Taylor, PhD, is Director of the Centre for Learning and Teaching at Dalhousie University, Halifax, Nova Scotia, Canada.

Dieter J. Schönwetter, PhD, is Director of Educational Resources and Faculty Development, Faculty of Dentistry, at The University of Manitoba, Winnipeg, Manitoba, Canada.

Donna E. Ellis, MA, is the Acting Director of the Teaching Resources & Continuing Education (TRACE) Office, University of Waterloo, Waterloo, ON, Canada.

Martha Roberts, PhD, is a Post-Doctoral Fellow in the Psychology Department of Carleton University, Ottawa, Ontario.

Appendix A

Pre-Program Survey

2002-03 EVALUATION OF THE CERTIFICATION PROGRAMS

Dear CHET or CUT Participant:

This questionnaire is designed to assist in the further development of the Certification in Higher Education Teaching (CHET) and Certificate in University Teaching (CUT) programs. Your participation is very important to the success of these programs and you are encouraged to respond thoughtfully and candidly. We are interested in your thoughts, feelings and actions as well as your expectations regarding CHET/CUT. The questionnaire is intended to be confidential. Results will be summarized and reported for groups.

This is the first of three data collection times. You will be asked to complete an exit questionnaire at the end of your certification program and one 18 months after graduation. The data from all three questionnaires will be combined into one large data set. In order to merge the data from the three collection times, we ask that you provide us with your name.

Instructions: Select the response that best answers the question and fill-in (pen or pencil) the corresponding bubbles. Please treat each item separately from every other item. There are no right or wrong answers to these items; we are simply interested in your first response. Do not spend too much time on any one item. Answer all questions. If unanswerable, leave item blank. The questionnaire takes between 20 – 30 minutes to complete.

Completion of this questionnaire is entirely voluntary and that withdrawal at any time will not affect your standing in the CHET or CUT program in any way. Thank you for providing this important information.

Dieter J. Schönwetter, Ph.D.
Associate Director
University Teaching Services
University of Manitoba

Donna Ellis, M.A.
Associate Director
Teaching Resources and Continuing Education
University of Waterloo

DEMOGRAPHICS

1. Name: _____

2. Department: _____

3. Visible minority group(s) you represent:
   _____

4. Year of Birth: 19 ___ ___

5. Is English your first language?   Yes   No

6. Gender: female   male

7. Current Degree being sought: Masters = 1   Ph.D. = 2   Post-Doc = 3   ① ② ③

8. Total number of terms/semesters completed in graduate studies (Masters + PhD): _____

9. Total number of courses completed in graduate studies (Masters + PhD): _____

10. Total number of post-secondary courses you have been a marker/grader: _____

11. Total number of post-secondary courses you have been a teaching assistant: _____

12. Total number of post-secondary courses you have been an instructor: _____

13. Total number of first authored publications: _____

14. Total number of co-authored publications (other than first): _____

15. Total number of refereed first authored conference presentations: _____

16. Total number of refereed co-authored conference presentations (other than first): _____

Using the scale below, rate the extent to which each of the following best describes you:

Very Low	Somewhat Low	Average	Somewhat High	Very High
①	②	③	④	⑤

17. Interest in teaching at a post-secondary level.   ① ② ③ ④ ⑤

18. Interest in presentation skills.   ① ② ③ ④ ⑤

19. Interest in research in a post-secondary institution.   ① ② ③ ④ ⑤

20. Interest in improving teaching.   ① ② ③ ④ ⑤

21. Importance of attaining a certification in teaching.   ① ② ③ ④ ⑤

22. Importance of Certificate completion on your university transcript.   ① ② ③ ④ ⑤

©2002 Schonwetter, Ellis, & Taylor

Appendix A (continued).

Answer the following by filling in the appropriate response in each of the two columns.

Very Low	Somewhat Low	Average	Somewhat High	Very High
①	②	③	④	⑤

		Rate the extent to which you are currently prepared for:	Rate the _importance_ of each to your academic career:
23.	Presenting your teaching philosophy.	① ② ③ ④ ⑤	① ② ③ ④ ⑤
24.	Presenting your teaching accomplishments.	① ② ③ ④ ⑤	① ② ③ ④ ⑤
25.	Discussing teaching with colleagues.	① ② ③ ④ ⑤	① ② ③ ④ ⑤
26.	Discussing teaching with potential employers.	① ② ③ ④ ⑤	① ② ③ ④ ⑤
27.	Presenting your research area.	① ② ③ ④ ⑤	① ② ③ ④ ⑤
28.	Presenting your research accomplishments.	① ② ③ ④ ⑤	① ② ③ ④ ⑤
29.	Discussing research with colleagues.	① ② ③ ④ ⑤	① ② ③ ④ ⑤
30.	Discussing research with potential employers.	① ② ③ ④ ⑤	① ② ③ ④ ⑤
31.	Reflecting on research issues.	① ② ③ ④ ⑤	① ② ③ ④ ⑤
32.	Writing academic publications.	① ② ③ ④ ⑤	① ② ③ ④ ⑤
33.	Understanding current _theories_ of teaching.	① ② ③ ④ ⑤	① ② ③ ④ ⑤
34.	Understanding _practical teaching strategies_.	① ② ③ ④ ⑤	① ② ③ ④ ⑤
35.	Understanding demands of _research_ in an academic career.	① ② ③ ④ ⑤	① ② ③ ④ ⑤
36.	Understanding demands of _teaching_ in an academic career.	① ② ③ ④ ⑤	① ② ③ ④ ⑤
37.	Understanding demands of _service_ in an academic career.	① ② ③ ④ ⑤	① ② ③ ④ ⑤
38.	Awareness of current research literature on student learning.	① ② ③ ④ ⑤	① ② ③ ④ ⑤
39.	Understanding issues in post-secondary teaching.	① ② ③ ④ ⑤	① ② ③ ④ ⑤
40.	Awareness of current research literature on effective teaching.	① ② ③ ④ ⑤	① ② ③ ④ ⑤
41.	Understanding your teaching strengths.	① ② ③ ④ ⑤	① ② ③ ④ ⑤
42.	Understanding your areas to improve in teaching.	① ② ③ ④ ⑤	① ② ③ ④ ⑤
43.	Asking students questions in the classroom.	① ② ③ ④ ⑤	① ② ③ ④ ⑤
44.	Responding to students' questions in the classroom.	① ② ③ ④ ⑤	① ② ③ ④ ⑤
45.	Using AV materials in the classroom.	① ② ③ ④ ⑤	① ② ③ ④ ⑤
46.	Using computers in the classroom.	① ② ③ ④ ⑤	① ② ③ ④ ⑤
47.	Developing a course.	① ② ③ ④ ⑤	① ② ③ ④ ⑤
48.	Preparing an individual class session.	① ② ③ ④ ⑤	① ② ③ ④ ⑤
49.	Providing examples in the classroom.	① ② ③ ④ ⑤	① ② ③ ④ ⑤
50.	Delivering content in the classroom.	① ② ③ ④ ⑤	① ② ③ ④ ⑤
51.	Keeping student attention in the classroom.	① ② ③ ④ ⑤	① ② ③ ④ ⑤

©2002 Schonwetter, Ellis, & Taylor

Appendix A (continued).

Answer the following by filling in the appropriate response in each of the two columns.

Very Low	Somewhat Low	Average	Somewhat High	Very High
①	②	③	④	⑤

		Rate the extent to which you are currently prepared for:	Rate the _importance_ of each to your academic career:
52.	Limiting disruptions in the classroom.	① ② ③ ④ ⑤	① ② ③ ④ ⑤
53.	Developing rapport with students.	① ② ③ ④ ⑤	① ② ③ ④ ⑤
54.	Assessing student learning.	① ② ③ ④ ⑤	① ② ③ ④ ⑤
55.	Selecting appropriate teaching techniques.	① ② ③ ④ ⑤	① ② ③ ④ ⑤
56.	Adjusting teaching techniques to improve student learning.	① ② ③ ④ ⑤	① ② ③ ④ ⑤
57.	Reflecting on your teaching performance.	① ② ③ ④ ⑤	① ② ③ ④ ⑤
58.	Reflecting on teaching techniques you use in the classroom.	① ② ③ ④ ⑤	① ② ③ ④ ⑤
59.	Preparing a teaching dossier.	① ② ③ ④ ⑤	① ② ③ ④ ⑤
60.	Dealing with time management.	① ② ③ ④ ⑤	① ② ③ ④ ⑤
61.	Writing clearly and succinctly.	① ② ③ ④ ⑤	① ② ③ ④ ⑤

The next set of 18 statements refers to your beliefs about teaching. Think of how you might feel if you were going to teach a _new course_ this semester. Please read each statement carefully and respond using the following scale. Note that the scale differs from the one used in the previous section.

Not at all true	A little true	Moderately true	Largely true	Complete true
①	②	③	④	⑤

WITH REGARD TO HAVING TO TEACH A NEW COURSE THIS SEMESTER:

62. I enjoy learning new things.	① ② ③ ④ ⑤
63. Before I start preparing to teach material in a course, I feel tense and anxious.	① ② ③ ④ ⑤
64. When preparing for a course, I feel bored.	① ② ③ ④ ⑤
65. Some topics are so enjoyable that I look forward to teaching them.	① ② ③ ④ ⑤
66. I feel queasy when I think of having to teach and to do all the work for a course.	① ② ③ ④ ⑤
67. The things I have to do for a course are often boring.	① ② ③ ④ ⑤
68. After I finish teaching, I feel satisfied that I know more than before.	① ② ③ ④ ⑤
69. When teaching a course, I worry that I won't be able to master all the material.	① ② ③ ④ ⑤
70. The content of course preparation is so boring that I often find myself daydreaming.	① ② ③ ④ ⑤
71. After preparing for a course, I feel relaxed and worry-free.	① ② ③ ④ ⑤
72. When teaching the material in a course, my heart rate increases because I get anxious.	① ② ③ ④ ⑤
73. When teaching, my thoughts are everywhere else, except on the course material.	① ② ③ ④ ⑤
74. Some topics are so fascinating that I am very motivated to continue teaching them.	① ② ③ ④ ⑤
75. While I am teaching, I sometimes look for distractions to reduce my anxiety.	① ② ③ ④ ⑤
76. The material in a course is so boring that it makes me exhausted even to think about it.	① ② ③ ④ ⑤
77. Because teaching is fun for me, I prepare the material more extensively than is necessary.	① ② ③ ④ ⑤
78. When I have problems with teaching the material in a course, I get anxious.	① ② ③ ④ ⑤
79. Often I am not motivated to invest effort in a boring course.	① ② ③ ④ ⑤

©2002 Schonwetter, Ellis, & Taylor

Appendix A (continued).

The following statements concern your beliefs about teaching expectancies. Read each item carefully and respond using the scale provided. Again, think of how you might feel if you were going to teach a <u>new course</u> this semester. Note that the scale differs from the one used in the previous section.

Strongly Disagree				Strongly Agree
①	②	③	④	⑤

WITH REGARD TO HAVING TO <u>TEACH A NEW COURSE</u> THIS SEMESTER:

80. My greatest personal accomplishments have come from hard work and persistence. ① ② ③ ④ ⑤
81. I have a great deal of control over my teaching performance in my courses. ① ② ③ ④ ⑤
82. Much of what happens in my life is beyond my control. ① ② ③ ④ ⑤
83. The more effort I put into teaching my courses, the better I do in them. ① ② ③ ④ ⑤
84. I have little interest in determining how well I do in teaching my courses. ① ② ③ ④ ⑤
85. No matter what I do, I can't seem to do well in teaching my courses. ① ② ③ ④ ⑤
86. What matters most is that I can influence what happens to me. ① ② ③ ④ ⑤
87. I prefer to think that life is what you make of it. ① ② ③ ④ ⑤
88. I see myself as largely responsible for my performance throughout my teaching career. ① ② ③ ④ ⑤
89. I often feel that my life is determined by others. ① ② ③ ④ ⑤
90. How well I do in my teaching is often the "luck of the draw." ① ② ③ ④ ⑤
91. Controlling how things unfold in my life is important to me. ① ② ③ ④ ⑤
92. Giving your best in your teaching makes little difference in the grand scheme of things. ① ② ③ ④ ⑤
93. There is little I can do about my teaching performance. ① ② ③ ④ ⑤
94. Things that happen in my life are largely determined by me. ① ② ③ ④ ⑤
95. When I do poorly, it's usually because I haven't given it my best effort. ① ② ③ ④ ⑤
96. I enjoy having control over the various things I do in my life. ① ② ③ ④ ⑤
97. It is important to me to be able to control how well I do in my teaching. ① ② ③ ④ ⑤
98. There is little you can do to avoid life's calamities. ① ② ③ ④ ⑤
99. Teaching evaluations are determined by things beyond my control. ① ② ③ ④ ⑤
100. I wish that I had a lot more influence over things in my life. ① ② ③ ④ ⑤
101. Getting good teaching evaluations is often the result of knowing how to play the game. ① ② ③ ④ ⑤
102. Being able to determine my teaching performance in my courses is important to me. ① ② ③ ④ ⑤
103. Much of what has happened in my life so far is my own doing. ① ② ③ ④ ⑤
104. In uncertain times, I usually expect the best. ① ② ③ ④ ⑤
105. If something can go wrong for me, it will. ① ② ③ ④ ⑤
106. I always look on the bright side of things. ① ② ③ ④ ⑤
107. I'm always optimistic about my future. ① ② ③ ④ ⑤
108. Things never work out the way I want them to. ① ② ③ ④ ⑤
109. I rarely count on good things happening to me. ① ② ③ ④ ⑤

©2002 Schonwetter, Ellis, & Taylor

Appendix A (continued).

The items below concern your feelings and thoughts about various things that have happened in your life during the last month. In each case, you are asked to indicate how often you felt or thought a certain way. Use the following scale for each item:

Never	Infrequently	Sometimes	Frequently	Very Often
①	②	③	④	⑤

During the last month, how often have you:

110.	been upset because of something that happened unexpectedly?	①	②	③	④	⑤
111.	felt that you were unable to control the important things in your life?	①	②	③	④	⑤
112.	felt nervous and "stressed"?	①	②	③	④	⑤
113.	found that you could not cope with all the things that you had to do?	①	②	③	④	⑤
114.	been angered because of things that happened that were outside of your control?	①	②	③	④	⑤
115.	found yourself thinking about things that you would have to accomplish?	①	②	③	④	⑤
116.	felt difficulties were piling up so high that you could not overcome them?	①	②	③	④	⑤

Please indicate the extent to which each of the following emotions describes how you feel about your **performance** in teaching, if you were required to teach a new course this semester.

Not at all									Very much so
①	②	③	④	⑤	⑥	⑦	⑧	⑨	⑩

WITH REGARD TO HAVING TO <u>TEACH A NEW COURSE</u> THIS SEMESTER:

117.	I am HOPEFUL.	①	②	③	④	⑤	⑥	⑦	⑧	⑨	⑩
118.	I feel GUILTY.	①	②	③	④	⑤	⑥	⑦	⑧	⑨	⑩
119.	I feel HELPLESS.	①	②	③	④	⑤	⑥	⑦	⑧	⑨	⑩
120.	I AM PROUD	①	②	③	④	⑤	⑥	⑦	⑧	⑨	⑩
121.	I feel ANGRY.	①	②	③	④	⑤	⑥	⑦	⑧	⑨	⑩
122.	I feel ASHAMED.	①	②	③	④	⑤	⑥	⑦	⑧	⑨	⑩
123.	I feel HAPPY.	①	②	③	④	⑤	⑥	⑦	⑧	⑨	⑩
124.	I feel REGRET.	①	②	③	④	⑤	⑥	⑦	⑧	⑨	⑩
125.	I DONT CARE.	①	②	③	④	⑤	⑥	⑦	⑧	⑨	⑩

Comparing yourself with others of similar experience and with your qualifications, how successful do you consider yourself?

Very unsuccessful									Very successful
①	②	③	④	⑤	⑥	⑦	⑧	⑨	⑩

126.	In your research?	①	②	③	④	⑤	⑥	⑦	⑧	⑨	⑩
127.	In your teaching?	①	②	③	④	⑤	⑥	⑦	⑧	⑨	⑩
128.	In your future academic career?	①	②	③	④	⑤	⑥	⑦	⑧	⑨	⑩

©2002 Schonwetter, Ellis, & Taylor

Appendix A (continued).

CHET/CUT Open-Ended Questions

1. How did you come to know about the CHET/CUT Program?

2. What most influenced or motivated you to sign-up for the CHET/CUT Program? Why?

3. How will your experience in the CHET/CUT Program contribute to your **professional** development?

4. How will your experience in the CHET/CUT Program contribute to your **personal** development?

Thank you for participating in this evaluation.

At your earliest convenience, please use the provided envelop to return your completed survey to your program centre:

©2002 Schonwetter, Ellis, & Taylor

Appendix B

Post-Program Survey

POST EVALUATION OF THE CERTIFICATION PROGRAM

Dear CHET or CUT Participant:
   This questionnaire is designed to assist in the further development of the Certification in Higher Education Teaching (CHET) and Certificate in University Teaching (CUT) programs. Your participation is very important to the success of these programs and you are encouraged to respond thoughtfully and candidly. We are interested in your thoughts, feelings and actions as well as your expectations regarding CHET/CUT. The questionnaire is intended to be confidential. Results will be summarized and reported for groups.

   This is the <u>second</u> of three data collection times. You will be asked to complete one more 18 months after graduation. The data from all three questionnaires will be combined into one large data set. In order to merge the data from the three collection times, we ask that you provide us with your name. You may choose to withdraw from this research project at any time. Your participation is completely voluntary.

   Instructions: Select the response that best answers the question and **fill-in** (pen or pencil) the corresponding bubbles. Please treat each item separately from every other item. There are no right or wrong answers to these items; we are simply interested in your first response. Do not spend too much time on any one item. Answer all questions. <u>If unanswerable, leave item blank</u>. This questionnaire takes approximately 20 – 30 minutes to complete.

   Completion of this questionnaire is entirely voluntary and that withdrawal at any time will not affect your standing in the CHET or CUT program in any way. Thank you for providing this important information.

Dieter J. Schönwetter, Ph.D.	**Donna Ellis, M.A.**
Associate Director	Associate Director
University Teaching Services	Teaching Resources and Continuing Education
University of Manitoba	University of Waterloo

DEMOGRAPHICS

1. Name: _____
2. Department: _____
3. Visible minority group(s) you represent: _____
4. Year of Birth: 19___ ___
5. Is English your first language? Yes   No
6. Gender: female   male
7. Current Degree being sought: Masters = 1   Ph.D. = 2   Post-Doc = 3   ① ② ③
8. How many months did it take to complete the CHET or CUT program? _____
9. Total number of terms/semesters completed in graduate studies (Masters + PhD): _____
10. Total number of courses completed in graduate studies (Masters + PhD): _____
11. Total number of post-secondary courses you have been a marker/grader: _____
12. Total number of post-secondary courses you have been a teaching assistant: _____
13. Total number of post-secondary courses you have been an instructor: _____
14. Total number of first authored publications: _____
15. Total number of co-authored publications (other than first): _____
16. Total number of refereed first authored conference presentations: _____
17. Total number of refereed co-authored conference presentations (other than first) _____

Using the scale below, rate the extent to which each of the following best describes you:

Very Low	Somewhat Low	Average	Somewhat High	Very High
①	②	③	④	⑤

18. Interest in teaching at a post-secondary level.	①	②	③	④	⑤
19. Interest in presentation skills.	①	②	③	④	⑤
20. Interest in research in a post-secondary institution.	①	②	③	④	⑤
21. Interest in improving teaching.	①	②	③	④	⑤
22. Importance of attaining a certification in teaching.	①	②	③	④	⑤
23. Importance of Certificate completion on your university transcript.	①	②	③	④	⑤

©2002 Schonwetter, Ellis, & Taylor

Appendix B (continued).

Answer the following by filling in the appropriate response in each of the two columns.

Very Low	Somewhat Low	Average	Somewhat High	Very High
①	②	③	④	⑤

	Rate the extent to which you are currently prepared for:	Rate the *importance* of each to your academic career:
24. Presenting your teaching philosophy.	① ② ③ ④ ⑤	① ② ③ ④ ⑤
25. Presenting your teaching accomplishments.	① ② ③ ④ ⑤	① ② ③ ④ ⑤
26. Discussing teaching with colleagues.	① ② ③ ④ ⑤	① ② ③ ④ ⑤
27. Discussing teaching with potential employers.	① ② ③ ④ ⑤	① ② ③ ④ ⑤
28. Presenting your research area.	① ② ③ ④ ⑤	① ② ③ ④ ⑤
29. Presenting your research accomplishments.	① ② ③ ④ ⑤	① ② ③ ④ ⑤
30. Discussing research with colleagues.	① ② ③ ④ ⑤	① ② ③ ④ ⑤
31. Discussing research with potential employers.	① ② ③ ④ ⑤	① ② ③ ④ ⑤
32. Reflecting on research issues.	① ② ③ ④ ⑤	① ② ③ ④ ⑤
33. Writing academic publications.	① ② ③ ④ ⑤	① ② ③ ④ ⑤
34. Understanding current theories of teaching.	① ② ③ ④ ⑤	① ② ③ ④ ⑤
35. Understanding practical teaching strategies.	① ② ③ ④ ⑤	① ② ③ ④ ⑤
36. Understanding demands of research in an academic career.	① ② ③ ④ ⑤	① ② ③ ④ ⑤
37. Understanding demands of teaching in an academic career.	① ② ③ ④ ⑤	① ② ③ ④ ⑤
38. Understanding demands of service in an academic career.	① ② ③ ④ ⑤	① ② ③ ④ ⑤
39. Awareness of current research literature on student learning.	① ② ③ ④ ⑤	① ② ③ ④ ⑤
40. Understanding issues in post-secondary teaching.	① ② ③ ④ ⑤	① ② ③ ④ ⑤
41. Awareness of current research literature on effective teaching.	① ② ③ ④ ⑤	① ② ③ ④ ⑤
42. Understanding your teaching strengths.	① ② ③ ④ ⑤	① ② ③ ④ ⑤
43. Understanding your areas to improve in teaching.	① ② ③ ④ ⑤	① ② ③ ④ ⑤
44. Asking students questions in the classroom.	① ② ③ ④ ⑤	① ② ③ ④ ⑤
45. Responding to students' questions in the classroom.	① ② ③ ④ ⑤	① ② ③ ④ ⑤
46. Using AV materials in the classroom.	① ② ③ ④ ⑤	① ② ③ ④ ⑤
47. Using computers in the classroom.	① ② ③ ④ ⑤	① ② ③ ④ ⑤
48. Developing a course.	① ② ③ ④ ⑤	① ② ③ ④ ⑤
49. Preparing an individual class session.	① ② ③ ④ ⑤	① ② ③ ④ ⑤
50. Providing examples in the classroom.	① ② ③ ④ ⑤	① ② ③ ④ ⑤
51. Delivering content in the classroom.	① ② ③ ④ ⑤	① ② ③ ④ ⑤
52. Keeping student attention in the classroom.	① ② ③ ④ ⑤	① ② ③ ④ ⑤

©2002 Schönwetter, Ellis, & Taylor

Appendix B (continued).

Answer the following by filling in the appropriate response in each of the two columns.

Very Low ①	Somewhat Low ②	Average ③	Somewhat High ④	Very High ⑤

	Rate the extent to which you are currently prepared for:	Rate the _importance_ of each to your academic career:
53. Limiting disruptions in the classroom.	① ② ③ ④ ⑤	① ② ③ ④ ⑤
54. Developing rapport with students.	① ② ③ ④ ⑤	① ② ③ ④ ⑤
55. Assessing student learning.	① ② ③ ④ ⑤	① ② ③ ④ ⑤
56. Selecting appropriate teaching techniques.	① ② ③ ④ ⑤	① ② ③ ④ ⑤
57. Adjusting teaching techniques to improve student learning.	① ② ③ ④ ⑤	① ② ③ ④ ⑤
58. Reflecting on your teaching performance.	① ② ③ ④ ⑤	① ② ③ ④ ⑤
59. Reflecting on teaching techniques you use in the classroom.	① ② ③ ④ ⑤	① ② ③ ④ ⑤
60. Preparing a teaching dossier.	① ② ③ ④ ⑤	① ② ③ ④ ⑤
61. Dealing with time management.	① ② ③ ④ ⑤	① ② ③ ④ ⑤
62. Writing clearly and succinctly.	① ② ③ ④ ⑤	① ② ③ ④ ⑤

The next set of 18 statements refers to your beliefs about teaching. Think of how you might feel if you were going to teach a <u>new course</u> this semester. Please read each statement carefully and respond using the following scale. Note that the scale differs from the one used in the previous section.

Not at all true ①	A little true ②	Moderately true Largely true ③	Complete true ④	⑤

WITH REGARD TO HAVING TO TEACH A NEW COURSE THIS SEMESTER:

63. I enjoy learning new things.	①	②	③	④	⑤
64. Before I start preparing to teach material in a course, I feel tense and anxious.	①	②	③	④	⑤
65. When preparing for a course, I feel bored.	①	②	③	④	⑤
66. Some topics are so enjoyable that I look forward to teaching them.	①	②	③	④	⑤
67. I feel queasy when I think of having to teach and to do all the work for a course.	①	②	③	④	⑤
68. The things I have to do for a course are often boring.	①	②	③	④	⑤
69. After I finish teaching, I feel satisfied that I know more than before.	①	②	③	④	⑤
70. When teaching a course, I worry that I won't be able to master all the material.	①	②	③	④	⑤
71. The content of course preparation is so boring that I often find myself daydreaming.	①	②	③	④	⑤
72. After preparing for a course, I feel relaxed and worry-free.	①	②	③	④	⑤
73. When teaching the material in a course, my heart rate increases because I get anxious.	①	②	③	④	⑤
74. When teaching, my thoughts are everywhere else, except on the course material.	①	②	③	④	⑤
75. Some topics are so fascinating that I am very motivated to continue teaching them.	①	②	③	④	⑤
76. While I am teaching, I sometimes look for distractions to reduce my anxiety.	①	②	③	④	⑤
77. The material in a course is so boring that it makes me exhausted even to think about it.	①	②	③	④	⑤
78. Because teaching is fun for me, I prepare the material more extensively than is necessary.	①	②	③	④	⑤
79. When I have problems with teaching the material in a course, I get anxious.	①	②	③	④	⑤
80. Often I am not motivated to invest effort in a boring course.	①	②	③	④	⑤

©2002 Schönwetter, Ellis, & Taylor

Appendix B (continued).

The following statements concern your beliefs about teaching expectancies. Read each item carefully and respond using the scale provided. Again, think of how you might feel if you were going to teach a <u>new course</u> this semester. Note that the scale differs from the one used in the previous section.

Strongly Disagree				Strongly Agree
①	②	③	④	⑤

WITH REGARD TO HAVING TO TEACH A NEW COURSE THIS SEMESTER:

81. My greatest personal accomplishments have come from hard work and persistence.   ① ② ③ ④ ⑤
82. I have a great deal of control over my teaching performance in my courses.   ① ② ③ ④ ⑤
83. Much of what happens in my life is beyond my control.   ① ② ③ ④ ⑤
84. The more effort I put into teaching my courses, the better I do in them.   ① ② ③ ④ ⑤
85. I have little interest in determining how well I do in teaching my courses.   ① ② ③ ④ ⑤
86. No matter what I do, I can't seem to do well in teaching my courses.   ① ② ③ ④ ⑤
87. What matters most is that I can influence what happens to me.   ① ② ③ ④ ⑤
88. I prefer to think that life is what you make of it.   ① ② ③ ④ ⑤
89. I see myself as largely responsible for my performance throughout my teaching career.   ① ② ③ ④ ⑤
90. I often feel that my life is determined by others.   ① ② ③ ④ ⑤
91. How well I do in my teaching is often the "luck of the draw."   ① ② ③ ④ ⑤
92. Controlling how things unfold in my life is important to me.   ① ② ③ ④ ⑤
93. Giving your best in your teaching makes little difference in the grand scheme of things.   ① ② ③ ④ ⑤
94. There is little I can do about my teaching performance.   ① ② ③ ④ ⑤
95. Things that happen in my life are largely determined by me.   ① ② ③ ④ ⑤
96. When I do poorly, it's usually because I haven't given it my best effort.   ① ② ③ ④ ⑤
97. I enjoy having control over the various things I do in my life.   ① ② ③ ④ ⑤
98. It is important to me to be able to control how well I do in my teaching.   ① ② ③ ④ ⑤
99. There is little you can do to avoid life's calamities.   ① ② ③ ④ ⑤
100. Teaching evaluations are determined by things beyond my control.   ① ② ③ ④ ⑤
101. I wish that I had a lot more influence over things in my life.   ① ② ③ ④ ⑤
102. Getting good teaching evaluations is often the result of knowing how to play the game.   ① ② ③ ④ ⑤
103. Being able to determine my teaching performance in my courses is important to me.   ① ② ③ ④ ⑤
104. Much of what has happened in my life so far is my own doing.   ① ② ③ ④ ⑤
105. In uncertain times, I usually expect the best.   ① ② ③ ④ ⑤
106. If something can go wrong for me, it will.   ① ② ③ ④ ⑤
107. I always look on the bright side of things.   ① ② ③ ④ ⑤
108. I'm always optimistic about my future.   ① ② ③ ④ ⑤
109. Things never work out the way I want them to.   ① ② ③ ④ ⑤
110. I rarely count on good things happening to me.   ① ② ③ ④ ⑤

©2002 Schönwetter, Ellis, & Taylor

Appendix B (continued).

The items below concern your feelings and thoughts about various things that have happened in your life during the last month. In each case, you are asked to indicate how often you felt or thought a certain way. Use the following scale for each item:

Never	Infrequently	Sometimes	Frequently	Very Often
①	②	③	④	⑤

During the last month, how often have you:

111. been upset because of something that happened unexpectedly?	①	②	③	④	⑤
112. felt that you were unable to control the important things in your life?	①	②	③	④	⑤
113. felt nervous and "stressed"?	①	②	③	④	⑤
114. found that you could not cope with all the things that you had to do?	①	②	③	④	⑤
115. been angered because of things that happened that were outside of your control?	①	②	③	④	⑤
116. found yourself thinking about things that you would have to accomplish?	①	②	③	④	⑤
117. felt difficulties were piling up so high that you could not overcome them?	①	②	③	④	⑤

Please indicate the extent to which each of the following emotions describes how you feel about your <u>performance</u> in teaching, if you were required to teach a new course this semester.

Not at all									Very much so
①	②	③	④	⑤	⑥	⑦	⑧	⑨	⑩

WITH REGARD TO HAVING TO <u>TEACH A NEW COURSE</u> THIS SEMESTER:

118. I am HOPEFUL.	①	②	③	④	⑤	⑥	⑦	⑧	⑨	⑩
119. I feel GUILTY.	①	②	③	④	⑤	⑥	⑦	⑧	⑨	⑩
120. I feel HELPLESS.	①	②	③	④	⑤	⑥	⑦	⑧	⑨	⑩
121. I AM PROUD.	①	②	③	④	⑤	⑥	⑦	⑧	⑨	⑩
122. I feel ANGRY.	①	②	③	④	⑤	⑥	⑦	⑧	⑨	⑩
123. I feel ASHAMED.	①	②	③	④	⑤	⑥	⑦	⑧	⑨	⑩
124. I feel HAPPY.	①	②	③	④	⑤	⑥	⑦	⑧	⑨	⑩
125. I feel REGRET.	①	②	③	④	⑤	⑥	⑦	⑧	⑨	⑩
126. I DONT CARE.	①	②	③	④	⑤	⑥	⑦	⑧	⑨	⑩

Comparing yourself with others of similar experience and with your qualifications, how successful do you consider yourself?

Very unsuccessful									Very successful
①	②	③	④	⑤	⑥	⑦	⑧	⑨	⑩

127. In your research?	①	②	③	④	⑤	⑥	⑦	⑧	⑨	⑩
128. In your teaching?	①	②	③	④	⑤	⑥	⑦	⑧	⑨	⑩
129. In your current academic career?	①	②	③	④	⑤	⑥	⑦	⑧	⑨	⑩
130. In acquiring an academic position?	①	②	③	④	⑤	⑥	⑦	⑧	⑨	⑩

With regards to the CHET/CUT Program, respond to each of the following three questions, using the scale below.

Not at all				Very much so
①	②	③	④	⑤

©2002 Schönwetter, Ellis, & Taylor

Appendix B (continued).

131. Did the program requirements add unreasonable amount of content to your existing graduate program?   ① ② ③ ④ ⑤
132. To what extent were the program requirements flexible.   ① ② ③ ④ ⑤
133. Did the program requirements extend the time required to complete graduate program?   ① ② ③ ④ ⑤

CHET/CUT Open-Ended Questions

1. What motivated you to complete the Program?

2. How has your experience in the CHET/CUT Program contributed to your **professional** development?

3. How has your experience in the CHET/CUT Program contributed to your **personal** development?

4. What element of the CHET/CUT Program most influenced you? Why?

5. What are some of the strengths of the CHET/CUT Program?

6. What were the least positive aspects of the CHET/CUT Program for you? Why?

©2002 Schönwetter, Ellis, & Taylor

Appendix B (continued).

7. What suggestions would you offer for improving the CHET/CUT Program?

8. If there is any aspect of your CHET/CUT Program experience that has not been addressed, please comment here.

Thank you for participating in this evaluation.

At your earliest convenience, please use the provided envelop to return your completed survey to your program centre:

Dieter J. Schönwetter, PhD
Associate Director
University Teaching Services
Centre for Higher Education Research and Development
220 Sinnott Building - 70 Dysart Rd.
University of Manitoba
Winnipeg, Manitoba
R3T 2N2

Donna Ellis, M.A.
Associate Director
Teaching Resources & Continuing Education
Math and Computer Building
University of Waterloo
Waterloo, Ontario,
N2L 3G1

©2002 Schönwetter, Ellis, & Taylor

Section III
Improving Graduate Assistants' Skills & Knowledge

Copyright © 2008, New Forums Press, Inc., P.O. Box 876, Stillwater, OK 74076. All Rights Reserved.

Chapter 4
Thinking Beyond the Department: Professional Development for Graduate Students of Color

Cathy Schlund-Vials
University of Connecticut, Storrs

Karen Cardozo
Amherst College

Mathew L. Ouellett
University of Massachusetts Amherst

Kirin Makker
Smith College

Over the past eight years, the Center for Teaching, University of Massachusetts Amherst has built an extra-departmental approach to mentoring and training for graduate students of color. The Graduate Students of Color Circle (GSOC) and its supplementary Mentoring Program create a collegial, culturally diverse, and cross-disciplinary future faculty preparation program.

Diversity and the Academy: The Case for a Focus on Graduate Students

For longstanding historical reasons, graduate education in the disciplines tends to focus on content rather than provide instruction about professional practices related to research, teaching, or publishing (Guillory, 2002). As a result of such institutional norms, graduate students often find themselves mystified about the academic tools of the trade (Graff & Hoberek, 1999; Nyquist et al., 2001). As Gerald Graff reveals, "...the message they get is that if you are any good, you will already know the essential secrets..." (Proceedings, 2000). While this institutional presumption negatively affects all graduate students, those from historically underrepresented groups (e.g., African Americans, Asian Americans, Native Americans, Latino/a Americans, and students from working class economic backgrounds) are likely to be disproportionately affected given that professional know-how depends, in the current system, upon access to informal cultural networks (Cardozo, 2006). As one recent report asks: Who loses when one is simply supposed to know how to be professional from watching one's parents or other role models?" ("Professionalization," 2002). While national and departmental practices have increasingly focused on the importance of professional development for graduate students (Gaff, et al., 2003; Pruitt-Logan, Gaff, & Jentoft, 2002), it will remain important to offer supplementary initiatives at the campus-wide level to ensure that students across the disciplines have access to information that can help them professionalize in diverse and challenging academic environments. Since 1995, the long-standing Teaching and Learning in the Diverse Classroom Faculty and TA Fellowship Program (TLDC) at the University of Massachusetts Amherst (UMA) has provided an opportunity for faculty and graduate teaching assistants to participate in a funded academic year-long teaching development seminar (Ouellett & Sorcinelli, 1995). As TLDC fellows, participants share information on teaching and learning; in the process, TLDC fellows collaboratively acquire concrete pedagogical skills to create effective, inclusive learning environments. While there have been many success stories related to outcomes of the TLDC program (Castaneda, 2004), over time we at the Center for Teaching (CFT) began to understand that the design, content, and processes of these forums served a consistent pattern of privileging the developmental needs and concerns of faculty participants (most often white) over the needs of graduate students (most often people of color).[1] The desire to establish a forum that addressed these concerns appropriately and in a timely fashion led to the creation of the CFT Graduate Students of Color (GSOC) seminar and, ultimately, its supplemental Mentoring Program. Ideally, of course, such activities would take place both centrally (in programs like the GSOC seminar) and in the departments, where discipline-specific training orients students to the norms and requirements of their particular fields. However, the cross-disciplinary nature of our program is valuable precisely because it helps graduate students distinguish the particular from the general: in such a forum students can learn which issues are discipline specific and which may serve as best practices across the disciplines. In this way, all students have an opportunity to learn about and thus benefit from non-discipline-specific professional development practices at work in other departments.

Graduate Students of Color Seminar

In 1998, the Center for Teaching launched the Graduate Students of Color (GSOC) seminar as a semester-long learning community offering informal near-peer mentoring and networking opportunities, career preparation, and teaching skills development developed by and offered for graduate students of color. Objectives for the seminar include bringing together graduate students of color from across disciplines, learning more about general teaching strategies, and discussing strategies for addressing the concerns and challenges specific to faculty of color within the classroom, department, and university. An additional goal involves introducing participants to senior faculty and campus administrators with a broad range of experiences as persons of color in academia.

From its inception, the GSOC seminar has functioned as a series of thematic workshops co-facilitated by a pair of advanced graduate students of color. Program continuity and growth have been achieved in large part because new seminar leaders are consistently paired with an experienced facilitator from prior years. By creating this structural bridge of institutional memory, the program has minimized the inefficiency of the "revolving door" structure that characterizes many higher education programs. Because many graduate students have participated for multiple years, the seminar in any given year also constitutes a healthy mix of new and returning participants, as well as a mix of levels from the first year to the dissertation stage.

In the early years of the GSOC seminar, four to five meetings were scheduled in a single semester. These meetings were structured primarily as a series of guest lectures by experienced faculty and administrators of color, speaking on primarily professional development or teaching-related topics. Many speakers say that they derive immense satisfaction from these connections to the next generation of scholars and from helping others learn from some of the difficulties they may have experienced. While these presentations were enthusiastically received, participant feedback consistently noted that there was insufficient time for group discussion in this limited framework. In answer to this critique, the program quickly expanded to a year-long format in which guest speaker sessions alternated with participant-only seminars, wherein the group might discuss a particular topic among themselves. For example, one session might be devoted to the topic of strategies utilized by faculty of color in predominantly white classrooms (this was the situation of almost all participants except in the rare instance where the instructor's particular subject area may have drawn a large number of undergraduate students of color) to establish authority and nurture mutual respect.

Naturally, such conversations necessarily slip back and forth between a focus on the experiences of academics of color and more universal concerns about the current training and preparation of future faculty. In a more pointed example of this, one participant in the seminar recently asserted that most of her students "had never been taught by a person of color." She often relied on other GSOC Seminar participants to help debrief her concerns that questions raised in class stemmed from dominant-held notions about her potential lack of intellectual credibility solely based on her racial group membership. At the same time, senior members of the group were able to point out that such biases may also be informed by age—that less experienced graduate teaching assistants of all racial backgrounds may suffer from challenges to their authority informed by undergraduate students' perceptions that their youth signifies inexperience.

Every year, GSOC participants also receive a set of print resources that functions as the seminar's "textbook"—a collection amplified over the years as new concerns have been raised. These include general articles on teaching as well as others specifically related to issues of diversity. In addition, participants receive materials on the teaching development services and resources available through the Center for Teaching. Thus, another important outcome of the seminar was that it served as a port of entry to the wide array of faculty development services available through the Center for Teaching. As with all learning communities sponsored by the Center for Teaching, individual consultations with CFT staff can be made by any GSOC participant to discuss specific teaching questions and issues. In addition to our most requested service, the Mid Semester Assessment Program (MAP), the CFT offers options such as classroom visits, videotaping of a class, course materials review, and instructor self-assessment. All consultations are confidential and voluntary. We have found that these consultation opportunities often expand well beyond the realm of classroom and teaching-related issues and into the broad realms of professionalization and career development.

As the current research suggests, participants in this program were hungry for information not only about teaching strategies, but also about completing the dissertation, preparing for the job market, and executing the balancing act of teaching, research, and service that awaited them as junior faculty members. In addition, many participants expressed their interest in learning more about the range of institutions within higher education, recognizing that the research-intensive environment may not be the type of institution at which they ultimately secure a faculty position. Despite the insufficient or unsystematic professional training that characterizes many graduate programs, we were able to address these concerns outside traditional departmental structures by organically broadening the program to include a mentoring initiative to complement the seminar.

The Graduate Students of Color Mentoring Program

Recent studies of graduate students from all backgrounds "show a strong desire for more information about potential careers, greater attention to teaching, better mentoring, and a closer relationship between doctoral preparation and the realities of faculty work" (Gaff, Pruitt-Logan, Sims, & Denecke, 2003; Golde & Dore, 2001; Lovitts, 2001; Nyquist, Austin, Sprague, & Wulff, 2001). Departmental structures attempt to facilitate a mentoring relationship through an advisor/advisee model; however, this model is inherently constrained by the power dynamic inherent in the process of evaluation, by departmental politics, and by disciplinary values. Such dynamics often prevent the graduate apprentice from freely asking for help, since such requests may imply professional vulnerabilities. These constraints disparately impact graduate students of color who must negotiate both stereotypes and unintentional forms of bias, and who likely experience social or intellectual isolation in departments where their cultural backgrounds and scholarly interests are significantly underrepresented (Moody, 2004).

In response to issues raised by the GSOC seminar, a supplementary mentoring initiative was developed which ultimately paired ten graduate students of color with ten faculty members. One of the most frequent issues raised by seminar participants concerned a lack of mentoring between faculty and graduate students. The participants mentioned that they often felt lost and frustrated within their departments and were uncertain as to how to proceed professionally within their respective fields, especially in understanding what to expect in different institutional contexts. Moreover, participants from the GSOC seminar remarked that it was difficult to ask advisors questions about their work because such a relationship was embedded within and circumscribed by departmental politics. For some graduate students of color the issue of mentoring can be further linked to a dearth of role models that can mirror their experiences. However, as several of our participants pointed out, some tension exists between the need for a mentor who can speak to the challenges faced by academics of color and one who can orient students to the discipline-specific scholarly norms upon which dissertation completion and tenure depend.

In our GSOC Mentoring Program, we began with an acknowledgement that the under-representation of faculty of color in the academy means that different mentors may serve different functions, and that people's needs for certain kinds of mentors may shift over time: for example, while students new to their graduate programs may benefit from mentoring by faculty of color both in and outside the department who have "been there" in the same cultural sense, these may not necessarily be the mentors who will guide participants through the academic job search or tenure process—modes in which discipline-specific values matter greatly and mentors savvy about the administrative process may be of greatest help.

Thus, while our program in most cases provides mentors of color, we emphasize that faculty and students alike must recognize that mentoring can be effective even when the mentor does not mirror the cultural background of the protégée. Given the statistical realities of under representation, and the correspondingly disproportionate burden placed on faculty of color to mentor students of color, it becomes important to consider mentoring beyond the "role model" paradigm. While seeing oneself reflected in a mentor remains a powerfully affirming experience, professional success depends both upon the willingness of faculty to actively mentor students unlike themselves and for students to cultivate mentors across the divisions of class, ethnicity, race, and gender. In order to proceed with the program, it was necessary to define mentoring for both students and faculty so that the most productive relationship could be fostered between the two groups. Though racial identification was a significant factor in initial conversations about mentoring that occurred through the GSOC seminar, what emerged from participant responses were other issues of community inflected by gender, international student status, and discipline.

Implementation and Assessment of the Mentoring Program

The Mentoring Program began in the spring semester of 2004 as an offshoot of the fall semester 2003 GSOC seminar. Five graduate students of color drawn from participants that had attended the seminar the previous year were asked to participate in the pilot semester. Like the GSOC seminar, this program was facilitated by a senior graduate student who worked in close collaboration with the two co-facilitators for the GSOC seminar. Out of the five participants, three were male and two were female; there were two international students included in this group; and the participants ranged from first year doctoral students to those finishing their dissertation projects.

Admittedly, the first semester of the Mentoring Program was filled with two major communication challenges. The busy schedules of faculty mentors were often matched by equally hectic graduate student schedules. The program was facilitated through electronic correspondence and GSOC seminar meetings. With regard to communication, mentors and their students often initiated communication electronically. In the early stages of launching the mentoring relationship, this was a generally useful strategy. However, we found that if the two people did not begin to spend time together in person relatively soon, the relationship languished and became impersonal and distant. We realized that constant communication between faculty mentor and graduate student was necessary to facilitate substantive dialogue and also that the Mentoring Program facilitator(s) needed to take a more active and directive role, particularly in encouraging personal contact early on in the relationships between faculty and graduate students.

In 2004-2005, the five students who had participated in the pilot program the spring before were invited to continue and five more graduate students of color were included. To recruit new students, email announcements were sent to departments and to specific graduate student organizations and listserves. Additionally, many "word of mouth" strategies were used as well. Participants included two international students and six women. All except one of the students was from the doctoral level in humanities disciplines; one student was a master's student in landscape architecture. Although attempts were made to recruit students from the sciences to participate in the program, the graduate students finally enrolled were not from these fields.

There are several reasons why the recruitment of science students remains difficult. First, graduate work in the sciences is generally far more collaborative than that in humanities disciplines and professional schools (e.g. the practice of co-authorship is common in the sciences, and still relatively rare in the humanities; science students may already be getting more on-site mentoring in the contexts of labs and research groups). Second, humanities students are far more likely to teach their own courses or sections than science students; as such, they may naturally be more drawn to the CFT programs as a higher priority. Finally, of course, the nature of a large university is such that humanities and science students do not necessarily mingle in the same physical spaces; as such the friendship and cultural networks needed to publicize and grow such a program have not extended as readily to the science departments.

As a starting point, participants were given parameters to develop a schema for choosing a mentor. For example, they were encouraged to think about the possibility of multiple mentors with each having a different role depending upon what stage one was at in her graduate career (as a first-year doctoral student, as one who has finished coursework, or a student about to enter the job market). Moreover, participants were encouraged to consider mentors outside their respective departments, for the reasons outlined earlier. Participants were then asked to assess their current academic and professional interests and goals. A list of potential faculty participants was gathered informally by queries to senior graduate student leaders, recalling faculty members with past connections to diversity initiatives conducted by the Center for Teaching, and via peer recommendations from faculty members of color from across the five local college campuses (University of Massachusetts Amherst and Amherst, Smith, Mount Holyoke, and Hampshire Colleges).

Most graduate student participants commented that they initially sought mentors who were from the same ethno-racial and/or gender background. However, alongside these identity constructions, participants stressed that ultimately they sought individuals who could provide excellent advice about the field in which they worked.

As may be predicted, the goals of each participant varied considerably depending on the academic advancement of the student towards her dissertation as well as personal interests. One student from American Studies commented,

> As a second year student, I am just beginning to navigate my path for research. In a mentor relationship, I am looking for someone who can offer suggestions about my work and where I can actively engage in open dialog about the nuances of academic research, projects and grants and being a woman of color in the academy. Also, I think a mentor will help me to break the solitude that writing often perpetuates.

A different student at the comprehensive exam stage explained,

> I am also looking for a friend, 'a brother in academia,' who can help guide me along, show me the ropes.... It seems that there are two different worlds that I'm leading: the academic and the non-academic. I have friends outside of academia and some friends inside the academic machine. I want a mentor who is able to flow between the two with little problem.

Each of the ten graduate students was successfully paired with a faculty member from the University of Massachusetts or one of the four nearby liberal arts colleges (Amherst, Hampshire, Mount Holyoke and Smith). To facilitate introductions, the Center for Teaching sent formal letters to faculty members requesting their involvement in the program. Once faculty had agreed to participate, the graduate student coordinating the program sent a further notice to faculty and students notifying them of their match in the program. Mentors were provided with modest honoraria to support their participation in the program. Teams were encouraged to meet as often as practical, but encouraged to meet at least five times during the year.

Assessment

Using a qualitative research design, in the fall semester 2005 we distributed a questionnaire to participants in the Mentoring Program. Additionally, we did an analysis of the formative and summative evaluations collected for the seminar in past years to identify issues across cohorts. Some themes did emerge from the survey and this review of prior evaluation sets. Clearly, the seminar provides an important and rare forum within which to explore and articulate the messages, conflicts, and challenges being experienced, as well as the joys, dreams and accomplishments valued within this group, even if not by others. In such a space, participants perceived that they could acknowledge with real understanding and empathy the significance of each other's successes, particularly the persistence and resilience required to complete the doctorate and to succeed in an academic career as people of color.

All those involved with the program expressed appreciation for its aims, and the relationships that had begun as a result of the program were often the basis for positive feedback for the initiative. Moreover, graduate student participants were able to further define their needs professionally and academically through the mentoring relationship. As another student explained at the mid-project point,

> I have met with [professor] in Sociology at UMass twice. We could share a number of things as internationals. He helped me to sharpen my ideas about my future career in the US academic world as an international student: how to prepare for my future (how to build up my career to be competitive in job market, publications to improve my CV, etc), how to adjust to a new cultural setting and how to overcome some barriers as an international. I got also insight directly

into my work because of our same interest in space theory (he even read my dissertation prospectus and gave some comments on it).

Another student noted, "I believe what I gained in the program will ultimately help me in ways I cannot anticipate at the moment; I feel better prepared for life as an academic."

Overall, graduate students perceived both opportunities as very successful, particularly for the students who participated during the pilot year and had a working relationship with their mentor already established for the second year. However, even the students who participated one year and were paired with a different mentor for the next one were highly pleased with the program, too. The students who regularly met with their mentors felt supported and encouraged. Generally, these students feel that their participation in the program has ultimately helped them to navigate their graduate school careers and potentially also their future careers as faculty of color in academia. Specific benefits included advice on job interviewing, preparing letters for fellowship applications, how to seek grant funding, the tracking down of teaching assistantships or research assistantship opportunities, dissertation topic guidance, editorial help, how to negotiate interdisciplinary interests, and other sorts of support.

Faculty participants were in general very pleased with the program and offered a variety of reasons. Some faculty felt that working with a student from outside of their department, but who had interests aligned with their own, fostered unanticipated positive results for both parties. One faculty member commented,

> I think the Mentoring Program was very useful to connect me with [student]. She is the kind of student I love to interact with but otherwise would not have the time, or would not even have met her. In addition to our one-on-one meetings, I invited her to meetings of the Asian and Asian American Studies program, which led to her being invited to teach the program's colloquium next year. I think the mentoring program is very valuable in many ways, but especially for connecting faculty and students of color.

In addition, some mentors found that participating in the program helped to educate them to the kinds of needs an advisee has beyond the scope of the dissertation. A mentor commented,

> Participating in a program like this made me think about my role as advisor and be more aware of 'looking out' for my advisee, in terms of conference and funding opportunities, significant books, new ideas, speakers coming to the area I may know of, and so on. It is easy to "drift" through an advisor/advisee relationship, especially in the years before a dissertation is underway. The Mentoring Program helps make advisors, and advisees, make the best of that relationship from early on.

In addition, there were some unanticipated benefits, such as a mentor meeting a student and making an effort to introduce the student to a colleague, thus developing another mentoring relationship; or a faculty member realizing how important mentoring is and subsequently making an effort to support other graduate students not directly involved in the program. One student commented,

> I've had one meeting thus far with [professor], and it felt productive and useful in terms of general advice about choosing courses, finding people to work with, etc. Also her involvement in Women's Studies and Asian American Studies is great because she can offer me specific advice as well on how to move between my interests.

Perhaps not unexpectedly, it is hard to overstate the contributions of the senior graduate student facilitators to the success of the program. They made countless contributions to participants' overall development as graduate students as well as to the relevance and essential strength of the GSOC and Mentoring Program. As near-peer mentors, these facilitators were often able to offer practical advice, institutional perspective and strategies for addressing a range of issues that went beyond the domain of good teaching.

Participants' biggest challenge in the Mentoring Program is establishing and maintaining consistent meetings. To reiterate, some students barely met face-to-face with their mentors because most exchanges took place via e-mail. In retrospect, both faculty and graduate student participants wished they had taken more advantage of direct forms of communication. At the close of the program, one faculty mentor commented,

> Unfortunately, I only met with [student] once. She is an incredibly busy woman and I think she also had some health problems. The one time we met, we had a good conversation and she said in an email that it was very helpful and wanted to meet again. But it did not happen.

Lessons Learned from the GSOC Seminar and Mentoring Programs

The social climate of most classrooms and academic departments reflect the social relations and perceptions of race of our broader United States society (Chesler, Lewis & Crowfoot, 2005). These values and beliefs impact on the educational experiences of all graduate students, but are often as pervasive and internalized as to make graduate students of color feel both simultaneously invisible and hyper-visible. The GSOC Seminar and Mentoring Program offers a supplementary model that reframes the prevailing institutional dynamics of individual competition and the under representation of students of color. These programs also offer insight into how one institution attempts to effect institutional change by going beyond traditional departmental activities. In its cross-disciplinary, multi-ethnic, and mixed-gender constitution, the seminar's participants generated a picture of the University unavailable within any single department.

References

Cardozo, Karen. (2006). Demystifying the dissertation. *Profession 2006*. New York: MLA.

Castaneda, C. (2004). *Teaching and learning in the diverse classroom: Faculty reflections on their experiences and pedagogical practices of teaching diverse populations.* New York: Routledge Falmer.

Chesler, M., Lewis, A., & Crowfoot, J. (2005). *Challenging racism in higher education.* New York: Rowman & Littlefield.

Gaff, J. (2000). Two cheers for professionalizing graduate students. *Publications of the Modern Language Association of America, 115*(5), 1192-93.

Gaff, J. G., Pruitt-Logan, A. S., Sims. L. B., & Denecke, D. (2003). *Preparing future faculty in the humanities and social sciences: A guide for change.* Washington, DC: American Association of Colleges and Universities, Council of Graduate Schools.

Graff, G., & Hoberek, A. (1999). Hiding it from the kids (with apologies to Simon and Garfunkel). *College English, 6*(2), 242-54.

Golde, C.M. & Dore, T.M. (2001). At Cross Purposes: What the experiences of doctoral students reveal about doctoral education (www.phd-survey.org). Philadelphia, PA: A report prepared for The Pew Charitable Trusts.

Guillory, J. (2002). The very idea of pedagogy. *Profession 2002*, 164-171. New York: MLA.

Lovitts, B. E. (2001) *Leaving the ivory tower: The causes and consequences of departure from doctoral study.* Lanham, MD: Rowman & Littlefield.

Moody, J. (2004). *Faculty diversity: Problems and solutions.* London: Routledge Farmer.

Nyquist, J. D., Austin, A. E., Sprague, J., & Wulff, D. H. (2001). *The development of graduate students as teaching scholars: A four-year longitudinal study* (Final Report, Grant #199600142). Seattle: University of Washington, Center for Instructional Development and Research.

Ouellett, M. L. & Sorcinelli, M. D. (1995). Teaching and learning in the diverse classroom: A faculty and TA partnership program. In E. Neal & L. Richlin (Eds.), *To Improve the Academy*: Vol. 14. *Resources for faculty, instructional, and organizational development* (pp. 205-217). Stillwater, OK: New Forums Press.

Proceedings of the Conference on the Future of Doctoral Education, University of Wisconsin, Madison, 15-18 April 1999. (2000). *PMLA, 115*(5): 1136-1276. New York: MLA.

Professionalization in perspective. (2002). *Report of the MLA Ad Hoc Committee on the Professionalization of PhDs, Profession 2002* (pp. 187-210). New York: MLA.

Pruitt-Logan, A. S., Gaff, J. G., & Jentoft J. E. (2002). *Preparing future faculty in the sciences and mathematics: A guide for change.* Washington, DC: Association of American Colleges and Universities.

Robbins, B. (1993). *Secular vocations: Intellectuals, professionalism, culture.* London: Verso.

Schmitz, B. (1992). *Core curriculum and cultural pluralism.* Washington, DC: American Association of Colleges and Universities.

Schmitz, B., Paul, S. P., & Greenberg, J. D. (1992). Creating multicultural classrooms: An experience-derived faculty development program. In L. Border & N. V. N. Chism (Eds.), *New directions in teaching and learning: No. 49. Teaching for diversity* (pp. 52-65). San Francisco: Jossey-Bass.

Cathy Schlund-Vials is an Assistant Professor in the Department of English and the Asian American Studies Institute, University of Connecticut, Storrs.

Karen Cardozo is a Visiting Five College Professor of Asian/American Studies at Amherst College.

Mathew L. Ouellett is the Director, Center for Teaching, University of Massachusetts Amherst

Kirin Makker is a Ph.D. Candidate in Planning at the University of Massachusetts Amherst and a Lecturer in Art at Smith College.

Copyright © 2008, New Forums Press, Inc., P.O. Box 876, Stillwater, OK 74076. All Rights Reserved.

Chapter 5
Beyond Language Skills: International Teaching Assistants' Experiences in US-Based ESL Programs

Seonhee Cho
Virginia Commonwealth University

Through interviews with non-native international teaching assistants from East Asia at three universities in the United States, this study examined the challenges they encountered and the strategies they developed in English as a Second Language (ESL) programs. The study focused primarily on ESL teaching contexts and individual international teaching assistants' subsequent experiences. Although they were inexperienced with the American educational system and American culture, lacked knowledge of course content, and were challenged by students' biases, the international teaching assistants in this study adapted to the culture, dealt with perceived student biases, and created successful teaching strategies. The findings showed that teaching in a different educational context involved a complicated process of observation and negotiation of meaning in the face of unfamiliar linguistic and cultural norms. Further, this study suggests an alternative approach to the education of international teaching assistants, which emphasizes that they are often inexperienced teachers in a new educational context rather than simply a linguistically deficient group with intelligibility problems in spoken English.

Research on non-native English speaking international teaching assistants in various academic disciplines has highlighted communicative competence, pedagogical skills, and cultural education (Hoekje & Williams, 1992; Salomone, 1998; Tyler, 1992; Williams, 1992; Yule & Hoffman, 1993). For instance, classroom discourse and interactions were analyzed (Tyler, 1992) and strategies and programs to help international teaching assistants were suggested in terms of increasing communicative competence (Williams, 1992). While a majority of US universities require oral English proficiency tests to screen qualified international teaching assistants, it has been reported that classroom communication requires more than language skills (Gorsuch, 2003). Program directors as well as international teaching assistants themselves, however, tend to identify pedagogical skills with language skills (de Berly, 1997). More recently, discipline-specific training using faculty or experienced teaching assistants within the student's department has been promoted (Byrd & Constantinides, 1992;

Gorsuch, 2006). The underlying notion of this new approach is that different academic disciplines have specific and preferred teaching styles, classroom interactions, and language use. Other studies (Compton, 2007; Gorsuch, 2003; Jenkins, 2000; Smith, Downey & Cox, 1999) warn about a simplistic view of issues of international teaching assistants because individual international teaching assistants bring varying degrees of prior experience such as teaching, social skills, culture, and even disciplinary knowledge to their departments. All of these issues factor into the effectiveness of international teaching assistants' teaching and willingness to communicate and to adjust into a new teaching environment. Missing from the previous studies, however, are international teaching assistants' voices and an examination of the specific educational contexts in which their teaching occurs.

Using a qualitative interview methodology, based on a context-specific and individual-based approach to issues of international teaching assistants, this study examined challenges faced by international teaching assistants and the teaching strategies they developed in ESL programs at three institutions.

Rationale for the Study

First, the number of international students pursuing their graduate degrees in US-based ESL (TESL, TESOL) programs has grown to the extent that international students outnumber US students in some universities (Johnson, 2003). Though not officially documented, it is likely that the number of international graduate students who are assigned teaching duties in American classrooms will increase proportionally. However, little is known regarding international teaching assistants' issues in ESL programs.

Secondly, non-native international teaching assistants in the ESL programs may have different challenges than international teaching assistants in other disciplines in that they teach English or ESL-related courses despite the fact that they are learners of English as a second language. Related to English language teaching, a number of studies (Canagarajah, 1999 b; Fairclough, 1989, 1992; Pennycook, 1989, 1994, 1999; Phillipson 1992; Tollefson, 1995) have triggered a critical dialogue regarding the construct of "native and non-native speakers" and its sociopolitical and ideological implications at a global and local level. Although non-native teachers are at an advantage because of their cultural and linguistic sensitivity and empathy to students' learning processes (Medgyes, 1999; Samimy & Brutt-Griffler, 1999), a common misconception suggests that "the ideal teacher of English is a native speaker" (Phillipson, 1992, p. 193). This misconception gives native English-speaking teachers an advantage over non-native teachers, regardless of the latters' qualifications (Canagarajah, 1999 a; Phillipson, 1992; Rampton, 1990). As such, non-native teachers may be construed as being less competent teachers than native teachers even though *what they know* may be more important than *who they are* (Samimy & Brutt-Griffler, 1999). Braine (1999) documents how such equity issues apply to non-native professionals in North America ESL contexts. Yet, none of these studies addresses the issues of international teaching assistants in the ESL programs specifically. The international teaching assistant predicament is different from that of ESL faculty or teacher educators in that international teaching assistants are still students and are not fully prepared for teaching in professional contexts.

As a third point, although being a good teacher takes more than language proficiency, a general belief among administrators, students, and even international teaching assistants themselves appears to be that good language speakers are good teachers (Plakans, 1997; Yule & Hoffman, 1990). This, however, may not be particularly true, as native teaching assistants were also reported to exhibit communication problems with their students (Smith, Downey & Cox, 1999). A fourth point is that quantitative research regarding issues of international teaching assistants tends to lose sight of the implications of the contexts within which they teach and their individual experiences as teachers. Regarding teaching contexts in ESL programs, the sites where individuals teach include university ESL programs, refugee centers, community colleges, and K-12 public schools (Ramanathan, Davies & Schleppegrell, 2001). According to Ramanathan, Davies & Schleppegrell (2001), TESOL graduate programs are offered in a variety of departments, including education, linguistics, and English. The location of these graduate programs dictates not only the focus of the program, but also the teaching context and the courses taught. The teaching contexts, course content, and learners' backgrounds which international teaching assistants must negotiate vary within the ESL programs themselves.

Finally, in terms of research, most previous studies are based on undergraduate students' evaluations of their international teaching assistants (e.g., de Berly, 1997; Plakans, 1997; Yule & Hoffman, 1993, Rubin 1992; Rubin & Smith, 1990), leaving the voices of the teaching assistants themselves relatively unheard. Further, the research conducted by ESL faculty (e.g., Gorsuch, 2006; Jenkins, 2000), using either classroom observations or interviews with international teaching assistants, may not adequately present the latters' viewpoints on their teaching experience due to power differentials between the researchers and the researched. Perceived power differentials might deter research participants from expressing their own views and candid opinions.

The current study attempted to alleviate power differentials by providing a different perspective: the researcher was a non-native graduate student like her research participants. Olesen (2000) indicated that an equal power relationship has a tendency to facilitate more open conversation regarding teaching experiences. On the basis of this rationale, this study explored, through in-depth interviews, the challenges and strategies of non-native international teaching assistants in US-based ESL programs, paying particular attention to how teaching contexts and individual situations play a part in their experiences.

Research Methodology

Research Participants and Teaching Contexts

The present study was a part of a larger one originally conducted to investigate the academic socialization processes of international graduate students. Nine research participants were recruited through *network sampling*. This sampling strategy involves asking each participant or a group of people to refer the researcher to other eligible participants. In doing so, researchers can obtain participants who can give relevant information (Merriam, 1998). Because five out of nine participants in the original study had experienced teaching as teaching assistants, this study focused on their narratives (see Table 1). To maintain participants' confidentiality, their names appear as pseudonyms.

The native languages and nationalities of the five participants varied: the group included three Chinese, one Japanese, and one Taiwanese. Time in their own graduate programs and in US varied from one to seven years. All five had taught in their home countries prior to their teaching assistantship in the United States.

When interviews were conducted, the five were pursuing their doctoral degrees in Teaching English as a Second Language at three large state-flagship universities in the midwestern and southern United States: Universities A, B, and C. Their graduate programs had different characteristics and, depending on the departmental focus, their assistantship sources were different. For instance, assistantships are offered in the English language program at University A, where international students take academic-specific

ESL courses as pre-matriculating courses for regular undergraduate programs, while at University B, which has a strong program in ESL composition, teaching assistantships are offered in regular English composition classes. At University C, teaching assistantships are offered through the ESL language institute where international students or domestic ESL students take ESL courses to improve their English skills.

Data Collection and Analysis

As this study inquired into the research participants' perceptions of and their reflections on their teaching, the researcher chose interviewing as the optimal method to collect data (McCracken 1988; Merriam, 1998). The initial interviews took between one hour and one and one-half hours each. Although a set of semi-structured questions was asked (See Appendix A), the participants' responses were not interrupted or guided (Fontana & Frey, 2000). Questions which needed further investigation or clarification during data analysis were asked through follow-up phone calls and emails. The collected data were transcribed verbatim and were analyzed through inductive and interpretive analyses in order to search for meanings and explanations of the phenomena being studied (Merriam, 1998; Shank, 2002). The following categories emerged from the analysis and guided the organization of this paper; 1) unfamiliarity with the US educational system and practices; 2) lack of knowledge about course content; 3) apparent student biases against international teaching assistants' non-native status; 4) adaptation to US culture and educational practices; (5) utilization of prior ESL learning experiences as well as prior native knowledge from participants' home countries; and (6) each non-native teachers' personal negotiation of what he or she perceived of as a socially constructed non-native teacher's identity.

Table 1: Background Information on Research Participants

	Yuka	Ling	Min	Mei	Bo
Gender	Female	Female	Male	Female	Male
Nationality	Japan	Taiwan	China	China	China
Native Language	Japanese	Mandarin	Hakka	Mandarin	Mandarin
Age	32	38	31	29	37
Current University Program	C	B	B	A	A
Years in the Program	4th year	4th year	4th year	2nd year	3rd year
Years in the NES Countries	7	7	4	3	3
Master's Degree	TESOL in the USA	Education in the USA	English Education in China	TESOL in New Zealand	ELT in UK
Undergraduate Degree	English Language & Literature	History	English Education	unknown	Teaching Language & Literature
Work Experience	5 years at private language institutions	3 years at a University in Taiwan	2 years at a University in China	2 years at a University in China	10 years at a University in China

Findings

Unfamiliarity with Educational Culture

Unfamiliarity with the US educational system and its academic culture appeared as one of the most salient themes that challenged international students in their teaching. It happened particularly with the teaching assistants who were in their early years in the US education system. For instance, Mei had just finished her first year in her doctoral program in TESOL at University A when the interview occurred, and her reflections on her experience during her first year of teaching were vivid. An assignment in the university's intensive language program shortly after her arrival, Mei was overwhelmed, as we can see in the following quote which expresses her frustration:

> Their whole way of doing lessons and preparing lessons is so different from what I did in China. In China, we like uh, if I [were] going to teach next week, I just prepare all the lessons for next week. Nothing more. But here, at the very beginning of the semester, you need to have the whole schedule for the whole semester. I don't know. It was the first time I have a look at that. How can I know where I actually start, where I should give grade, where I should give a test? It was just so frustrating.

Although there were coordinators available to help her, she did not know where to begin or what to ask: "Because my mind is just blank, if you're just empty, you cannot ask any questions."

Though somewhat different, Bo's experience in the same program also showed how his lack of knowledge and inexperience with American classroom systems and practices challenged him. As noted earlier, the University A program offered academic-specific ESL courses as pre-matriculating courses for international students. Bo described his experience as demanding:

> In terms of my teaching, student background I have to know. But I don't know. This is one challenge, right? Another example is that what kind of American classroom is like. I have no idea. Right? I have never been to America. So I have to learn base just because you know, when I first got here, I was asked to teach. All of these going together become a challenge to me.

Min taught an English composition course in the University B program. He mentioned that his unfamiliarity with American pop culture hindered communication between him and his students during his first year of teaching. While he was assigned to teach English composition, he had difficulty understanding when students talked to each other. As he described it, "Because they talk about movies, they talk about TV shows. I couldn't [understand] because I couldn't get a chance to watch it." Although he was confident about his English skills, he had difficulty understanding aspects of American pop culture that he had never experienced growing up in China.

Being perceived of as communicatively less competent than their native counterparts and lacking both the formal educational and informal popular culture experiences necessary appears to make international instructors feel handicapped. It is also critical to note that when the international teaching assistants faced something new that they had never experienced, they failed to understand or even to request help. Mei's inability to ask for help during the first few weeks mirrors Krase's (2003) account of an international student (Hanna) in her first year. Even when her professor offered help, Hanna could not take advantage of it because she did not know what to ask. The availability of faculty assistance without specific guidance and contact may not be accessible for newly-arrived international teaching assistants who do not have any experiences on which to base questions or for help. Lack of a cultural and educational context seems to create a communicative mutism on the part of instructor new to the culture.

Lack of Knowledge about Course Content

The international teaching assistants' lack of knowledge about the course content also challenged them in teaching. As a teaching assistant, Bo was teaching an English for Academic Purposes course in the university's English language program and an introductory linguistics course in his department. The former course was to prepare international students for their mainstream courses, while the latter was a regular course for undergraduate students in his department. He observed that both courses challenged him a great deal but for different reasons. For instance, in the former, he was assigned to teach psychology. Unfortunately, Bo had never studied psychology prior to his teaching assignment. He had earned his bachelor's and master's degrees in language and English language teaching, not in psychology. He stated, "How can I express myself in the field of psychology in English?" Another course that he taught was the required introductory linguistics course that most American undergraduate students in the program have to take. Although Bo had taken a linguistics course, he found the difference between knowing the course content as a student and understanding the content well enough to teach it as an instructor challenging.

Similarly, when Ling in the University B program was assigned to teach English composition, she found herself in an ironic situation because she was not a good writer herself and did not enjoy writing:

> Because when I was in my country and when I was a college student, my English writing was terrible . . . . And then, for some reason, I was in that program and I became a TA and had to teach students composition. You know, I was totally overwhelmed. I didn't even know how to write.

Accordingly, her lack of confidence was not limited to her lack of language skills—teaching an unfamiliar and even disliked subject is not easy for any teacher.

These findings echo Compton's (2007) claim that international teaching assistants were more willing to communicate when they were familiar with the content presented. Similarly, an international teaching assistant's response who participated in Jenkins' (2000) study showed that topic familiarity or the lack thereof can respectively facilitate or hinder conversation. For instance, an international teaching assistant in the math department could not follow his colleague's explanation of his daughter's education, while he could comprehend the conversation regarding math. The results of this present study parallel other studies that confirm the significance of course content familiarity in international teaching assistant education and in international teaching assistants' success as teachers.

Dealing with Students' Perceived Biases toward Non-native Teacher Status

Even if the challenges of the international teaching assistants of this study did not solely originate from their English language proficiency, the reality of teaching in an ESL context reminded them of their non-native status. Particularly, students' evaluation of their teaching always included comments on their non-native English accents and their so-called unintelligibility. In Mei's case, some of the students' written comments on her teaching at the end of the semester were quite disheartening. As she described it:

> Some of them mentioned that I'm not experienced enough which I think . . . that's my first year. And some of them, just one student, that's the evaluation, that I got last year. I guess that the student has some prejudice against me. He said that my accent is bad and my teaching is bad, everything is bad.

In spite of a few students' negative comments, however, Mei attributed them to her inexperience in her new teaching community. As for the criticism about her being non-native, including her foreign accent, she also ascribed it to potential student biases rather than taking it personally. She mentioned that the rest of her students gave her positive feedback: "They said that I'm really caring about them and easygoing, this kind of thing."

Similarly, Yuka, in the program at University C, also experienced student complaints about the difficulty they had understanding her. As for students' responses to Yuka's teaching in the university language program, she observed some students who came to class and expressed prejudice against non-native English teachers. She stated, "Some students come with bias. I learned the bias. They change their mind and they change their perceptions about non-native teachers. But some don't. That's what I learned." When one of her students wrote in a teaching evaluation that he would not want to take her class anymore, she was very hurt. She did suspect, however, that this student was the one who had failed the class previously, and assumed that he was blaming her for his current failure. From this experience, she realized she could not satisfy all students and believed that a native teacher might have the same response from students.

Ling's experience regarding students' biases about her non-native status was similar. In fact, she had opportunities to observe her native colleagues' classes and realized her classes were as good as theirs. In spite of her effort to make her English understandable and her class more organized, however, she received negative feedback about her accent. Ling expressed her frustrations about being a non-native teacher:

> I feel that being non-native speaking TA in the United States is very challenging because you can never change your skin color and change language tongue. That's always blamable. Right, because there are always students who do not want to learn and if they fail, they're gonna blame, 'That's all your fault because you cannot speak English well. I don't understand. I don't know what you're talking about.' That's really disappointing, actually.

Although she perceived that her well-prepared class could be conducive to her students' learning, Ling's accent (which she did not believe that she could change), was a consistently negative point in her students' evaluation of her teaching. She realized that no matter how hard she tried to make her class more understandable, there were always some students who complained about her oral English. Ling's experience of students' feedback led her to believe that some students were more than willing to blame their failure on the international teaching assistant. As she put it: "Those students who skip classes and who don't turn in papers complain about my English." Ling was also critical about the TA evaluation survey item: "Do you clearly understand instructors' teaching?" She thought this question could mislead students to judge non-native teachers' speaking ability primarily by their accents.

For these reasons, the international teaching assistants in this study perceived students' negative comments on their teaching as students' biases and believed that students blamed their own poor academic performance on their international teaching assistants' language problems. The international teaching assistants did not believe that students' negative comments on their teaching accurately described what they really had accomplished in terms of teaching. These perceptions of students' negative comments in course evaluations, however, resonate with the research findings of Plakans' study (1997) on the relationship between undergraduate students' attitudes toward international teaching assistants and their background characteristics. In her study, traditional-aged male students (18-24 years old) with an expected GPA in the C range had a low opinion about their international teaching assistants' teaching and had rare interactions with their international teaching assistants even when they needed help. For these students, international teaching assistants' non-standard English seemed to be a reason to justify their poor academic performance. Similarly, Rubin and Smith's (1990) and Rubin's (1992) studies reported students' biases related to international teaching assistants' ethnicity in their evaluations of teaching effectiveness and comprehensibility of lectures. Thus, it would appear that international teaching assistants' claims of students' biases should not be dismissed.

Adapting to Teaching in the American Classroom

All the international teaching assistants in this study strove to adapt to American educational practices and to American classroom culture. For instance, Mei's teaching experience during the first semester was overwhelming because she was new to the US system of education and still had to teach students using American educational practices. In the beginning, it was not easy for Mei to create engaging activities and to encourage her students to do group and peer work. She compared her native Chinese educational culture with her new environment:

> In China, we give lectures to students so students sit there and listen and they do their exercises and teachers correct their exercises. But here I realize that I have to make things more interesting for students. I need to invent exercises for students to involve them. And also I need to encourage group work and peer work.

Mei's professor, after observing her teaching, suggested integrating more group activities and explained the reason for the importance of those activities. Because the international students she was teaching were going to study in an American classroom, where students' group work and participation are appreciated and valued, Mei needed to prepare her students accordingly. After the conference, Mei took her supervisor's advice and tried to integrate more student-centered activities and group work. After the second observation, her supervisor said to her, "O.K., you have improved." Mei was very encouraged by her professor's positive feedback.

Like Mei, Bo, also from China, was aware of differences in academic cultures in China and the US. He stated, "I have to do something different from what I did back in China. For example, here in this culture, students' participation is emphasized. So I have to do something to encourage them to participate in my teaching." He mentioned that his English Language Teaching education in Britain also helped him to believe that students' participation is essential in language education. On the other hand, students' spontaneous questions were challenging to him. Although he had thoroughly prepared for his class, he felt nervous when he faced students' unexpected questions.

Bo's candid account revealed his inner conflicts between what he knew he should do and what he was actually doing. Through a teaching education course, he learned that teachers should admit when they did not know the answer, but it was not easy for him to do so. He attributed this to his native Chinese cultural influence:

> They [Chinese] say 'face' is important. They say, if you don't know the thing, you're not qualified to be a teacher. So I'm still influenced by that kind of culture thing. So I know that it's not good thing. If I haven't gotten very clear understanding of students' questions, but still I pretend to understand it and I can answer it anyway.

Like Bo's awareness of his native cultural influences on his teaching, Wen and Clément (2003) described the concept of "face" in Chinese educational settings. According to their explanation, teachers who are figures of authority in the classroom are expected to show their mastery of the subject; if they do not, they feel they may lose their credibility and their reputation. It is, however, worth noting that Bo recognized his native cultural influences and tried to adjust to the practices of his new teaching community. He described how he handled students' questions that he could not answer: "Sometimes I just imitate or follow American teacher's way. 'Oh! that's a good question'." In addition, the activities that he had not implemented in his class were student presentations. Bo explained the reason: "They speak fast. And I can't follow them, how do I respond to that?" For this reason, he often gave quizzes and exams to his students. Nevertheless, he believed that his many years of teaching experience in China were very helpful in terms of how to manage a classroom, how to build good teacher and student relationships, and how to motivate students to learn.

Bo also displayed professionalism and a sense of responsibility in his teaching: "You know, in class, you have 20-30 students. In first semester, I had 35 students in class. If my teaching is not so good, I mean, their future will be affected. I'm responsible for 35 students that way. So that's why teaching to me is very important." Although he perceived that it was more important for him to finish his doctoral degree successfully and as soon as possible, teaching ruled his life, often making him uncertain about his emotions: "Today, I'm very happy because of my teaching. Today I'm very sad because of my teaching."

Ling at University B stated that she had been secretly observing her professors' teaching styles while she was taking classes. As she put it: "I'm kind of observing different professors' performance and try to copy or imitate some teaching strategies— something like that." Coming from a very competitive educational culture in Taiwan where students tend not to share their ideas and opinions, Ling noticed that US educational culture was more encouraging of peer interactions on the academic level. Another strategy that Ling utilized thoroughly preparing for classes and using visual aids:

> I have to organize, and then list all the points that I'm gonna lecture today and give students handouts since I'm afraid that they can not understand my English. So I usually have to do a lot of preparations before I teach.... I'm trying to use other ways to make up the weaknesses and you know, to help students understand more.

As earlier noted, Min had difficulty understanding students' conversations due to his lack of exposure to American popular culture. Min, however, over time not only could understand his students better, but also learned how to engage his students. He explained: "[Now] I know about American culture. In the class, I can relate, make jokes, talk more easily, related to things that students themselves are interested in or familiar with."

As illustrated above, the international teaching assistants in this study not only were aware of the culturally embedded educational practices, but also actively negotiated the terrain between their native educational cultures and their new environment. They further developed strategies that worked best for their individual situations and put a great deal of effort into preparation for teaching.

Maximizing the Benefits of a Non-native Background

The international teaching assistants in this study also utilized their former experiences as an English second language learner in their teaching. Further, they took advantage of their native knowledge in explaining cultural and linguistic examples. Their status helped them to bond with international students in their courses. For instance, Yuka's case showed that her experience as an Asian female instructor helped her to make connections with other Asian female students at University C's intensive English program. She stated that she helped students in ways that might have been difficult for native English speaking teachers:

> Sometimes, actually, young Asian women, uh, students, Chinese, Korean, Taiwanese students seem to be, seem to think that I'm very approachable. So they opened up their mouth more easily with me. Maybe, just my impression. I don't know. They approached me very easily and asked questions. And the whole class, I think, a little more participating because I was very patient with students. I could wait until students said something.

Yuka's own ESL learning experiences allowed her to be more patient. Bo also utilized his knowledge about the Chinese language while he was teaching linguistics in order to help students understand language varieties. He perceived that his knowledge about Chinese contexts and Chinese languages could be used as a resource. Similarly, Mei, who taught crosscultural studies, used numerous examples of Asian culture of which she was knowledgeable, providing both an insider's perspective and helping students link to other cultures.

As we can see from these examples, while the international teaching assistants adapted to their new environments, they were not just passive recipients of US cultural norms and languages. They also brought their insiders' perspectives as second language learners and native informants of different languages and cultures into their classes which appeared to be of benefit to the students.

Conclusions and Implications for International Teaching Assistant Education

Although each teaching context, student body, and course content in which the international teaching assistants taught varied, the challenges that they experienced were similar. More important, as the findings of this study showed, the international teaching assistants' limited language skills were not the main challenges they faced despite a common belief that lack of language proficiency is the biggest obstacle to international teaching assistants' effective teaching. Non-language aspects such as unfamiliarity with American educational culture and practices, lack of knowledge about course content, and the perceived students' biases were equally challenging.

The international teaching assistants in this study felt uneasy in a teaching context with which they were not familiar. As noted earlier, Mei, in particular, was frustrated by having to plan a multi-month syllabus—which she did not know how to do. Without knowing students' levels, what to teach and what to grade, it was not an easy task for her to design a syllabus for the entire course. Furthermore, without having prior experience with how American classrooms function, she had to teach a pre-matriculated course for international students. It is important to note that Mei did not feel able to ask for help even when the program coordinators were available. When she was given a new task, which she had not experienced nor observed before, she did not know how to ask for help. These findings suggest that what new international teaching assistants need is the time to observe and increase their participation in a community of practice to become more familiar with the new environment (Lave & Wenger, 1991). More specifically, active observation during their first semester on campus and reflection on the courses they will be teaching later (see Gorsuch, 2006) will help international teaching assistants develop discipline-specific language and pedagogical skills as well as knowledge of American educational culture.

In relation to course content, the international teaching assistants felt insecure and uneasy when they were assigned to teach courses that they had not previously taught or in which they were not knowledgeable. This finding demonstrates that international teaching assistants' course content knowledge plays a pivotal part in their teaching, although this aspect has previously been overshadowed by a focus on communicative competence in international teaching assistant education. While this study does not dismiss the fact that proficient language skills are vital in teaching, the portrayal of international teaching assistants' issues as a lack of language skills undermines important factors such as unfamiliarity with American educational culture and lack of course content knowledge; both should be enhanced in international teaching assistant education.

All of the international teaching assistants in this study had taught English in their home countries before they joined US programs. In their home countries, where a majority of English teachers are non-native English speakers, their non-native status was never an issue. However, when they were relocated to American ESL contexts where native teachers are the norm, they became painfully aware of their non-native status. Although they perceived students' biases against their non-native status and non-standard English as a harsh reality, none of them was devastated by a few students' negative comments on their teaching. Instead, they identified those comments as their students' failure rather than their own, while assuming that similar feedback could happen in any educational context with both native and non-native ESL teachers.

The international teaching assistants in this study made significant efforts to make their classes more prepared and organized to overcome the challenges they faced. Further, they used their native knowledge in terms of culture and language to help their students understand other linguistic and cultural features in their classes. Their ESL learning experience also helped them to be patient and sympathetic with their own ESL students. This indicates that they did not perceive themselves simply as non-native international teaching assistants, but rather as instructors who need to be actively engaged with students and who could rise to the challenge of addressing problems faced by instructors in ESL programs.

Suggestions

Based on the findings, this study suggests an alternative approach to international teaching assistant education. As Thomas (1999) claims, "Although stories of unintelligible foreign teaching assistants abound, the fact remains that there are good teachers and 'not-so-good' teachers" (p.6). The direction of international teaching assistant screening and training processes should move away from a simplistic view of dealing with a linguistically and culturally "deficient" group where teaching contexts and varying degrees of individual experiences are overlooked. First, the attention to international students' teaching issues should be shifted from a communicative competence approach to an approach that focuses on helping inexperienced teachers adjust to a new educational context.

Second, international students need time to adjust to the American educational system; it is crucial that they observe similar classrooms (Gorsuch, 2006), become familiar with American students' daily culture (see Altinsel & Rittenberg, 1996), participate in a discipline-specific mentoring program, and benefit from their mentor's classroom observation feedback. Because most international teaching assistant trainers have a background in ESL teaching and do not have another content expertise, departments hosting international teaching assistants should support building international teaching assistants' course content knowledge and language acquisition either through cooperation with international teaching assistant trainers or through a mentoring program within the department (see Gorsuch, 2006; Jenkins, 2000).

Most important, international teaching assistant issues should not be approached at an institutional level from a "deficit" position. Yook and Albert's (1999) study showed that undergraduate students trained in intercultural issues had a more positive attitude toward international teaching assistants' non-standard English accents and forms than non-trained groups of students. Therefore, in order to benefit both international teaching assistants and their students, this study suggests implementing a two-way model of cultural training rather than continuing the traditional unilateral training imposed only on international teaching assistants.

As for the international teaching assistants, they should be encouraged to perceive themselves as a valuable resource on campus to provide different perspectives and diverse cultural knowledge. They also should be allowed to speak up for themselves, instead of simply accepting their limitations which are a result of existing social structures. In this process, raising critical awareness of new social and educational contexts and practices is crucial. This will further lead international teaching assistants themselves to adapt to their new environments, develop content expertise, and learn to create effective teaching strategies.

As a final point, international teaching assistant education should become a shared responsibility of the department, international teaching assistant trainers, and international teaching assistants. Training should include not only international teaching assistants but also all parties involved so that American undergraduates can appreciate and learn from their international instructors.

Limitations and Recommendations for Further Research

While this study examined international teaching assistants' perspectives regarding the challenges they faced and the strategies they tried, it has a few limitations. Although generalization is not the concern of a qualitative study

(Denzin & Lincoln, 2000; Hatch, 2002; Merriam, 1998; Shank, 2002), the sample size of this study was limited. Thus, the findings might not be transferable to other contexts. In addition, as this research explored only international teaching assistants' voices, their students' viewpoints on bias and failure are not explored. Regarding researcher bias, my particular viewpoint as a non-native scholar working in the US educational system is neither perfect nor entirely objective, leaving interpretation of my conclusions up to readers.

There are some questions which emerged in the process of this research, some of which I leave open for further exploration. Some of the challenges that the international teaching assistants experienced are similar to those any novice teacher might experience in a similar situation regardless of his or her native or non-native status. For instance, other novice teachers may experience a lack of confidence as a consequence of unfamiliarity of course content, inexperience in a new educational setting, and discomfort with students' ungrounded complaints. To discriminate more clearly between the kinds of challenges international teaching assistants and native teaching assistants face, a follow-up study should include native teaching assistants. In addition, the scholarship related to issues of international teaching assistant should move toward building positive role models for international teaching assistants by shedding light on their strengths and abilities to adapt to and build effective strategies for teaching in American classrooms.

References

Altinsel, Z. & Rittenberg, W. (1996, March). *Cultural support for international TAs: An undergraduate buddy program.* Chicago, IL: The Conference of Teachers of English to Speakers of Other Languages. (Eric Document Reproduction Service No. ED407918)

Braine, G. (Ed.) (1999). *Non-native speakers in English language teaching*. Mahwah, NJ: Erlbaum.

Byrd, P., & Constantinides, J. C. (1992). The language of teaching mathmathics: Implications for training ITAs. *TESOL Quarterly, 26,* 163-167.

Canagarajah, A. S. (1999a). Interrogating the "native speaker fallacy": Non-linguistic roots, non-pedagogical results. In G. Braine (Ed.), *Non-native educators in English language teaching* (pp.77-92). Mahwah, NJ: Erlbaum.

Canagarajah, A. S. (1999b). *Resisting linguistic imperialism in English teaching*. New York: Oxford University Press.

Compton, L. K. L. (2007). The impact of content and context on international teaching assistants' willingness to communicate in the language classroom. *TESL-EJ, 10*(4), 1-20.

de Berly, G. (1997). *Sources of conflict in an international teaching assistant training programs.* (ERIC Document Reproduction Service No. ED423777)

Denzin, N. K., & Lincoln, Y. S. (2000). Introduction: The discipline and practice of qualitative research. In N. K. Denzin & Y. S. Lincoln (Eds.), *Handbook of qualitative research* (pp.1-28). Thousand Oaks, CA: Sage.

Fairclough, N. (1989). *Language and power*. New York: Longman.

Fairclough, N. (Ed.). (1992). *Critical language awareness*. New York: Longman.

Fontana, A., & Frey, J. H. (2000). The interview: From structured questions to negotiated text. In N. K. Denzin & Y. S. Lincoln (Eds.), *Handbook of qualitative research* (pp.645-672). Thousand Oaks, CA: Sage.

Gorsuch, G. J. (2003). The educational cultures of international teaching assistants and US universities. *TESL-EJ, 7*(3), 1-17.

Gorsuch, G. J. (2006). Discipline-specific practica for international teaching assistants. *English for Specific Purposes, 25,* 90-108.

Hatch, J. A. (2002). *Doing qualitative research in education settings*. Albany: State University of New York Press.

Hoekje, B., & Williams, J. (1992). Communicative competence and the dilemma of international teaching assistant education. *TESOL Quarterly, 26,* 28-54.

Jenkins, S. (2000). Cultural and linguistic miscues: A case study of international teaching assistant and academic faculty miscommunication. *International Journal of Intercultural Relations, 24,* 477-501.

Johnson, K. (2003, March). *Re-examining curricula in MA TESOL programs*. Paper presented at the Meeting of the Teaching English to the Speakers of Other Languages, Baltimore, MD.

Krase, E. (2003). *Socio-cultural interactions and ESL graduate student enculturation: A cross-sectional analysis*. Unpublished doctoral dissertation, University of Tennessee, Knoxville.

Lave, J., & Wenger, E. (1991). *Situated learning: Legitimate peripheral participation*. New York: Cambridge University Press.

Lincoln, Y. S., & Guba, E. G. (2000). Paradigmatic controversies, contradictions, and emerging confluences. In N. K. Denzin & Y. S. Lincoln (Eds.), *Handbook of qualitative research* (pp.163-168). Thousand Oaks, CA: Sage.

McCracken, G. (1988). *The long interview*. Thousand Oaks, CA: Sage.

Medgyes, P. (1999). Language training: A neglected area in teacher education. In G. Braine (Ed.), *Non-native educators in English language teaching* (pp.177-195). Mahwah, NJ: Erlbaum.

Merriam, S. B. (1998). *Qualitative research and case study applications in education*. San Francisco: Jossey-Bass.

Olesen, V. L, (2000). Feminisms and qualitative research at and into the millennium. In N.K. Denzin & Y.S. Lincoln (Eds.), *Handbook of qualitative research* (pp. 215-256). Thousand Oaks, CA: Sage.

Pennycook, A. (1989). The concept of method, interested knowledge, and the politics of language teaching. *TESOL Quarterly, 23,* 589-613.

Pennycook, A. (1994). *The cultural politics of English as an international language*. New York: Longman.

Pennycook, A. (1999). Introduction: Critical approaches to TESOL. *TESOL Quarterly, 33,* 329-348.

Phillipson, R. (1992). *Linguistic imperialism*. New York: Oxford University Press.

Plakans, B. S. (1997). Undergraduates' experiences with and attitudes toward international teaching assistants. *TESOL Quarterly, 31,* 95-119.

Ramanathan, V., Davies, C. E., & Schleppegrell, M. J. (2001). A naturalistic inquiry into the cultures of two divergent MA-TESOL programs: Implications for TESOL. *TESOL Quarterly, 35*, 279-305

Rampton, M. B. H. (1990). Displacing the 'native speaker': Expertise, affiliation, and inheritance. *ELT Journal, 44*, 97-101.

Rubin, D. L. (1992). Nonlanguage factors affecting undergraduates' judgments of nonnative English-speaking teaching assistants. *Research in Higher Education, 33*, 511-531.

Rubin, D. L., & Smith, K. A. (1990). Effects of accent, ethnicity, and lecture topic on undergraduates' perceptions of non-native English speaking teaching assistants. *International Journal of Intercultural Relations, 14*, 337-353.

Salomone, A. M. (1998). Communicative grammar teaching: A problem for and a message from international teaching assistants. *Foreign Language Annals, 31*, 552-566.

Samimy, K.K., & Brutt-Griffler, J. (1999). To be a native or non-native speaker: Perceptions of "non-native" students in a graduate TESOL program. In G. Braine (Ed.), *Non-native educators in English language teaching* (pp. 127-144). Mahwah, NJ: Erlbaum.

Shank, G. D. (2002). *Qualitative research: A personal skills approach.* Upper Saddle River, NJ: Merrill Prentice Hall.

Smith, L. G., Downey, R. G., & Cox, K. S. (1999, June). *The international GTA problem: A new approach.* Seattle, WA: The Annual Forum of the Association for Institutional Research. (ERIC Document Reproduction Service No. ED433770)

Thomas, J. (1999). Voices from the periphery: Non-native teachers and issues of credibility. In G. Braine (Ed.), *Non- native educators in English language teaching* (pp. 5-12). Mahwah, NJ: Erlbaum.

Tollefson, J. W. (Ed.). (1995). *Power and inequality in language education.* New York: Cambridge University Press.

Tyler, A. (1992). Discourse structure and the perception of incoherence in international teaching assistants' spoken discourse. *TESOL Quarterly, 26*, 713-729.

Wen, W. P., & Clément, R. (2003). A Chinese conceptualization of willingness to communicate in ESL. *Language, Culture and Curriculum, 16*, 18-33.

Williams, J. (1992). Planning, discourse marking, and the comprehensibility of international teaching assistants. *TESOL Quarterly, 26*, 693-711.

Yook, E. L., & Albert, R. D. (1999). Perceptions of international teaching assistants: The interrelatedness of intercultural training, cognition, and emotion. *Communication Education, 48*, 1-17.

Yule, G., & Hoffman, P. (1990). Predicting success for international teaching assistants in a US university. *TESOL Quarterly, 24*, 227-243.

Yule, G., & Hoffman, P. (1993). Enlisting the help of US undergraduates in evaluating international teaching assistants. *TESOL Quarterly, 27*, 323-327.

Seonhee Cho, Ph.D., is an Assistant Professor of ESL/FL Education in the Department of Teaching and Learning at the Virginia Commonwealth University.

Appendix A
Interview Guide Questions

1. Could you tell me about yourself . . . such as academic background and work experience?

2. Tell me about your teaching experience as a graduate teaching assistant.
    a. What courses have you taught?
    b. What challenged you the most?
    c. What did you enjoy the most?
    d. How was your relationship with your students?
    e. How about with your relationship with your mentoring supervisor (or coordinator)?
    f. What strategies do you use to overcome the challenges?

3. Do you have anything else to tell me about your teaching experience?

Copyright © 2008, New Forums Press, Inc., P.O. Box 876, Stillwater, OK 74076. All Rights Reserved.

Chapter 6
International Teaching Assistants and Student Retention in the Sciences

Mary C. Wright, Joel Purkiss, Christopher O'Neal, & Constance E. Cook
University of Michigan

Concern about international teaching assistants (ITAs) is particularly acute in STEM fields because of high rates of undergraduate student attrition and the presence of large numbers of international graduate student teachers. With a quantitative analysis, we examine two primary research questions: (1) Even when ITAs are screened for language proficiency and receive extensive pedagogical training, are undergraduate students less satisfied with their international teachers than with their domestic teaching assistants? (2) Do ITAs affect undergraduate students' plans to stay in or leave the sciences, either positively or negatively? Although students are less satisfied with their ITAs in the sciences, we find no significant impact on grades, retention, or attrition. Based on these findings, we offer suggestions for teaching assistant development programs.

Recent moves in the South Dakota legislature to refund undergraduates' tuition if students documented that their instructors did not "speak English clearly and with good pronunciation" point to the challenges that international teaching assistants (ITAs) face in the American classroom (Gravois, 2005). Concern about the "ITA problem" is particularly acute in the STEM (science, technology, engineering and math) fields, where approximately half of the undergraduates who enter higher education with plans to major in the sciences switch to non-science majors before graduation (Seymour & Hewitt, 1997) and where international representation among graduate students is particularly high (Institute of International Education, 2006). Many universities have implemented ITA training programs, but even at universities with these programs, student complaints persist. The question of interest here is, in spite of undergraduate students' complaints, does ITAs' teaching affect students' persistence in their majors differently than that of domestic teaching assistants? This article contrasts research on student satisfaction with research on retention statistics, to better pinpoint the source of challenges ITAs and domestic TAs face in the classroom and to make programmatic suggestions for TA training.

Using course grades and final exam scores as measures, prior research has shown nonnative English-speaking TAs to be as effective in STEM classrooms as native English speakers if they are adequately prepared for teaching and are screened for language proficiency (Borjas, 2000; Jacobs & Friedman, 1988; Norris, 1991). Some research suggests that language screening improves ITAs' student ratings (Papajohn, 2006), but students' complaints about ITAs are well-documented (Davis, 1991; Rubin, 1992; Rubin & Smith, 1990; Smyrnious, 1995), and questions could be raised about the long-term impact of students' discontent on their decisions to abandon a STEM major. Therefore, an important question to be investigated is whether ITAs' teaching, even when they are well screened for language proficiency, has an impact on both student satisfaction in a course and on subsequent retention in the major.

Seymour and Hewitt (1997) found that undergraduates who have left the sciences infrequently attribute "language difficulty with foreign faculty or TAs" as a reason for their decision. Three percent of those who left indicated it was a factor in their switching decisions, while 30% labeled it "a concern." However, it may be that students do not fully understand the impact that a TA has on their learning. Indeed, other research has shown that TA instructional roles, particularly how TAs shape the lab climate, have a more significant impact on student retention than undergraduates realize (O'Neal, Wright, Cook, Perorazio & Purkiss, 2007). A quantitative analysis that controls for a number of other possible influences is needed to better understand the impact of ITAs on American classrooms.

Additionally, little research has looked at the opposite question: could an ITA's classroom presence benefit student learning? (Norris., [1991] is an important exception, finding that students in the sciences with nonnative English-speaking TAs had higher final course grades.) Additionally there is an extensive literature on the educational benefits of interactional diversity, or how college students' engagement with diverse peers can lead to greater intellectual and personal outcomes (Antonio, Chang, Hakuta, Kenny, Levin, & Milem, 2004; Gurin, 1999; Hu & Kuh, 2003; Milem, 2003). Even though much of the previous research on ITAs has focused on whether they are "as good" as native-English-speaking TAs, a more interesting question might examine whether the interactional diversity present in the instructional relationship leads to increased retention among undergraduates.

In this study, we primarily utilize a quantitative methodology that controls for many possible influences on students' choices of majors in order to better understand the impact of ITAs on undergraduate attrition in the STEM disciplines. We have two primary research questions: (1) Even when they are screened for language proficiency and receive extensive pedagogical training, are students less satisfied with ITAs? (2) Does ITAs' classroom presence affect, either positively or negatively, undergraduate students' plans to stay in or leave the sciences?

Institutional Context

This study takes place at a large Midwestern research university with a little over 2,000 TAs. In the science departments in this study, TAs account for over half (52-85%) of student contact hours.

All of the TAs in the three science departments studied here – biology, chemistry and physics – receive at least twenty hours of pedagogical training before or concurrent with their first teaching assignment. Much of this training happens within the department.

Additionally, rather than screen all international TAs for language proficiency, this university administers an oral English test only to those whose undergraduate degree program was not conducted in English. Therefore, in the following sections, we refer to "English-educated TAs" (i.e., educated in the U.S. or in international undergraduate institutions where English was the medium of instruction) and "non-English-educated TAs," or TAs who have passed an oral English language proficiency test but who were not educated in English.

Study Methodology

To determine the role of ITAs in undergraduate attrition from the sciences, in January 2004, we surveyed all undergraduates at a large, Midwestern university who had taken the seven gateway courses for prospective majors in chemistry, biology, and physics in Fall 2003. The survey asked students about their intention to major in the sciences (or have a career in the health sciences) before the class they had just taken, as well as after they had taken the course (i.e., when they took the survey). The complete survey is presented in the Appendix.

A web-based survey tool was used to create and distribute the survey. Because the survey tool allowed us to track individual responses, individuals' responses were paired with demographic data (sex, race/ethnicity, class, and course grade) obtained from the university registrar. Out of 3,656 undergraduate students surveyed, 2,669 students responded to the survey (a 73% response rate), and nearly half (47%) of students who responded to the survey also offered a qualitative response. Of the 2,669, most were first- and second-year students (2,102 or 78.8% of respondents). We focused our analysis on first- and second-year students only because they were not yet committed to a major. About half (46.7%) of these respondents were first-year students, and a small majority (53.3%) were sophomores. Nearly half (49.4%) were female, and only a small minority (10.2%) were under-represented non-Asian minorities.

A separate survey collected demographic data on the 113 TAs teaching in the sampled sections, as well as data on TAs' evaluation of their training. This survey is presented in the Appendix. Of the 113 TAs in our study, 80 (70.8%) were English-educated and 33 (29.2%) were non-English-educated.

Data Analysis

Our independent variable was the linguistic educational status of the TA, that is, was the TA's undergraduate degree from a program that utilized English as the medium of instruction?

In the regression models, we used the following control variables:
- The gender of the TA
- Was the TA an under-represented minority in the sciences?
- Was the TA a new graduate student?
- Was this the TA's first term of teaching?
- Did the TA report that she planned to pursue a faculty position, a proxy variable for the degree to which teaching related to the TA's future plans?
- Did the TA feel that the training prepared her well, in order to control for the perceived quality of a TA's training? (As noted above, all TAs received at least 20 hours of preparation.)
- Difficulty of the course, measured by average student grade
- Effects of the discipline or of different departmental training, as measured by the department associated with the course

Student Satisfaction

TA language background was a key factor that affected student satisfaction. On student ratings, undergraduates are asked to give their overall evaluation of their instructors.[1] English-educated TAs (4.12) scored significantly higher than their non-English-educated colleagues (3.77) on a rating scale of one (lowest) to five (highest). Of the non-English-educated TAs, those with more experience as TAs scored slightly higher than their less experienced colleagues (3.83 vs. 3.72) but the difference was not significant.

Eighteen TAs scored at or below the fifteenth percentile of students' ratings of all of the TAs in this study. Of those eighteen, fourteen (78%) were ITAs: eleven who were not English-educated and three who were educated abroad in English. In qualitative comments from the TA survey, three of these 18 poorly evaluated TAs noted that they did not feel confident in their teaching because of their struggles with classroom English language skills. For example, one illustrative quote notes, "Sometimes I feel difficult [sic] due to the language barrier." However, in spite of these struggles, the non-English-educated TAs felt that the instructional experience would help their professional

---

[1] The question asks students to respond to the question, "Overall, this is an effective instructor."

development: "It's a good practice for speaking English and for teaching. My aim is to join the academy in the future and this experience is necessary for me."

In the qualitative portion of the student survey, the number of students (79) commenting pejoratively on their TA's language facility was fairly small but it was the most frequent type of negative comment made about TAs. Qualitative comments describe the communication difficulties students experienced. For example, one white female sophomore noted,

> I had an extremely difficult time conversing with my TA. He spoke minimal English and thus could not understand what my group members or I were asking. He actually gave us incorrect information and had problems with troubleshooting.

Another female first-year student found that her TA "decreased my interest because it made me realize how a career in this area is kind of difficult when you're not fully able to understand a person in the same field (partially due to [not] knowing the same language)."

Student Retention

While it is clear that students were more dissatisfied with non-English-educated TAs, did this discontentment translate into a decision to leave the sciences? Across all TA sections, an average of 75% of students stayed interested or became even more interested in a science career, and 12% became less interested. (The remainder were disinterested in science to begin with and stayed that way over the course of the term.) In a simple bivariate analysis, there was no significant difference in the retention and attrition rates of undergraduate students between English-educated TAs and non-English-educated TAs (Table One).

In fact, in non-English-educated TAs' sections, more students reported plans to stay in or become a science major (a mean of 77.8% in non-English-educated TA sections vs. 74.0% in English-educated TA sections), although again, the difference is not statistically significant (t=0.907, p-value=0.366). Similarly, non-English-educated TAs had a *lower* rate of planned student attrition, but also not at a level of significance (mean difference=1.7%, t=-0.613, p-value=0.541). In sum, results suggest TAs with non-English-language background do not affect students' plans to major in the sciences.

Controlling for the TA and course characteristics listed above, a multivariate analysis of the relationship between TA English language background and STEM retention obtains similar findings. Results indicate that when controlling for other relevant factors, TAs' English-language background still has no significant effect on students' planned STEM retention or attrition. (Given a p-value > 0.10 in both cases, there is no convincing evidence of any effect.)

Only non-demographic variables had a significant effect on the outcome variables. Interestingly, the average student grade in the course was significantly and positively associated with retention. For attrition, there was also a small disciplinary effect, with the rate of attrition in physics TAs' sections being somewhat lower than in biology TAs' sections.

Discussion and Implications for TA Training

The results of this study echo Seymour and Hewitt's (1997) findings, although we find even less of an effect than their prior research. Although students express dissatisfaction with ITAs' communication abilities, ITAs do not have a significant impact on students' educational plans, compared to the effect native English-speaking TAs have. There are several possible explanations for this finding, with concomitant practical implications, some targeted to undergraduates and others to TAs.

First, some research indicates that stereotypes or lack of learner readiness to adapt to different communication styles leads many undergraduates to evaluate ITAs poorly (Oppenheim, 1996; Rubin, 1992; Rubin & Smith, 1990). In other words, it may be that undergraduates perceive that ITAs' communication styles have more of an impact on their learning than they actually do. Workshops or new student orientation units that address these misconceptions

Table 1. Bivariate Analysis of the Relationship between TAs' English-Language Background and Percentage of TAs' Students who Plan to Continue (Retention) or Leave (Attrition) a STEM Major

	RETENTION		ATTRITION	
	English-Educated TAs	Non-English-Educated TAs	English-Educated TAs	Non-English-Educated TAs
Number of TAs	*80*	*33*	*80*	*33*
Retention & Attrition	% of TAs' students planning to *continue* a STEM major		% of TAs' students planning to *discontinue* a STEM major	
	English-Educated TAs	Non-English-Educated TAs	English-Educated TAs	Non-English-Educated TAs
Mean*	74.0%	77.8%	12.5%	10.7%
(S.D.)	(21.6%)	(16.5%)	(15.3%)	(8.2%)
Median	75.8%	81.8%	10.0%	9.5%
Minimum	0.0%	33.3%	0%	0%
Maximum	100%	100%	100%	37.5%

* Retention % and attrition % do not sum to 100, because students who did not begin with plans for a STEM major were not included in the analysis.

may provide some helpful tools for undergraduates to better conceptualize their relationships to their ITAs. Additionally, engagement of undergraduates in the training of ITAs also can help broaden students' perceptions of their international instructors (Wright & Bogart, 2006).

Second, the findings on attrition/retention presented here highlight the continued need for language screening and professional development for TAs, as it may be the same training that accounts for the lack of significant attrition. However, the differences in student ratings between TAs educated in English

Table 2. Multivariate Analysis of the Relationship Between TA English-Language Background and STEM Retention or Attrition: Summary of Multiple Linear Regression Results.

	Retention[1]			Attrition[2]		
	Beta	SE	p-value	Beta	SE	p-value
TA CHARACTERISTICS						
TA's Primary Language of Undergrad Education (Non-English)	-.032	.062	.103	-.069	.043	.631
TA's Sex (female)	-.004	.044	.822	.104	.030	.350
TA's Race/Ethnicity (all others)	.019	.052	.969	-.016	.035	.902
Is the TA a First-Term Grad Student? (yes)	-.061	.044	.879	.062	.030	.583
Is this the TA's First Term as a TA? (yes)	.139	.048	.578	-.187	.033	.107
"My TA training prepared me well" rating by TA.	.200	.026	.223	.055	.018	.641
"I plan to pursue a faculty position" rating by TA.	-.094	.021	.091	.178	.014	.143
SUBJECT AND COURSE CHARACTERISTICS						
How hard is the course this TA taught? (avg. student grade)	.405	.112	.001**	-.018	.076	.882
Chemistry Course? (yes)[3]	.095	.058	.507	-.259	.039	.077
Physics Course? (yes)[3]	.239	.061	.086	-.516	.042	.000***
	$R^2=.225$ $Adj.R^2=.122$			$R^2=.204$ $Adj.R^2=.098$		

*** $p < 0.001$ ** $p < 0.01$ * $p < 0.05$

[1] If p-value≥0.05, no effect on retention can be assumed. When p-value<0.05, a positive *Beta* indicates *increasing* retention, while negative indicates *decreasing* retention.
[2] Likewise, if p-value≥0.05, no effect on attrition can be assumed. When p-value<0.05, positive *Beta* indicates *increasing* attrition, and negative indicates *decreasing* attrition.
[3] Biology Course is the excluded category.

and TAs not educated in English also point to the need for additional programs. Student ratings can have a significant impact on a graduate student's career, especially when they play such a key role in future TA appointment decisions and, often, a graduate student's application for a faculty position. Programs that may be of assistance include orientation programs that explicitly address effective classroom communication skills needed to teach a diverse student body, as well as ways to develop rapport with undergraduates. Micro teaching is one often-used tool for this objective; other workshop formats to enhance clarity and climate are offered in Ross and Dunphy's (2007) volume, *Strategies for Teaching Assistant and International Teaching Assistant Development*. (Ideas include workshops on analysis of effective TA presentations, student learning styles, and diversity awareness.) Additionally, early intervention structures, which solicit feedback from all TAs so that additional assistance can be targeted to those who are struggling, can offer support before an instructional problem becomes intractable.

Third, the findings presented here indicated that all TAs would benefit from training on student retention. With such close contact to their undergraduates, TAs can play a key role in helping to retain students, at both the departmental and university level. Sample workshops are offered by O'Neal, Wright, Cook, Perorazio, and Purkiss (2007), as well as Bolgiano and Horton (1993). Possible workshops presented in these articles include presentations of retention data and case studies that engage TAs in the role they can play to address the problem (especially their role in creating a positive lab climate), resources for TAs to introduce possible science careers to undergraduates, grading strategies to make expectations explicit, and ways to give effective feedback.

Finally, more research is needed on how interactional diversity plays out when the racial, ethnic or cultural differences are between the instructor and the student (rather than among students). This research shifts the frame of ITA scholarship away from the potential drawbacks toward the possible benefits of having an ITA. Although ITAs may not have a significant impact on retention, are there other ways that they might contribute to undergraduate education? As universities look to redesign the undergraduate experience to internationalize the curriculum and to provide students with a more global perspective, ITAs may be an overlooked resource to address these goals.

References

Antonio, A. L., Chang, M. J., Hakuta, K., Kenny, D. A., Levin, S., & Milem, F. M. (2004). Effects of racial diversity on complex thinking in college students. *Psychological Science, 15*(8), 507-510.

Bolgiano, C.F., & Horton, G.R. (1993). Effective use of trained teaching assistants in improving the retention of university students. *The Journal of Graduate Student Teaching Assistant Development 1*(2), 67-74.

Borjas, G. J. (2000). Foreign-born teaching assistants and the academic performance of undergraduates. *American Economic Review, 90*(2), 355-359.

Davis, W. (1991). International teaching assistants and cultural differences: Student evaluations of rapport, approachability, enthusiasm and fairness. In J. Nyquist, R. Abbott, D. Wulff, & J. Sprague (Eds.), *Preparing the professoriate of tomorrow to teach* (pp. 446-451). Dubuque, IA: Kendall Hunt.

Gravois, J. (2005, April 8). Teach impediment: When the student can't understand the instructor, who is to blame? *Chronicle of Higher Education*. Retrieved January 15, 2008 from http://chronicle.com/weekly/v51/i31/31a01001.htm

Gurin, P. (September, 1999). Expert report. "Gratz et al. v. Bollinger et al." No. 97-75321 (E. D. Mich.); "Grutter, et al. v. Bollinger, et al." No. 97-75928 (E. D. Mich.), *Equity & Excellence in Education, 32*(2), 36-62.

Hu, S., & Kuh, G.D. (May-June, 2003). Diversity experiences and college student learning and personal development. *Journal of College Student Development, 44*(3), 320-334.

Institute of International Education (2006). *Open doors*. Retrieved February 15, 2008 from http://opendoors.iienetwork.org/.

Jacobs, L.C., & Friedman, C.B. (1988). Student achievement under foreign teaching associates compared with native teaching associates. *Journal of Higher Education, 59*(5), 551-563.

Milem, J. (2003). The educational benefits of diversity. In M.J. Chang, D. Witt, J. Jones, & K. Hakuta (Eds.), *Compelling interest: Examining the evidence on racial dynamics in higher education* (pp. 126-169). Palo Alto, CA: Stanford University Press.

Norris, T. (1991). Nonnative English-speaking teaching assistants and student performance. *Research in Higher Education, 32*(4), 433-448.

O'Neal, C., Wright, M., Cook, C., Perorazio, T, & Purkiss, J. (2007). The impact of teaching assistants on student retention in the sciences: Lessons for TA training. *Journal of College Science Teaching, 36*(5), 24-29.

Oppenheim, N. (1996, April 8-13). *Undergraduates learning from nonnative English-speaking teaching assistants.* Paper presented at the Annual Meeting of the American Educational Research Association, New York, NY. (ERIC Document Reproduction Service No. ED 394418)

Papajohn, D. (2006) Student perceptions of the comprehensibility of international instructors. *Journal on Excellence in College Teaching, 17*(1&2), 97-121.

Ross, C., & Dunphy, J. (Eds.). (2007). *Strategies for teaching assistant development and international teaching assistant development: Beyond micro teaching.* San Francisco: Jossey-Bass.

Rubin, D. (1992). Nonlanguage factors affecting undergraduates' judgments of nonnative English-speaking teaching assistants. *Research in Higher Education, 33*, 511-531.

Rubin, D.L., & Smith, K.A. (1990). Effects of accent, ethnicity, and lecture topic on undergraduates' perceptions of nonnative English-speaking teaching assistants. *International Journal of Intercultural Relations, 14*, 337-353.

Seymour, E., & Hewitt, N.M. (1997). *Talking about leaving: Why undergraduates leave the sciences.* Boulder, CO: Westview Press.

Smyrnious, G. (1995). When it comes to my major, it matters if you are foreign or not. *Reading Improvement, 32*(4), 227-35.

Wright, M.C., & Bogart, P. (2006, October 12). *Mutual benefits: Developing intercultural learners and ITAs.* Paper presented at the Annual Conference of the Professional & Organizational Development Network, Portland, OR.

Mary C. Wright is an Assistant Research Scientist and an Assistant Director at the Center for Research on Learning in Ann Arbor. She received her Ph.D. in Sociology and an M.A. from the Center for the Study of Higher and Postsecondary Education, both at the University of Michigan.

Joel Purkiss is the Associate Director of Curriculum Evaluation at the University of Michigan Medical School and a Lecturer for the Department of Sociology. He has a Ph.D. in Sociology from the University of Michigan, Ann Arbor.

Christopher O'Neal an Assistant Director at the Center for Research on Learning and Teaching in Ann Arbor. He received his Ph.D. in Ecology from the University of Michigan in 2001.

Constance E. Cook serves as the Associate Vice Provost at the University of Michigan, and also Executive Director of the Center for Research on Learning and Teaching. She is Clinical Professor in the School of Education.

Correspondence concerning this article should be addressed to Mary C. Wright, who is at the Center for Research on Learning and Teaching, University of Michigan, 1071 Palmer Commons, Ann Arbor, Michigan, 48109. Email may be sent to mcwright@umich.edu.

Appendix

Undergraduate Survey

Please answer the following questions about your experience as a student in [course] in the 2003 Fall Term. The survey will take less than five minutes and all individuals' answers will be confidential.

1. Please indicate your agreement with the following statements:

	Definitely not	Probably not	Unsure	Probably so	Definitely so
a. BEFORE the Fall 2003 term, I planned to major in science, engineering or math.					
b. As of NOW, I plan to major in science, engineering or math.					
c. BEFORE the Fall 2003 term, I planned to pursue a career in a health field (such as medicine or nursing).					
d. As of NOW, I plan to pursue a career in a health field.					
e. For the Winter 2004 term, I plan to enroll in a science, engineering or math course.					
f. After the Winter 2004 term, I plan to continue enrolling in science, engineering or math courses.					

2. How have the following factors influenced your choice of major and/or career?

	Decreased my interest in science career	No influence	Increased my interest in science career
a. The professor for this science course			
b. The Graduate Student Instructor (TA) for this course			
c. The environment or climate of the lecture for this course			
d. The environment or climate of this lab section			
e. My grade in this science course			
f. My grades in math			
g. Learning more about a career or major outside of science			
h. Other (please specify in the box below)			

(Continued on next page.)

Appendix (continued).

4. If your TA increased or decreased your interest in a science career or major, please explain why.

5. Any other comments?

TA Survey

Please answer the following questions about your experience as a Graduate Student Instructor (TA) in the 2003 Fall Term. The survey will take less than two minutes and all individuals' answers will be confidential.

1. My TA training at the [University] prepared me well for teaching.

Strongly Disagree	Disagree	Neutral	Agree	Strongly Agree

Please explain:

2. I feel confident about my teaching ability.

Strongly Disagree	Disagree	Neutral	Agree	Strongly Agree

Please explain:

3. I believe that my TA experience will be helpful to me in my future career.

Strongly Disagree	Disagree	Neutral	Agree	Strongly Agree

Please explain:

4. I plan to become a faculty member when I complete my [University] graduate degree.

Strongly Disagree	Disagree	Neutral	Agree	Strongly Agree

Please explain:

5. I began graduate school at [the University] in (term/year):

Chapter 7
Integrating Teaching & Technology: Facilitating Student-Centered Teaching for Graduate Students at a Research University

Neeraja Aravamudan, Susanna Calkins, Mary Schuller, & Dreana Rubel
Northwestern University

This study focuses on a graduate student Teaching and Learning with Technology program (TLTP) designed for teaching assistants and future faculty members at a private research-intensive university located in the Midwest. We investigate how TLTP participants conceived of the relationship between teaching, technology and student learning. In particular, this study investigates the ways that graduate students experience teaching, learning, and technology as interrelated practices, and how these perceptions can be developed through an intensive teaching, learning, and technology program. We offer a model to better understand how teaching, learning and technology interact along two dimensions: the approach to teaching dimension (in which the focus of instruction is teacher-centered or student-centered) and the technology usage dimension (in which the focus of technology is either content-oriented or process-oriented).

Introduction

As technology continues to facilitate change in higher education (Albright, 1998; Baldwin, 1998), and as college students increasingly anticipate technology in the classroom (McEuen, 2001), the critical nexus between technology, teaching, and learning has received great attention by educators (Baylor & Ritchie, 2002; Gandolfo, 1998). The extent to which technology accentuates, promotes, or enhances student learning has been a particular point of interest given the larger paradigm shift that has overtaken institutions in recent decades: the move from the idea that colleges exist to provide instruction (the instruction paradigm) to the idea that colleges exist to produce learning (the learning paradigm) (Albright, 1998; Barr & Tagg, 1995). This paradigm shift corresponds with recent research about teaching beliefs held by academics in higher education. This research suggests that there are two broad orientations towards teaching and learning: teacher-centered/content-oriented teaching, which emphasizes the transmission of content and a surface approach to student learning, and student-centered/learner-oriented teaching, which emphasizes students' deeper approaches to learning and promoting conceptual change (Kember, 1997; Prosser & Trigwell, 1999; Trigwell & Prosser, 2004).

This study focuses on a graduate student Teaching and Learning with Technology program (TLTP) designed for teaching assistants and future faculty members at a private research-intensive university located in the Midwest. We sought to investigate how TLTP participants conceive of the relationship between teaching, technology, and student learning. In particular, this study investigates the ways that graduate students experience teaching, learning, and technology as interrelated practices. We conducted the study to provide insight into how graduate students perceive the relationship and how their perceptions can be developed through an intensive teaching, learning, and technology program. We offer a model to better understand how teaching, learning and technology interact along two dimensions: the approach to teaching dimension (in which the focus of instruction is teacher centered or student centered) and the technology usage dimension (in which the focus of technology is either content oriented or process-oriented).

Technology and the Learning Paradigm

The transformative nature of technology in teaching and learning is often touted in the literature (Surry & Land, 2000; Thiele, Allen, & Stucky, 1999). At the same time, many researchers echo the proposition that technology in itself can not *transform* teaching and learning (Hall, 2002), even though technologies such as the Internet, multi-media, distance education, and on-line learning environments may *encourage* student-focused approaches to teaching. Even the best technology tools can not supplant good teaching or a well-designed course (Albright, 1998; Ip & Naidu, 2001; Katz, 2003; Lu, Yu, & Liu, 2003; Richardson, 2003). Instructors need to be taught *how* to integrate technology into their teaching so that their students are meaningfully engaged and able to learn more fully (Hokanson & Hooper, 2004: 14).

In addition, there are many challenges to the effective integration of technology into a well-designed course. While traditional technologies (e.g. overhead projectors, videos, slides) are regularly utilized in today's college classrooms, emerging and innovative instructional technologies have been adopted more slowly by educators (Cooley & Johnston, 2001). Faculty members often lack the time to experiment with new technologies or to seek training in instructional technology (Chizmar & Williams, 2001). Furthermore, faculty members' interest in developing classroom technologies is often inhibited by a lack of financial incentives such as course release time, monetary awards, software and hardware support, and credit towards salary, promotion, and tenure (Chizmar

& Williams, 2001). On the other hand, as Gibbs, Major, and Wright (2003) found, faculty members are more motivated to use instructional technologies in their teaching when they have sufficient time, financial incentives, and formal reward and support structures. Institutional support provided by faculty development programs further encourage faculty acceptance of technology in teaching and learning settings (Fleming, Lipscomb, Light & Nielsen, 2004).

Technology and Graduate Student Development

How graduate students and teaching assistants elect to use traditional and emerging instructional technologies has yet to be addressed in a systematic way. Albright (1998) found that faculty attitudes towards technology influence how TAs decide to adopt technology for use in the classroom, which can have a deep impact if faculty members are not convinced that technology will enhance their teaching. This contention fits with other studies that have shown that the attitudes that faculty take towards their own teaching can deeply impact the practices of their TAs (Austin, 2002; Chism & Warner, 1987; Marincovich, Prostko & Stout, 1988; Nyquist, Abbott, Wulff, & Sprague, 1991).

Even more significantly, there is often a lack of attention paid to graduate teaching—let alone teaching with technology—that can impede the professional development of graduate students and TAs (Hardré, 2005; Marincovich, Prostko, & Stout, 1998; Tice, Gaff, & Pruitt-Logan, 1998). As such, it is vital for graduate students, especially TAs and future faculty members, to be supported at an institutional level through programs like the graduate TLTP discussed in this study. These programs assist them in their endeavor towards integrating technology into their course design, and ultimately to engage them in conversations about teaching and learning. These conversations, when properly supported and conducted, develop their concepts of teaching towards a more learner-centered model.

Methods & Procedures

TLTP Program Design

In a partnership, the university's Teaching and Learning Center (TLC) and Center for Academic Technologies (AT) developed and taught a six-week teaching and learning with technology program (TLTP) for graduate students. The TLTP was developed in response to several emerging needs within the graduate student population. First, graduate students felt ill-prepared as TAs and as future faculty to design effective learning environments using technology. In particular, graduate students expressed a lack of familiarity with new technologies, including the new distributed learning tools such as the course management system (CMS) and other software applications offered on our campus. Second, many graduate students have recognized that mastering technological skills can provide them with a competitive advantage in their employment search and future careers. Third, TAs are increasingly expected by senior faculty members to manage the instructional technology components of their classes, a trend common on many campuses (Albright, 1998). Fourth, graduate students often receive little to no training on teaching at the college level without the assistance of specialized training programs designed for TAs, such as those provided by the campus TLC (Chism & Warner, 1987; Marincovich et.al. (1998); Nyquist & Sprague, 1998; Nyquist & Wulff, 1996).

Drawing on Chickering & Gamson's (1987) seven principles for good practice in undergraduate education and Bloom's (1956) Taxonomy of Educational Objectives, the program provides graduate students with an opportunity to develop student-centered approaches to teaching and to create a course or section that integrates technology—primarily the university's CMS—into the course design. The program's focus on the capabilities of CMS is in keeping with the emerging perspective that CMS offer a crucial development in the evolution of the academy, by promoting access to both instruction and student learning (Katz, 2003; Lu, Yu & Liu, 2003). The program was designed to facilitate the critical and reflective use of technology to support teaching and learning, and to challenge and broaden the students' own conceptions of teaching and learning. Thus, in the program, students are introduced not only to teaching with technology, but also to teaching and learning in general.

During the TLTP, facilitators model a blended course—a course that uses both on-line and face-to-face interactions—by using both in-class and online assignments so that participants could design a blended course of their own. Participants were expected to attend all program sessions, read assigned materials, submit critical reflections, participate in on-line and in-class discussion sections, complete several case studies outside of class, provide regular feedback using surveys, and design a lesson or component of a course. The original five-week series of 150-minute sessions roughly followed the course design process. By the end of the program, students were expected to develop learning objectives for a lesson, utilize learner-centered instructional methods, align these methods with their original objectives, incorporate appropriate instructional technologies throughout their lesson design, create an assessment plan appropriate for their learning objectives; and evaluate the effectiveness of their design in achieving their lesson outcomes.

In 2005, after looking at the participant feedback and our own experience as instructors, we realized that in trying to ensure that we provided participants with a clear introduction to teaching and learning, we had not clearly made the connection between technology and teaching. Specifically, we wanted participants to leave the program with not only a stronger awareness of the range of technology tools but also with a clearer understanding of when (or if) to use technology in specific learning contexts to achieve particular objectives. To achieve this aim, we modified our program design in 2005 to include more explicit discussions of why we used technology when we did during our workshops. We also consistently asked our participants to consider not only *what* technology tool they would use to achieve an objective, but *why* that particular tool was appropriate. We explained our own decision-making process when we opted to integrate technology into our program, to model the process for our students.

Study Design

Participants

In 2003, 2004, and 2005, 32 graduate students (9, 13, and 10 respectively) participated in the program. Of these 32 participants, 19 were women (5, 7, and 7 respectively) and 13 were men (4, 6, 3). Participants represented a range of schools and disciplines, including the College of Arts and Sciences (Chemistry, English, Geology, Foreign Languages, Geology, History/Religion, Liberal Studies, Linguistics, Mathematics, Neuroscience, Psychology, Sociology), and the Schools of Engineering (Chemical/Biological and Civil/Mechanical Engineering), Communications (Communication Studies, Media/Technology/Society, and Theatre); Business (Management/Organizations) and Music. Program participants reported varied levels of prior teaching experience before participating in the program. Several reported that they had less than one year of teaching experience or had been a teaching assistant for a year or less. Others reported more significant teaching experience, whether serving as a TA for multiple terms, facilitating teaching and learning workshops, or teaching their own courses. While we drew some illustrative data from all three years to demonstrate the evolution of our program and methodology, we focused our study on our most recent cohort of ten participants (2004-2005).

Interviews

The current study evolved from pilot data we collected during the first two years of the program (2003 & 2004), which helped us recognize the need to analyze the intersection between technology and teaching. The interviews we conducted were semi-structured, using both open and closed-ended questions, and lasted approximately 25-35 minutes. The interviews were designed to elicit how participants understood and approached teaching; to probe how participants viewed the connections among technology, teaching, and learning; to assess the program's effectiveness; and to gauge participant satisfaction. The focus of our questions was to gauge the program's effect on *how* participants *experience* and *use* technology in their teaching. In particular, we wanted to see if participants would move away from thinking of "technology" as something to add to a course to thinking of teaching with technology as a process intimately tied to specific learning contexts. The interviews were fully audio-taped and transcribed.

In the pre- and post- interviews, we asked participants to consider the relationship between teaching and technology. Participants described what they considered to be "good" and "bad" uses of technology, and explained how they had used or hoped to use technology in their teaching. Participants were also asked to respond to two case studies concerning the use of technology in teaching. The case studies were the same in both the pre- and post- interviews so that we could track how participants' made decisions about the use of technology in teaching and whether those decisions changed before and after the program. In the first case, participants were asked to imagine that they were teaching a large introductory course comprised of majors and non-majors and students ranging from freshmen to seniors. Participants were then asked to describe how they would use technology, if at all, when they realized after a few classes that about half the students seemed very bored with the class while the other half seemed very interested. In the second case, participants were asked to suppose that they were teaching a small, upper-level seminar, required for majors, with large amounts of reading. Participants were asked to explain how they would incorporate technology into the class, if they chose to do so, and why they would use that technology and approach.

In pairs, the four of us separately coded every relevant item in the 2005 data by focusing on participant responses to questions related to technology and teaching. Two of us were involved in implementing the TLTP, and 2 of us were not. We focused our analysis on the types of technology that our participants did or would use in the classroom, such as email, discussion boards, on-line surveys & quizzes, and the reasons and context for why a specific technology would be utilized (e.g. record keeping, to get feedback, or to gauge student interest). Three of us then coded each participant as teacher-centered or learner-centered, by following criteria for each orientation well-established in literature (Kember, 1997, Prosser & Trigwell, 1999). Any variation among coders was discussed until we reached consensus.

Results

Motivation for Participation

Over all three years, participants indicated a number of reasons for their interest in participating in the program. The categories of responses were identified from the following question, "What made you interested in signing up?" The categories included: (1) career advancement (assisting them in a future job search); (2) the development of teaching with technology skills; (3) the development of technology skills (without mentioning teaching explicitly); (4) the development of teaching skills (without mentioning technology explicitly); and (5) inherent interest and the opportunity for peer feedback. In 2005, four of the ten participants explicitly indicated that developing their technology skills was their primary reason for participating in the program. The remaining categories were equally distributed. Two participants identified career advancement, two identified the development of teaching with technology skills, and two more emphasized the development of teaching skills as the reason they had sought out the program.

Experience of Teaching, Learning, and Technology

The analysis of our 2005 participant data disclosed a range in how our participants experienced the relationship of teaching and technology with respect to student learning. We found a wide range in how our participants could envision the use of technology in teaching. Some of these approaches could be characterized as teacher-focused/content-oriented with an emphasis on information transmission, while other approaches could be viewed as student-centered/learner-oriented with an emphasis on conceptual change (Kember, 1997; Prosser & Trigwell, 1999; Trigwell & Prosser, 2004).

Intersecting with these two broad orientations to teaching and learning, we also saw a range in how instructors sought to use technology in their courses. On one end of this technology usage continuum we placed less sophisticated content-oriented approaches that used technology mainly to add content to the course or to improve organization and administration; on the other end we placed more sophisticated process-oriented approaches that used technology to promote interaction with material and/or other students. This framework illustrates that technology does not inherently increase student engagement or learning, but that it is *how technology is used in particular learning contexts* that matters most (See Figure 1 below).

To test the usefulness of our model and to measure the effectiveness of

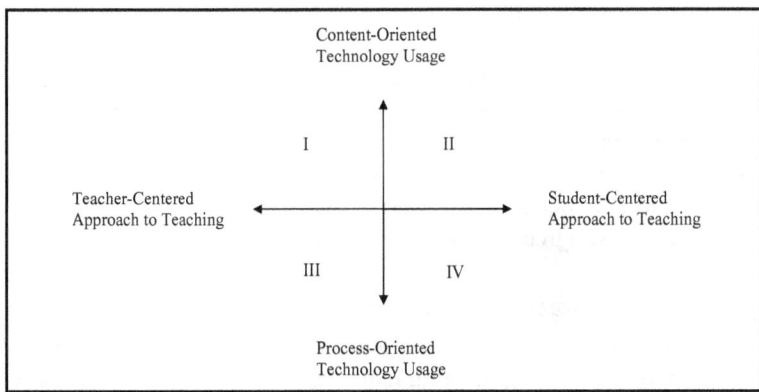

Figure 1: A Model of Teaching & Learning with Technology

our program, we used the above framework to place participants on the two continuums before and after the program. We did not look to place participants at specific points along the continuums but rather to group them by quadrants.

Teacher-Centered/Content-Oriented Approaches to Teaching with Technology

In the teacher-centered/content-oriented quadrant, we found two instructors who initially understood technology in teaching merely as a means to improve course efficiency and to keep the class generally organized. We characterized these instructors as teacher-centered in their conception of teaching who also used technology in only a very basic, content-oriented, way. By using online tools to provide students with easier access to course documents and grades, these instructors were able to reduce in-class time spent on administrative tasks. They used email to improve communication outside of class and the CMS to provide access to additional course materials, such as websites or journal articles. These instructors did not seek to integrate these materials into course objectives, assignments or assessments, or to directly engage the students. For example, in her pre-program interview, a Civil Engineering graduate student explained how the CMS allowed her to be more efficient in what she covered in class:

> I think [technology offers] a fast and easy way to communicate like that's one thing. But now, I don't have many materials [to bring to class]. I want to cover a lot of material like text books…but not every book gives every thing perfectly. So, I say…the way you can do it, you can have many references and now there are so many web sites and everything. So, I think I can cover a lot, I can discuss a lot, but that time you can just use the Blackboard [CMS].

The other graduate student spoke favorably of a professor who relied heavily on a CMS in supplying questions and information about assignments to the class. As she explained:

> I think that what was helpful that she [the former instructor] did and I see myself start doing it, she put basic questions out there; the different chapters and then she gave some information also about the readings. I think it's almost like giving Cliff's notes except through computer. She hit some of the high points that people should pick out of those readings and then ask questions about that section whether we agree with her view or not.

While these instructors seem to appreciate how technology allows the class to cover and access more material, they did not view technology as a means for supporting or transforming learning. Instead, technology was considered a means to focus on basic administrative tasks. They are teacher-centered, emphasizing coverage of material with little to no acknowledgment of where the students are in their own learning process. The emphasis is on conveying information versus interacting with the students in a meaningful way.

Teacher-Centered/Process-Oriented Approaches to Teaching with Technology

Other instructors used technology to promote student interaction with course content or the instructor, but did not look to ensure that this interaction led to deeper understanding which is why we shifted these instructors on the technology usage continuum but not the approaches to teaching continuum. For example, several instructors used video clips to spark student interest in the material or required that students respond on a discussion board to ensure that they are doing the reading. When asked how she would use technology in an upper-level class with lots of reading, a Communication Studies graduate student said:

> …I would still use technology in terms of grade distribution; keeping track of grades, keeping track of attendance, using emails sometimes as a tool to send documents or material. …I may use something like email where I would send them paper that has the themes or ideas or the things that I want them to be thinking about for each of the meetings. I tell them 'come prepared to discuss these ideas; jot some ideas down or think about this before class and expect to be participating in a discussion for the whole class time.'

While this participant still uses the CMS for administrative tasks, she wants to do more than to simply provide additional information to students, by seeking to use technology to spark student thinking about the material. Yet, she is still teacher-centered, because she is not looking for ways to let students guide their own learning, nor is there any indication that she is trying to promote conceptual change in her students. Instead technology is a tool to ease the teacher's burden of communicating information and ideas to the students.

Even though these instructors used fairly sophisticated types of technologies, such as online surveys and quizzes, their intention was to check interest in particular course topics or readings, rather than to ascertain how well the students were learning the material. One instructor in our study, a second Communication Studies graduate student, did seem to understand the concept of course design and sought to use technology to support her course objectives and to improve her teaching. She states:

> I think that technology is really a means, just a means, for … more effective teaching. I think it becomes a problem when people see it as an end and just want to use it for the sake of using it and don't really have end goal—teaching

end goal and the learning end goal in mind. So, I see technology as a means to better teaching.

In the same interview, she explained that in an upper-level class with a large amount of required reading, technology could be a means to improve communication between teacher and student:

> I'll ask the students prior to the class to sort of submit their notes on the readings for that week electronically in class and I would collate them along with my notes and sort of chain them together to show ... where the students were on base and where they're off base. And then work that way in a seminar, work through the notes with these upper level students to explain the reading better. That would give me a sense of what they know and what they don't know or what they are understanding and what they are not understanding and hopefully insure that they cover the material that needs to be covered and give them the understanding.

In her perspective, technology could serve as a useful means to gather feedback from students in order to improve her teaching methods (as opposed to explicitly improving their learning). Although she advocates the use of technology to improve communication between instructor and student, her approach is still teacher-centered because her intention is to improve the transmission of information from the teacher to the student.

Student-Centered/Content-Oriented Approaches to Teaching with Technology

On the other hand, several instructors demonstrated a fairly strong tendency towards student-centered teaching although again there was a gradation in how and why technology was employed. For example, one instructor, a third Communications graduate student, expressed an interest in improving learning but did not connect her use of technology to this interest. While she generally displayed a keen interest in developing their students' critical thinking skills, which is why we characterized her as student-centered/content-oriented, she employed fairly low levels of technology that focused on course administration, such as posting numerous links and articles, without integrating the technology into assignments or assessments. As she explained:

> One of the assignments that the students have been expected to participate in is in -class debate where half the class is on one side of gun control and the other half of the class is on the [other] side. In order to work together, we need to communicate by email such that ten people on one side of the debate know what they are talking about. So, in order to facilitate discussion outside of class, we set up an email list where we can exchange ideas and then at some point they have to communicate some of those to the other sides.

She is very student-centered, clearly wanting the students to take ownership of their own learning. Yet, she still uses technology for only basic tasks, rather than to support or complement her student-centered approach to teaching. It is as if the use of technology and teaching are disconnected practices, rather than interdependent and linked activities that could facilitate or enhance student learning.

Student-Centered/Process-Oriented Approaches to Teaching with Technology

Other instructors used technology to improve learning by encouraging interaction among students. To promote such interaction, they used discussion boards in which students question each other about assigned readings, had students interact with online simulations, or used online surveys to gauge student learning. For example, when a graduate student in the social sciences was asked what impact the program has had on his current or future teaching, he stated:

> I think that one of the things I'm going to be doing is using [a] more interactive style not just using like a web site as a place to offer students information but hopefully get the students to interact with each other and with me over the web and using that as another media of communication.

Later in the interview, when asked to explain an effective use of technology, he said:

> This [technology] is sort of to make available to students, especially materials that may not be generally available. But also to encourage collaborative learning, cooperative learning by getting students online to produce work and then talk about their work in a sort of out of the classroom context with other students.

He rejected the idea that technology in teaching consists mainly of adding content to a course, preferring instead to use technology as a way to let students engage in each others' work and the material outside of class. He focused instead on letting participants interact with the material and each other, beyond simply reading a text online or reproducing information that he has presented in class. Similarly, another Engineering graduate student explained:

> I think good uses [of technology] are trying to create a setup where it's beneficial to the students; it promotes more discussion, it promotes more interest in learning. Setting up some sort of extra motivations for the class in terms of like different articles to read or different activities that might help benefit learning but not necessarily impact on the grade.

This participant is clearly student-centered in the way that his attention is focused on the students' learning rather than achieving his own ends as a teacher. His use of technology centers around motivating students to engage with the material and helping students understand the process of problem-solving rather than just the mechanics of solving equations.

Two instructors displayed a fairly sophisticated approach to using teaching to support student-centered learning objectives. They employed strategies that ranged from having students create websites that synthesize online research they have conducted independently or in groups, to using collaborative tools (e.g. track changes in a word processing program), to having students engage in peer feedback. When asked about the relationship between technology and teaching after participating in the program, one Engineering graduate student explained how technology can promote student-centered teaching and student learning:

> I think some good examples are examples that facilitate discussion; and make it easier for students to collaborate and to expand their learning outside of class; anything that helps sort of guide students' learning and kind of give them that sort of first push and help them develop their interest in the subject is a good example of teaching as well.

The emphasis is on helping students develop independent interests and to serve as a guide in the process rather than directing students' learning.

Similarly, a History graduate student described the relationship between technology and teaching as a complementary relationship:

> I would describe.... technology [as] hopefully complementing teaching and learning. So that as I said in the beginning that you are to make sure that the goals and objectives are closely aligned with technology....

In describing the range of participants in terms of both their approaches to learning and their orientation to technology usage, we can better explain how technology and teaching intersect. To measure the effectiveness of teaching with technology programs in training graduate students (or others) to teach, we cannot only examine how participants' conceptions of teaching and learning change. As shown above, participants may shift to a more student-centered approach to teaching without a corresponding shift in their understanding of how technology usage can be used to support such learner-centered approaches. Our program looks to not only cause a shift in participants' approaches to teaching but also their orientations to technology usage. It is this distinction that we looked to address in our latest offering of this program. The following section reveals initial results from our analysis.

Change in Participants

Pre-participation and post-participation interviews were conducted for 9 of the 10 individuals in the program. Using the methodology described above, we determined that 7 of our participants could be characterized as teacher-focused and 2 as student-centered at the outset of the program. Of those 7 teacher-centered participants, 6 conceived of using technology in teaching primarily for basic administrative tasks and low-level interaction with course material. The 2 participants we categorized as student-focused also used technology primarily for course upkeep and administration, although they viewed technology as potentially a way to promote student learning.

In the post program interviews, we characterized 3 participants as teacher-focused and 6 participants as learner-focused. Of those 6, all the participants conceived of technology as a means to promote interaction among students and as a means of supporting learning objectives. Of the 3 participants characterized as teacher-focused in their orientation, none of them viewed technology as simply a tool to promote classroom efficiency, but rather as a means to gain feedback from students about their teaching. We found that 4 of our participants moved from teacher-centered to student-centered approaches to teaching, which we found to be a promising indicator of the success of our program.

Table 1 below provides a summary of the changes described above, and visually depicts that the program did have an impact on participants across both continuums. From the table we can see participants shifted not only from a teacher-centered to a student-centered approach to teaching but also from content-oriented to process-oriented focus on technology usage. Given the small sample size, we recognize these findings are not generalizable about the program's effectiveness, but we wanted to use this preliminary data to illustrate how our model can be used to measure change in participants in teaching with technology programs.

Discussion & Implications

The goal of our study was not to measure program effectiveness, but rather to understand how our participants' conceived of the relationship between teaching, learning, and technology, and how those conceptions could be developed and enhanced. The illustrative nature of the categories help us de-

Table 1: Overall Participant Change

	Pre-Program	Post-Program
I: Teacher-Centered/Content-Oriented	6	
II: Teacher-Centered/Process-Oriented	1	3
III: Student-Centered/Content-Oriented	2	
IV: Student-Centered/Process-Oriented		6

termine how program participants initially understand the relationship between teaching, student learning, and technology, and how they might develop their understanding of all three by the end of the program.

We offer this framework as both a descriptive model and normative tool. We suggest that while many graduate instructors may initially take a teacher-focused, content-oriented approach to teaching, in which technology is viewed as administrative tool, they can be encouraged to move to a student-centered approach to teaching in which technology is integrated into teaching as a means to facilitate student learning and to promote conceptual change. Indeed, recent research shows a correlation between instructor approaches to teaching and student approaches to learning, so that teacher-focused teaching (information transmission) correlates with students' surface approaches to learning, and learner-focused teaching (promoting conceptual change) correlates with deeper approaches to learning. (Gow & Kember 1993; Kember & Gow, 1994; Light, 2004; Prosser & Trigwell, 1999).

While our data suggest important interactions among technology, teaching, and student learning, our findings are preliminary. Nevertheless, we believe this framework provides a meaningful way of capturing variation in how graduate instructors conceive of the relationship among teaching, learning, and technology. Our study suggests important differences between using technology to support teacher-centered goals and using it to support student-centered goals.

We hope this model will prove useful to developers and instructors in providing a more nuanced way to think about teaching with technology. Subsequent efforts to train instructors on using technology to teach can use this model as a framework for designing their own programs, helping participants shift from thinking of technology as an end in itself to thinking of technology as a means to promote deep learning. Ultimately, this framework could help evaluate the success of other Teaching, Learning, and Technology programs similar to our own.

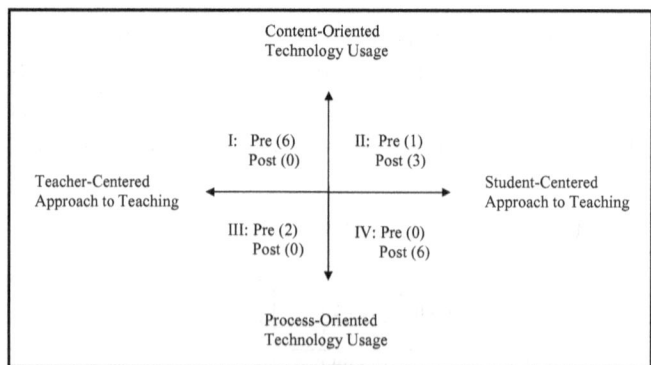

Figure 2: Overall Participant Change

While our research is suggestive, there is clearly room for deeper understanding. Future studies need to more clearly distinguish between how people think about teaching, learning and technology and the actual strategies they use in their teaching to accomplish these aims. Someone may conceive of using technology in a particular way, but use an approach that does not correlate with this conception. Articulating these variations can help us better understand how technology can be used and misused, and may provide stronger guidelines for others looking to provide instructors with a framework beyond 'Technology as Tool.'

References

Akerlind, G.S. (2003). Growing and developing as a university teacher: Variation in meaning. *Studies in Higher Education, 28*(4), 375-390.

Albright, M.J. (1998). Technology and TA training. In M. Marincovich, J. Prosko, F. Stout (Eds). *The professional development of graduate teaching assistants* (pp. 195-212). Bolton, MA: Anker.

Austin, A.E. (2002). Preparing the next generation of faculty. Graduate school as socialization to the academic career. *Journal of Higher Education, 73*(1), 94-122.

Baldwin, R. G. (1998). Technology's impact on faculty life and work. In K. H. Gillespie (Ed.), *New directions for teaching and learning: No. 76. The impact of technology on faculty development, life, and work* (pp. 7-21). San Francisco: Jossey-Bass.

Barr, R.B. & Tagg, J. (1995, November-December). From teaching to learning; a new paradigm for undergraduate education. *Change Magazine*, 13-25.

Baylor, A.L & Ritchie, D. (2002). What factors facilitate teacher skill, teacher morale, and perceived student learning in technology-using classrooms? *Computers and Education, 39*, 395-414.

Biggs, J. (1987). *Student approaches to learning and studying*. Melbourne: Australian Council for Educational Research.

Bloom, B. S. (1956). Taxonomy of educational objectives: The classification of educational goals. In B. S. Bloom (Ed.), *Handbook I: Cognitive domain*. White Plains, NY: Longman.

Chickering, A. W., & Gamson, Z.F. (1987). Seven principles for good practice in undergraduate education. *AAHE bulletin, 39*(7), 3-7.

Chism, N. & Warner, S.B. (1987). Institutional responsibilities and responses in the employment and education of teaching assistants. Columbus: The Ohio State University.

Chizmar, J.F. & Williams, D.B. (2001). What do faculty want? *Educause Quarterly, 1*, 18-24.

Cooley, N. & Johnston, M. (2001). Professional development: The single most important IT challenge in the United States. *Journal of Faculty Development, 18*(1), 35-41.

Fleming, V.M., Lipscomb, S., Light, G., & Nielsen, B. (2004). Teaching for learning with technology: A faculty development initiative at a research university. *Estudios Sobre Educacion, 7*, 7-20.

Gandolfo, A. (1998). Brave new world? The challenge of technology to time-honored pedagogies and traditional structures. In K. H. Gillespie (Ed.), *New directions for teaching and learning: No. 76. The impact of technology on faculty development, life, and work* (pp. 23-38). San Francisco: Jossey-Bass.

Gow, L. & Kember, D. (1993). Conceptions of teaching and their relationship to student learning. *British Journal of Educational Psychology, 63,* 20-33.

Gibbs, J. E., Major, C.H., & Wright, V.H. (2003). Faculty perception of the costs and benefits of instructional technology: Implications for faculty work. *Journal of Faculty Development, 19*(2), 77-88.

Hall, R. (2002). Aligning learning, teaching and assessment using the web: An evaluation of pedagogic approaches. *British Journal of Educational Technology, 33*(2), 149-158.

Hardré, P. L. (2005). Instructional design as a professional development tool-of-choice for graduate teaching assistants. *Innovative Higher Education, 30*(3), 163-173.

Ho, A. (2000). A conceptual change approach to staff development: A model for programme design. *International Journal for Academic Development, 5*(1), 30-41

Hokanson, B. & Hooper, S. (2004, November-December). Levels of teaching: A taxonomy for instructional design. *Educational Technology,* 14-22.

Katz, R. N. (2003). Balancing technology and tradition: The example of course management systems. *Educause, 4,* 48-59.

Kember, D. (1997). A reconceptualisation of the research into university academics' conceptions of teaching. *Learning and Instruction, 7*(3), 255-275.

Kember, D. & Kwan, K.P. (2000). Lecturers' approaches to teaching and their relationship to conceptions of good teaching. *Instructional Science, 28,* 469-490.

Light, G. & Cox R. (2001). *Learning and teaching in higher education: The reflective professional.* London: Paul Chapman.

Lu, J., Yu, C.S., & Liu, C. (2003). Learning style, learning patterns, and learning performance in a WebCT-based MIS course. *Information & Management, 40,* 497-507.

Marincovich, M., Prostko, J. & Stout, F. (1998). *The professional development of graduate teaching assistants.* Bolton, MA: Anker.

Marton, F. & Booth, S. (1997). *Learning and awareness.* Mahwah, NJ: Lawrence Erlbaum.

McEuen, S. F. (2001). How fluent with information technology are our students? A survey of students from Southwestern University explored how FIT they see themselves. *Educause Quarterly, 4,* 8-17.

Nyquist, J.D., Abbott, R.D., Wulff, D.H. & Sprague, J. (Eds.). (1991). *Preparing the professoriate of tomorrow to teach.* Dubuque, IA: Kendall/Hunt.

Nyquist, J.D. & Wulff, D. H. (1996). *Working effectively with graduate student assistants.* Thousands Oaks, CA: Sage.

Prosser, M., & Trigwell, K. (1999). Understanding learning and teaching: The experience in higher education. *British Educational Research Journal, 25*(4), 564-565.

Richardson, J.T.E. (2003). Approaches to studying and perceptions of academic quality in a short web-based course. *British Journal of Educational Technology, 34*(4), 433-442.

Surry, D.W. & Land, S. M. (2000). Strategies for motivating higher education faculty to use technology. *Innovations in Education and Training International, 37*(2), 145-153.

Thiele, J.E., Allen, C., & Stucky, M. (1999). Effects of web-based instruction on learning behaviors of undergraduate and graduate students. *Nursing and Health Care Perspectives, 20,* 199-203.

Tice, S. L., Gaff, J.G., Pruitt-Logan, A.S. (1998). Building on faculty development. *Liberal Education, 84*(1), 48-54.

Trigwell, K., & Prosser, M. (2004). Development and use of the Approaches to Teaching Inventory. *Educational Psychology Review*, *16*(4), 409-424.

Acknowledgments

The authors wish to thank the anonymous reviewers and the editor for their useful comments. In addition, we would like to thank Gregory Light for his encouragement of this project, Melissa Luna and Melissa Quinby for their assistance with interviews, Remi Akinyemi for transcription assistance, and Marina Micari for her editorial assistance.

Neeraja Aravamudan received her Ph.D. in Sociology from Northwestern University. She directs programming for graduate students at different levels across the university. She was one of the designers and instructors of the Teaching & Learning with Technology Program discussed in this article.

Susanna Calkins received her Ph.D. in History from Purdue University. She currently directs the faculty development programs at the Searle Center for Teaching Excellence.

Mary Schuller received her MS Ed. in Higher Education Administration from Northwestern University. She managed the training and support for various instructional technologies. She was one of the designers and instructors of the Teaching & Learning with Technology Program discussed in this article.

Dreana Rubel received her Bachelors in Anthropology from Northern Illinois University. She oversees operations at the Searle Center for Teaching Excellence.

Copyright © 2008, New Forums Press, Inc., P.O. Box 876, Stillwater, OK 74076. All Rights Reserved.

Chapter 8
Examining Kinesiology GTAs' Perceptions of a Videotape Instructional Analysis and Consultation Process

Jared A. Russell
Auburn University

Historically, graduate teaching assistants (GTAs) have served an important function in carrying out the instructional mission of many universities and colleges. Accordingly, recent decades have seen an increase in programs and activities to prepare and support GTAs more effectively in their teaching role. The purpose of this ethnographic case study was to examine the perceptions of twenty-seven kinesiology GTAs as they took part in an innovative GTA instructional development and evaluation process which combined videotape instructional analysis and consultation. Findings suggest that indeed such a process can positively affect GTA instructional development and self-perceptions of instructional effectiveness.

The fact that graduate teaching assistants (GTAs) serve a vital instructional role in higher educational settings is apparent when one examines the teaching loads and number of undergraduate students affected by the instruction of GTAs. Wert (1998) pointed out that "graduate teaching assistants provide instruction for roughly 40% of the undergraduate courses in research and comprehensive universities, and they have teaching responsibilities in approximately 60% of the introductory courses taken by first- and second-year undergraduates" (p. xvii). This reality is particularly the case for kinesiology graduate academic programs in which GTAs are the instructors-of-record for a significant percentage of course offerings in physical activity and wellness programs (PAWPs) or what some institutions call basic, service, or collegiate physical education programs (Russell & Chepyator-Thomson, 2004). Despite the obvious importance of the instructional development of their GTAs, kinesiology graduate academic programs have been slow, or perhaps reluctant, to allocate scholarly, human, and financial resources to implementing appropriate instructional development and support processes for their GTAs (Savage & Sharpe, 1998). Consequently, kinesiology GTAs often find themselves in a "sink-or-swim" situation and are afforded very little consistent and relevant instructional support or training (Rikard & Nye, 1997). As a result, the quality of instructional experiences that undergraduate students receive may be significantly reduced (Housner, 1993; Russell & Chepyator-Thomson, 2004). Decades previously, Sage (1984) commented on this troubling trend in physical activity and wellness programs:

> With graduate programs came the practice of turning over basic instruction classes to graduate teaching assistants thus relegating basic instruction to the least experienced and to a group whose highest priority, understandably, was their own education and not the physical education of others. (p. 118)

A review of the limited scholarly inquiries into kinesiology GTA instructional development, and specifically GTAs in physical activity and wellness programs, revealed three main areas of focus: examinations of the impact of non-conventional instructional curriculum on student engagement and learning (Pennington, Manross, & Poole, 2001); institutional or administrative reviews of GTA program frameworks or models (Mondello, Fleming, & Focht, 2000); and questionnaire-driven descriptive accounts of student enrollment or demographic trends (Leenders, Sherman, & Ward, 2003). In light of this existing research, I have chosen to answer the call of researchers Savage and Sharpe (1998), Housner (1993) and Landers (2003) for more research directed to the proper methods of not only preparing GTAs for their roles as PAWP instructors, but also for their future teaching responsibilities as members of the professoriate. The exploratory research project discussed in this article examined the perspectives of kinesiology GTAs regarding the use of a videotape instructional analysis followed by a consultation process as an instructional development, socialization, and evaluation tool.

The PAWP GTA Videotape Instructional Analysis and Consultation Process

In the fall of 2003, the Department of Kinesiology allocated resources to develop, implement, and evaluate the effectiveness of a videotape instructional analysis and consultation (VIAC) process to enhance the instructional development of its kinesiology GTAs. Videotape instructional analysis when combined with formative consultation has long been reported in the research as a viable means of evaluating and improving GTA instructional effectiveness (Chism, 1998; Paulsen & Feldman, 1995; Prentice-Dunn & Pitts, 2001). Moreover, GTAs have opportunities to receive valuable evaluative feedback concerning their teaching in an environment conducive to facilitating formative rather than summative dialogues regarding their development as instructors. The VIAC model, based on strategies and principles advocated by faculty development research (Black & Kaplan, 1998; Meyers & Prieto, 2000; Prentice-Dunn, Payne, & Ledbetter, 2006) is cyclical in nature and consists of three key phases: planning, implementation, and reflection.

Phase I

Pre-observation Conference: The objective of this planning phase is for the GTA and instructional leader to meet and discuss the instructional goals of the proposed lesson, potentially viable strategies for student learning, possible management of logistical issues, and any relevant general concerns. Prior to meeting the GTA completes and submits the pre-observation paperwork (see Appendix A) that provides a general outline of his or her perspective concerning the lesson to be observed. The conference lasts approximately 30 minutes to one hour.

Phase II

Implementation: The GTA implements the self-observation process by videotaping his or her classroom teaching. The primary focus of the exercise is to capture the GTA's instructional practices, strategies, and interactions with the students. To do this effectively the GTA wears a light-weight microphone system. Taping begins 10 minutes before and ends 10 minutes after the actual class meeting time. Once recording is complete, the GTA provides the instructional leader with a copy of the lesson which they both review and evaluate. A time is arranged for the post-observation conference within a week of the video and audio-recorded lesson.

Phase III

Post-observation Conference: The objective of this reflective phase is to provide the GTA with formative, supportive, and corrective evaluative feedback concerning his or her teaching. More importantly, the evaluated videotaped lesson facilitates a dialogue focused on what actually occurred in the classroom setting compared to how the GTA perceived the events in the classroom. It is the examination of the potential discrepancy between the two that allows the GTA to grow as an instructor. Prior to the conference the GTA completes and submits a post-observation reflective assignment (see Appendix A) that explores his or her perceptions of the lesson and the achievement of proposed instructional goals. The conference lasts approximately one to one and one-half hours.

Research Purpose and Questions

The purpose of this study was to examine the perceptions of kinesiology GTAs regarding the use of videotape instructional analysis and consultation as a means of providing formative instructional development, evaluation, and support. Two research questions guided this study:
1. What are the GTAs' perceptions of the VIAC process in regard to improving their instructional self-efficacy and awareness?

2. In particular, what aspects of the VIAC process did GTAs consider most helpful in improving their immediate teaching performance?

Methods

An ethnographic case study approach was deemed most appropriate for this research (Merriam, 2002). Ethnographic research focuses on obtaining and effectively presenting the participants' "voices" as the lens by which the reader can interpret and make meaning of the beliefs, attitudes, perceptions, and values that a particular group or "case" of individuals within a specific cultural setting uses to contextualize their behaviors (Creswell, 2003). Furthermore, case studies, which are bounded by time, space, location, and context, have been shown to be a highly effective method of evaluating the cultural or organizational behaviors of instructional programs and settings (Merriam, 2002).

Context of Study

This research was conducted in a major southeastern university over a period of three academic years. Specifically, GTAs employed by the Department of Kinesiology to teach introductory level courses in the Physical Activity and Wellness Program (PAWP) served as participants. The Department of Kinesiology offers master's and doctoral degrees in the disciplines of exercise science, physical education teacher education, health promotion and behavior, and respective sub-disciplines. The PAWP offers the student body elective courses ranging from individual and team sports such as basketball, kayaking, and aerobics to content-oriented courses such as wellness and weight-control. PAWP courses carry a two-hour academic credit weight and are graded using a letter grade (A, B, C, D, F) system.1

Participants

Twenty-seven (N = 27) GTAs took part in this research. Sixteen of the participants were master's students while the other eleven were doctoral candidates. The departmental teaching assistantship guidelines stipulated that each GTA teach a minimum of three 15-week courses each academic term as instructor-of-record.

Data Collection

VIAC pre- and post-consultation assignments. As part of the VIAC process GTAs were required to complete pre- and post-observation paperwork that focused on their teaching expectations and strategies concerning their instructional evaluation. The assignments were used as the foundation for the discussions between the GTAs, peers, or the instructional leader during the consultation phase of the VIAC process. Excerpts from these documents served as data to support relevant thematic categories.

Semi-structured individual and focus group interviews. Semi-structured interviews were utilized as the primary data collection method for this research. The goal of the interviews was to facilitate an open dialogue and exchange ideas concerning topics relevant to the GTAs' perceptions of the VIAC as part of the current PAWP's instructional development and support processes. Participants took part in a minimum of three individual interviews during the duration of this research. Each focus group was comprised of a minimum of six GTAs of varied years of experience. Twelve focus-group sessions took place under the supervision and direction of the primary researcher. Each participant took part in at least two of the twelve focus-group sessions. All sessions were audiotaped, videotaped, and transcribed verbatim within two weeks. Participants were provided a transcript of their individual or focus-group session and given the opportunity to provide feedback regarding the accuracy of the presentation of their comments. Typically, interviews lasted approximately ninety minutes. Please refer to Appendix B for the interview guide.

Reflective journals. Each novice GTA was required to enroll in the semester-long seminar on College Teaching. As part of the seminar's course work GTAs were required to maintain a weekly journal that documented their instructional and socialization experiences. At the conclusion of the semester, the primary researcher asked the GTAs to provide their journals for inclusion in this research study's analysis process.

Participants' confidentiality. Upon agreeing to participate in this research each GTA, as part of obtaining informed consent, was asked to provide the primary researcher with a pseudonym to utilize throughout the duration of the research process and any subsequent presentation of findings. The purpose of acquiring and using a pseudonym was to maintain the confidentiality of the participant's identity and statements. Only the primary researcher was privy to information linking each pseudonym with the GTA.

Data Analysis

The data analysis process followed traditional methods associated with the qualitative approach (Creswell, 2003; Merriam, 2002). Specifically, the process involved ongoing analysis of the data throughout the research process and the systematic organization and review of interview transcripts, reflective journal accounts, and participant responses to open-ended questions found on the VIAC's pre- and post-observation paperwork. Data analysis processes occurred concurrently with data collection, enabling the primary researcher to identify tentative themes that provided a context for future data collection opportunities. Data acquired were analyzed by constructing tentative coding categories, constant comparison between participant responses across data sources, engaging in analytic induction, and the identification of current thematic categories. Moreover, a content analysis process was used to construct and code themes from reflective journal entries. The concluding result of this process was an authentic, detailed, and comprehensive account of the perspectives and narratives of the GTAs under investigation.

Credibility of Findings and Interpretations

Multiple strategies were implemented to attend to the issue of data trustworthiness and credibility effectively (Creswell, 2003; Merriam, 2002): *Member checks* were performed with each interviewee within two weeks of the actual interview. At this time participants were encouraged to check their transcripts for accuracy of content and to point out discrepancies or errors. The primary researcher established *prolonged time and exposure* with the GTAs within their work environment through consistent supervisory interactions, observations, interviews, and meetings across a three-year period. Throughout the findings section evidence is provided of the *triangulation of data* from multiple participant response sources. Fellow Department of Kinesiology faculty served as *peer debriefers* to the primary researcher. They assisted and enhanced the accuracy and clarity of themes, interpretations, and the final account of this research. *Negative case or discrepant data* are included in the findings section which provides the reader evidence of divergent participant perspectives and insights being documented as a result of rigorous data analysis and comprehensive presentation.

Researcher's Subjectivity Statement

By its inherent nature, qualitative research calls for investigators to be fully transparent concerning their engagement in the ongoing process of data collection, analysis, and interpretation (Creswell, 2003; Merriam, 2002). The role of the researcher as the primary data collection instrument requires the acknowledgment of personal biases, assumptions, and beliefs at the onset of the study. I began this study with the perspective that graduate academic programs must provide their GTA with focused, developmentally appropriate, and hands-on supervision to enhance their instructional effectiveness. Furthermore, I argue that it is imperative that the GTA instructional leader be allowed to participate in the research or program evaluation process due to the perspective and context he or she can provide to the overall research findings. Currently, my faculty responsibilities include the development and evaluation of processes designed to enhance the overall instructional effectiveness and socialization of program GTAs. Subsequently, this research is an effort to fulfill those obligations and responsibilities.

Research Limitations and Generalizability

This exploratory study sought to provide pragmatic solutions and recommendations concerning the use of the VIAC process as a means of providing kinesiology GTAs with formative instructional leadership and support. The goal was not to develop, test, or support a hypothesis regarding this research focus. In light of the inherent nature of qualitative research, findings and interpretations presented are particularistic to the participants and setting under investigation (Creswell, 2003). Subsequently, the transferability and generalizability of findings from the "case" under investigation in this work to another setting are limited.

Presentation of Findings

The following thematic categories present this study's findings as relevant to the implementation and evaluation of the VIAC process. An interpretive analysis of the interview transcripts and GTA reflective journals identified multiple themes in the data that best characterized the perceptions of the participants in regard to the research focus under investigation. Through the use of quotes and journal excerpts, the researcher seeks to present the GTAs' "voices" as a means of describing and supporting provided thematic interpretations.

Research Question 1: What are the GTAs' perceptions of the VIAC process in regard to its impact on their instructional self-efficacy and awareness?

Theme 1: GTAs reported a greater sense of instructional confidence, preparedness, and motivation to teach effectively. The participants acknowledged that the consistent and formal instructional interactions with the instructional leader, particularly the pre- and post-evaluation consultations, helped facilitate their development of a greater sense of instructional preparedness and subsequently confidence. Dolby, a racquetball course instructor, wrote in his reflective journal:

> Getting to meet with you when I need to is great and helpful. I like being able to run ideas past you before I try them. In my master's program we never met with the supervisor to talk about teaching in a positive manner just only about problems . . . and what to do with problem students. I feel much better about my teaching and confident in how I can make my class go smoothly because I can talk to you or my peers about potential barriers to getting the lesson content to my students in an effective manner. (Dolby, Veteran GTA, PhD candidate)

Another key factor in the GTAs' development of greater instructional preparedness and confidence was the availability of the evaluative checklist items to develop, implement, and self-evaluate their daily lessons. The GTAs reported that regardless of whether or not they were involved in the VIAC process they often used the evaluative checklist as a template and self-assessment "gauge" for their daily lessons. This practice speaks to the changing of the GTAs' perceptions and motivations concerning effectively preparing and implementing lessons as well as reflecting on their teaching. Karla, a jogging for fitness course instructor, noted a dramatic change in her efforts and motivation to become an effective and critically reflective teacher during a focus-group interview:

> OK let me be honest . . . I feel much better about my teaching now than I did at the start or even at my old program [master's program]. Coming from exercise science with no background or willingness to teach as a career was hard at first. Now I often catch myself REFLECTING on what happened in the class and making necessary adjustments for the next lesson. As the semester has progressed I actually feel more confident and prepared to teach a great and dynamic lesson than when I started. That's a big step for me . . . whether people know it or not. (Karla, Novice GTA, PhD candidate)

Theme 2: GTAs expressed a sense of appreciation and professionalism as instructors due to participating in the VIAC process. Collectively the GTAs expressed a sense of appreciation for the efforts that the department chair and GTA instructional supervisor were making to ensure that they were provided with sufficient instructional support. A common theme among the GTAs, specifically the doctoral candidates, was the lack of exposure to formative instructional development processes at their master's degree graduate academic program. Raynard, a wellness course instructor, stated during an interview:

> In my master's program no one cared how we [the GTAs] were doing as long as the grades were turned in on time and no one got hurt in our classes. Talk about being left out on your own to sink-or-swim. I'm not used to all this attention!!! It is good to have someone to talk to about teaching and just being a graduate student. I'm glad this department has such a stable program in place to help the GTAs. We don't need a lot—just a little support and a place to vent. (Raynard, 3rd Year GTA, PhD candidate)

Additionally, the GTAs saw themselves as an intricate and valued component in the department's instructional teaching ranks. Consequently, they recognized the necessity not only to represent themselves as excellent teachers, but also to represent the department as a place where students could expect the best instructional experiences possible. In a post-evaluation conference, Shirley, a tennis course instructor, discussed her perspectives on maintaining a high level of professionalism as an instructor:

> I'm a professional and I carry myself as such . . . I'm here to do a job and not be any more and definitely not less than the best teacher and representative of this department I can be. The department puts so many resources into our training it is a shame to do less than your best when you teach . . . I don't want to be known around campus by my students as the teacher who gives easy A's or

doesn't know what she is doing . . . I want to be known as a good teacher. (Shirley, 2nd Year GTA, master's candidate)

Theme 3: GTAs expressed that initially the VIAC process raised their level of anxiety about teaching. The final theme illustrated the possible practical obstacles GTAs and instructional leaders may face when implementing the VIAC process. A common theme among the GTAs, primarily during the first two evaluative cycles, was an over-emphasis or focus on the negatives in their teaching. Consequently, the GTAs reported the VIAC process actually raised their sense of anxiety about teaching. However, it is important to note that by the conclusion of the semester the participants' perceptions of the VIAC process were overwhelmingly supportive. The following quote by Melody, a water aerobics instructor, highlighted the general perception of the GTAs concerning their anxiety during their initial videotaped lessons:

> I have been teaching in pre-college settings for five years but I haven't ever been videotaped. This was major change for me. I'm used to just talking about what happened not actually seeing it and trying to make sense of it for someone else. I was scared all the way through the process and it showed . . . I can see it all over the tape. I was anxious to get it over with and I began to rush. Then to sit down and watch it all over again just brought back those same feelings. (Melody, 1st Year GTA, PhD candidate)

Lastly, an additional recommendation that was expressed consistently was the GTAs initial resistance to the multiple videotaped lessons during their first semester. In light of this issue, Roy, a softball instructor, provided recommendations during a post-observation conference for improving the VIAC and GTA instructional development processes:

> Multiple evaluations can be draining. I have a teaching background and I could go without some of the feedback because I know about reflections and assessment. I guess others can learn from my experiences during discussions but I can't get much from them . . . I think new GTAs with no or limited backgrounds [in teaching] should have to do more of this stuff [VIACC process] not people like me. Give me some training on innovative ways to teach tennis and softball, etc. The basics of how to teach should be left for the other guys. (Roy, 1st Year GTA, PhD candidate)

Research Question 2: In particular, what aspects of the VIAC process did GTAs consider to improve their immediate teaching performance?

Theme 1: GTAs were able to discern the differences between actual and perceived teaching performance in regard to their awareness of general principles and practices associated with instructional effectiveness.

With the availability of the VIAC evaluation checklist the GTAs had clearly defined general standards and expectations for appropriate and effective instructional behaviors, strategies and practices. Initially, the GTAs only focused on meeting the evaluative objectives for the sake of completing a satisfactory evaluation via the VIAC process. However, as the semester progressed and the GTAs became more comfortable with their instructional responsibilities, they began to utilize the evaluative objectives as a means of framing their lessons on a daily basis. This represented a change in mind-set from just "getting through the evaluation" to making these principles a part of their overall teaching philosophy and practices. The VIAC process not only assisted the GTAs with planning and self-assessing their lessons and prompting reflection concerning their teaching but it also facilitated an appreciation for the art of teaching. In her reflective journal, Mercedes, an aerobics course instructor, acknowledged this transition:

> Now I plan every lesson . . . at least in my mind around the objectives. I find myself thinking about each class after the students leave and saying to myself 'did I hit that point or reach that objective.' This is whether I'm being evaluated, observed or not. I think doing the evaluations and seeing everyone else's [peer GTAs] tapes has changed my thinking about my teaching . . . I haven't had a 'perfect lesson' but I definitely think about why or why not a whole lot now. (Mercedes, 2nd Year GTA, master's candidate)

Theme 2: Videotaped lessons allowed for consultations that were more conducive to identifying effective pedagogical practices, habits, and dispositions. The principal benefit of using videotape instructional effectiveness analysis techniques was that it allowed for a clear showing of the GTAs' teaching during subsequent consultations between the GTAs and the instructional leader. More specifically, the use of videoclips allowed the instructional leader to facilitate formative discussions, analysis, and dialogue concerning specific instructional issues that were pinpointed during viewing. For example, Mark, a swimming for fitness course instructor, was enlightened by his peers on his reluctance to use students' names during instruction and how that habit negatively affected his teaching effectiveness. He stated during a focus-group interview:

> I'm embarrassed to be a pedagogy PhD student who can't do the simplest things associated with teaching. The tape clearly showed that I wasn't using students' names or even speaking to all of the students in the class on a regular basis. I thought I was doing a good job with that but clearly I wasn't . . . I know the students' names but I'm so slow to articulate them that I miss those quick "teaching moments" because I can't pronounce or remember the student's full name. (Mark, 1st Year GTA, PhD candidate)

The GTAs expressed that by actually seeing themselves on video,—many for the first time—they were more accepting and understanding of the evaluative feedback they were receiving. More specifically, the use of videoclips allowed for the delivery of concrete evidence of *how* and *when* the GTAs demonstrated or did not demonstrate effective instructional practices or strategies. Stephen, a basketball course instructor, discussed his perceptions of the VIAC process during an interview:

> The feedback makes a lot of sense now ... I can see myself doing the good, bad, and ugly. It's live in color. You can't miss it—the mistakes and successes. I've never been videotaped before ... but this process is extremely helpful to me so that I can get a grip on what I need to do and how I should be conducting myself in the classroom. Not only do I know what I did in the classroom right or wrong but the comments help me to rationalize why I did it and what I can change to be a better teacher. (Stephen, 1st Year GTA, master's candidate)

To summarize, evidence supports the conclusion that the VIAC process positively facilitated the GTAs' instructional development and self-efficacy as college-level teachers. Particularly, the GTAs expressed a sense of appreciation, value, and professionalism in regards to their roles as instructors within the context of the department's instructional teaching force. As part of the VIAC process, the evaluative checklist, pre- and post-evaluation conferences, and classroom discussions during group analyses of peer GTA teaching were noted as being helpful in increasing the GTAs' awareness of effective teaching practices and strategies. Some apprehension concerning aspects of the VIAC process was reported by the GTAs during their initial instructional evaluation episodes. However, the consensus was that as an instructional development tool the VIAC process was meaningful, relevant, and effective at assisting in the preparation and support of the GTAs' instruction.

Discussion and Conclusions

In order to encourage GTAs to appreciate and grow in their teaching it is necessary to engage them actively in a process of critical examination using evidence of their teaching as the foundation. The current study's results both support and extend general knowledge regarding GTA instructional development, supervision, and evaluation. Overall, the primary finding was that the VIAC process was an effective method of facilitating and supporting formative discussions regarding teaching between GTAs, their instructional leader, and in some cases their peers. More specifically, results indicated that the VIAC process addressed three key areas identified in the existing literature as being fundamental (Meyers, 2001; Prentice-Dunn, Payne, & Ledbetter, 2006; Prentice-Dunn & Pitts, 2001; Wulff, Austin, et al, 2004) to assisting GTAs develop their instructional skills: consistent formative leadership and supervision; meaningful and authentic evaluative feedback; and the development of positive dispositions concerning teaching as a valued craft.

In conclusion, it is the researcher's hope that other graduate academic programs choose to develop instructional development and support processes that are tailored for their GTA and departmental needs. The VIAC process was an effective model for our setting but each program's needs are based on factors such as program size, initial instructional experience of the GTAs, and the availability of resources (both financial and human). Philosophically, graduate academic programs must address a pivotal question when conceptualizing their respective GTA instructional development and support mechanisms: Is the focus of our graduate teaching assistantship experience to prepare a competent departmental instructional labor force in exchange for financing student graduate studies? Or are we focused on preparing our graduate students to value and excel as instructors as they progress towards becoming possible future members of the professoriate in kinesiology? For too long, GTAs have had to live through episodes of "instructional abandonment" and "sink-or-swim" as part of their graduate teaching experience, yet his is not the philosophical basis of the graduate teaching assistantship. The graduate teaching assistantship is meant to be a time when faculty engage talented graduate students in mentorship experiences focused on the principles and practices of effective research and teaching. The VIAC process is a viable means for GTAs' peers, faculty, and the GTA instructional leadership to provide beginning university teachers with the necessary guidance, mentorship, and formative supervision to allow them to grow into a generation of faculty who value and excel in the art of teaching.

References

Black, B., & Kaplan, M. (1998). Evaluating TAs' teaching. In M. Marincovich, J. Prostko, & F. Stout (Eds.), *The professional development of graduate teaching assistants* (213–234). Bolton, MA: Anker.

Chism, N. V. N. (1998). Evaluating TA programs. In M. Marincovich, J. Prostko, & F. Stout (Eds.), *The professional development of graduate teaching assistants* (pp. 249–262). Bolton, MA: Anker.

Creswell, J. W. (2003). *Research design: Qualitative, quantitative, and mixed methods approaches* (2nd ed.). Thousand Oaks, CA: Sage.

Housner, L.D. (1993). Research in basic instruction programs. *The Journal of Physical Education, Recreation and Dance, 64*(6), 53–58.

Landers, D. (Ed.). (2003). The academy papers: Preparing future faculty [Special Issue]. *Quest, 55*(1).

Leenders, N. Y., Sherman, W.M., & Ward, P. (2003). College physical activity courses: Why do students enroll, and what are their health behaviors? *Research Quarterly for Exercise and Sport, 74*(3), 313–318.

Merriam, S. B. (Ed.). (2002). *Qualitative research in practice: Examples for discussion and analysis.* San Francisco: Jossey-Bass.

Meyers, S. A. (2001). Conceptualizing and promoting effective TA training. In L. R. Prieto, & S. A. Meyers (Eds.), *The teaching assistant training handbook: How to prepare TAs for their responsibilities* (pp. 3-23). Stillwater, OK: New Forums Press.

Meyers, S. A., & Prieto, L. R. (2000). Training in the teaching of psychology: What is done and examining the differences. *Teaching of Psychology, 27*(4), 258–261.

Mondello, M., Fleming, D., & Focht, B. (2000). The organization, administration, and operational procedures of an elective physical education program at a research one university. *The Physical Educator, 57*(2), 77–83.

Paulsen, M. B., & Feldman, K. A. (1995). *Taking teaching seriously: Meeting the challenge of instructional improvement* (ASHE-ERIC Report No. 2). Washington, DC: George Washington University.

Pennington, T. R., Manross, D., & Poole, J. (2001). Exploring alternative assessment in college physical activity classes. *Physical Educator, 58*(4), 206–210.

Prentice-Dunn, S. & Pitts, G. S. (2001). The use of videotape feedback in GTA training. In L. R. Prieto, & S. Meyers (Eds.), *The teaching assistant training handbook: How to prepare TAs for their responsibilities* (pp. 89–102). Stillwater, OK: New Forums Press.

Prentice-Dunn, S., Payne, K. L., & Ledbetter, J. M. (2006). Improving teaching through video feedback and consultation. In W. Buskist & S. F. Davis (Eds.), *Handbook of the teaching of psychology* (pp. 295-300). Malden, MA: Blackwell.

Rikard, G.L., & Nye, A. H. (1997). The graduate instructor experience: Pitfalls and possibilities. *The Journal of Physical Education, Recreation and Dance, 68*(5), 33–37.

Russell, J. A., & Chepyator-Thomson, J.R. (2004). Help wanted!!! Perspectives of physical education graduate teaching assistants on their instructional environment, preparation and needs. *Educational Research Journal, 19(2)*, 251–280.

Sage, G. H. (1984). The quest for identity in college physical education. *Quest, 36*(2), 115–121.

Savage, M. P., & Sharpe, T. (1998). Demonstrating the need for formal graduate student training in effective teaching practices. *Physical Educator, 55*(3), 130–137.

Wert, E. (1998). Foreword. In. M. Marincovich, J. Prostko, & F. Stout (Eds.), *The professional development of graduate teaching assistants* (pp. xvii–xxi). Bolton, MA: Anker.

Wulff, D. H., Austin, A. E., Nyquist, J. D., & Sprague, J. (2004). The development of graduate students as teaching scholars: A four-year longitudinal study. In D. H. Wulff, & A. E. Austin (Eds.), *Paths to the professoriate: Strategies for enriching the preparation of future faculty* (pp. 46-73). San Francisco: Jossey-Bass.

Jared A. Russell, Ph.D., teaches in the Department of Kinesiology at Auburn University.

Appendix A
VIAC Process Pre- and Post-Observation Consultation Questions

Pre-Observation Questions
1. What are the instructional goal(s) and/or objectives of this lesson?
2. How do you plan to meet the identified instructional goals and/or objectives?
3. What potential **positive** instructional/environmental variables might influence your lesson?
4. What potential **negative** instructional/environmental variables might influence your lesson?
5. Identify any pre-observation concerns you have?

Post-Observation Questions
1. What were the instructional goal(s) and/or objectives of this lesson?
2. Think about the instructional positives of your lesson.
   a. From a learning perspective, which aspects of the class went well?
   b. Which instructional goals or objectives were met? Why?
   c. Identify factors that influenced you lesson positively.
3. Think about the instructional weaknesses of your lesson or of possible areas for improvement.
   a. Which aspects of your lesson were not valuable in relation to student learning?
   b. Which instructional goals and objectives were not obtained? Why?
   c. Identify factors that influenced your lesson negatively.
3. Based on this experience, how do you plan to improve your instruction?
4. Do you wish to add anything to your comments concerning this evaluation experience?

Appendix B
Interview Guide: Individual and Focus-Group Interview Questions

1. In regards to your instructional development, what are your perceptions of the PAWP's current use of end-of-semester student course evaluations?
2. What are your general perceptions of the VIAC model in regard to your instructional socialization and development?
3. In particular, what aspects of the VIAC model did you perceive to improve your immediate teaching performance?
4. What aspects of the VIAC model were not beneficial in regard to your instructional socialization and development?
5. How can the VIAC model be changed to meet your instructional socialization, support and development needs better?
6. What administrative assistance do you perceive to be necessary for your development as an effective instructor?

Section IV
Bridging the Transition to Beginning Faculty Positions

Chapter 9

The Background Experiences of Early-Career Science Faculty in Research, Teaching, and Service

Kenneth S. Sagendorf
United States Air Force Academy

Successful college faculty should be effective teachers, competent researchers, and active participants in academic life (Adams, 2002). However, early-career college faculty members may not be prepared for the many and varied responsibilities they will face as members of the academy. This study documents the background experiences in teaching, research and service of 30 early-career college faculty in the sciences (biology, chemistry, earth sciences and physics) at institutions across the United States. Early-career science faculty also rated their preparation for and support provided in their current academic positions. At least seventy-five percent of the faculty in this study had conducted, presented and co-authored research. Furthermore, 60% of the faculty in this study had taught lecture classes and 80% had taught laboratory classes prior to becoming a faculty member. This study shows that relative to previous studies, there may be an increase in teaching-related experiences prior to joining the academy. However, the college science faculty in this study had few other common experiences, especially in teaching and service. This research supports a continued need for 1), broadening doctoral education to improve the preparation of new college faculty, especially in teaching and service and 2), making and or improving the support available to early-career faculty in their current positions, giving special attention to the disparity of background experiences, gender and institution-type of employment.

Introduction and Background

Although there are many paths into the professoriate, graduate, and especially doctoral, education remains the primary preparation of new college faculty members. More than half of the doctoral degree recipients in the United States seek an academic position during their career (Golde & Dore, 2000). Kathrynn Adams (2002) states that, "institutions expect the faculty they hire to be effective teachers, competent researchers, and active participants in academic life." In their 2004 book, *Paths to the Professoriate*, Nyquist and Wulff list some of the skills and abilities that new college faculty will need. They include: the awareness of ethical responsibilities of researchers, knowledge of teaching and learning processes, the ability to incorporate technology into instruction, the ability to collaborate with different groups and being responsible academic citizens at their institution. These general statements apply across many fields but omit specific discipline-related experiences. Often, early-career college faculty face a period of adjustment where issues of isolation, time management and judgment by peers and supervisors provide distractions from honing the necessary skills to be a successful academic (Menges, 1999).

Not only will a new college *science* faculty member need to have all of these skills, but they will also need to include "teaching, mentoring, advising, carrying out research, writing proposals and papers, lecturing and presenting professional talks, managing budgets and supervising people, serving on committees and professional societies and so on" (Schwartz, Archer, El Ashmawy, Lavalee & Eikey, 2003). Rick Reis (1997) points out that job advertisements for assistant professors in the sciences have gone from asking about a candidate's *potential* for teaching and research excellence to requiring *documentation and/or evidence* of excellence and success in these important areas. Deciding how to create, manage and fund a laboratory is another skill that may be required of a science faculty member. These changing demands raise several questions: What prepares one to become a successful new college faculty member in the sciences? What are the common experiences that new college science faculty members share? What areas may be lacking in their preparation?

In spite of reports calling for improved doctoral preparation in the sciences (e.g., COSEPUP, 1995; Committee on Undergraduate Science Education, 1997; Committee on Graduate Education, 1998), finding data on the background experiences of early-career college science faculty remains difficult. The purpose of this research is to document the research, teaching and service background experiences of early-career, first-year college faculty members in the sciences. Although early-career faculty have previously been studied, the studies have been limited to single institution, single discipline faculty (e.g., Fink, 1984) or multiple institution, multiple discipline studies (e.g., Boice, 1992). The current study is also multiple institution but only includes a specific group of early-career faculty in the sciences in their first year at their current institution. The inventory of background experiences provided by this research can identify areas where the preparation of future college science faculty needs to be improved.

Methods

Subjects

Potential participants were identified by contacting Provosts and Deans of Faculty at institutions across the country. The Provosts or Deans of the Faculty were identified through a web search and contacted via email. The email asked for their assistance in either identifying newly-hired faculty in the sciences or recruiting their participation. For the purpose of this study, the sciences were considered as: Biology, Chemistry, Earth Sciences, and Physics and their subdisciplines. Institutions representing Doctorate-granting and Master's universities, Baccalaureate and Associate's colleges (Carnegie Foundation, 2006) were included. Once the faculty members were identified, they were individually sent an email explaining the project and what their participation would involve. If they agreed to participate, they were mailed hard copies of the survey, consent information and return mailing envelopes.

Instrument

Despite the growing body of literature on this topic, there was no single reference that could identify the background experiences in teaching, research and service of an early-career college faculty member in the sciences. A new survey was developed based on the previous research conducted on new or prospective college faculty members from a broad range of disciplines (Rice, Sorcinelli and Austin, 2000; Menges, 1999; Reis, 1997; Fiebleman, 1993; Boice, 1992; Whitt, 1991; Astin, Corn and Dey, 1991; National Center for Education Statistics, 1989; Turner and Boice, 1987; Fink, 1984a, 1984b).

Within each area of the survey (teaching, research and service), respondents were asked to identify their previous experiences by choosing them from a list. In addition, there were two five-point Likert-scale questions which asked them to rate their satisfaction with their preparation for their current faculty position and to rate the support they felt they were currently receiving at their institution. The survey questions for each area can be found in Table 1.

The survey was piloted with first-year faculty in the Chemistry and Physics departments at the researcher's home institution. Feedback was provided through a face-to-face interview with each pilot survey respondent. Based on this feedback, the survey was adjusted to better address the concerns of early-career college faculty members in the sciences.

Statistical Analyses

Since the purpose of the study was to document the experiences of early-career college faculty in the sciences, the results from each yes/no question (the presence of experiences) and each Likert-scaled question were reported as a percentage of respondents. In order to more fully explain the results, Pearson's chi-square (X^2) analyses were used to assess frequency counts. A one-way Analysis of Variance (ANOVA) was used to determine if significant differences existed among the responses to all Likert-scaled questions. Factors studied included gender, scientific discipline, ethnicity, tenure status, post-doctoral experience and institution type. Where significant differences existed and there were more than two groups, a Tukey post-hoc analysis was employed to identify where the differences occurred.

In all cases, SPSS Version 14.0 (SPSS, Inc., Chicago, IL) was used. Statistical significance was accepted for all analyses at the $p = 0.05$ level.

Table 1. Survey Questions Asked of First-Year Faculty Members Regarding Teaching, Research, Service, Preparation, and Support

---

TEACHING
1. Please mark all that represent your **teaching** experience(s) prior to your current position.
   - [ ] Graduate Teaching Assistantship
   - [ ] Primary school teacher (K-6)
   - [ ] Grading
   - [ ] Secondary school teacher (7-12)
   - [ ] Course design
   - [ ] Exam creation
   - [ ] Teaching laboratories
   - [ ] Syllabus construction
   - [ ] Student advising
   - [ ] Teaching discussion sections
   - [ ] Teaching lecture courses
   - [ ] Curriculum development
   - [ ] Developing and articulating a teaching philosophy
   - [ ] Professional development courses/workshops
   - [ ] Creating a teaching portfolio
   - [ ] Other (please describe) _____

RESEARCH
1. Please mark all that represent your **research** experience(s) prior to your current position.
   - [ ] Research assistantship
   - [ ] Conduct research
   - [ ] Publish research findings (sole author)
   - [ ] Publish research findings (co-author)
   - [ ] Research apprenticeship
   - [ ] Present research at professional meetings
   - [ ] Submit grant proposals
   - [ ] Review research papers for professional journals
   - [ ] Attend research seminars/workshops
   - [ ] Developing/Articulating a research agenda
   - [ ] Other (please describe)

SERVICE
1. Please mark all your prior experience(s) in departmental or professional **service**.
   - [ ] Member of disciplinary/professional society or association
   - [ ] Service on departmental committees
   - [ ] Service on institution-wide committees
   - [ ] Apply expertise to service in the community
   - [ ] Other (please describe) _____

Using the following scale, please circle how **prepared** you feel for (teaching, research or service) in your current position.

Not at all Prepared		Somewhat Prepared		Extremely Prepared
1	2	3	4	5

Please use the following scale to circle your satisfaction with the **support** you are receiving for (teaching, research or service) in your current position.

Not at all Satisfied		Somewhat Satisfied		Extremely Satisfied
1	2	3	4	5

Results

Forty-nine faculty were identified as newly-hired early-career faculty in Biology, Chemistry, Physics or Earth Sciences at their respective institutions. Of these, thirty faculty agreed to participate (61% response rate). They represented sixteen different colleges and universities and four scientific disciplines: Biology, Chemistry, Earth Sciences and Physics. These were the main disciplinary areas and include any subdisicplines that were submitted. The faculty were employed at institution types ranging from Associate's colleges to Doctorate-granting universities (Carnegie Foundation, 2006). Table 2 provides demographic information of the subjects.

Twenty-three of the thirty respondents were in their first faculty position. The remaining seven survey participants indicated this was not their first faculty position but no other information was given. Any differences by this variable are discussed later. All of the study participants were new to their current institution and in their first year. Twenty-two of the thirty faculty in this study were in a tenure track position. Of the eight respondents that were not in tenure track positions, five were non-tenure track assistant professors (appeared to be on temporary contracts), held post-doctoral positions, visiting positions, instructor, and adjunct positions. There were statistically no significant

Table 2: Relevant Demographic Information about Study Participants Reported as Number of Subjects (N=30)

Gender	Male 17				Female 13									
Ethnicity	African American 3				Asian 1				Hispanic 3			White/Caucasian 22		Black 1
Citizenship	Native U.S. Citizen 21				Naturalized U.S. Citizen 2				Permanent U.S. Resident 2			Temporary U.S. Resident 5		
Birth Year*	1959 1	0	0	0	1964 1	1	1	3	1968 3	0	1	1972 0 2	6 2	1976 4 1 3
Academic Title	Assistant Professor 27				Instructor 1				Post-Doctoral Teaching Fellow/ 1			Visiting Assistant Professor 1		
Department	Biology 12				Chemistry 7				Physics 6			Earth Sciences 5		
Highest Degree Earned	Ph.D. 25				Ph.D. (A.B.D.) 2				M.S. 3					
Tenure Status	Tenure Track 22				Non Tenure Track 8									
Institutional Type	Associate's College 5				Baccalaureate College 6				Master's College/Univ. 12			Doctorate Granting Univ. 7		

* = one subject omitted their answer to this question making n=29 for this variable differences between tenure track and non-tenure track faculty in this study regarding any of the variables examined in this study.

Twenty-five of the respondents had completed their Ph.D. studies, two were A.B.D. and three had completed an M.S. degree. Those with an M.S. degree were employed at an Associate's college or as an instructor at a Baccalaureate college.

A majority of the participants were male (n=17). Twenty-two individuals listed themselves as Caucasian, while nearly one-third third (n=7) of the study population was comprised of traditional minority groups (African-American, Asian and Hispanic). Additionally, nearly one-third of the survey respondents consisted of individuals with international backgrounds (n=9, Table 2).

The average age of survey respondents was 35.7 years, with one person omitting their date of birth (Table 2). In order to illustrate how new the individuals were to being a faculty member at their institution, Figure 1 indicates the date of the respondents' faculty appointment. Twenty-two of the 30 survey participants were appointed during June to September of 2004. No one that was included in the survey had an earlier faculty appointment date.

The percentage of newly-hired first year science faculty reporting their experiences in teaching is shown in Table 3. Similarly, Tables 4 and Table 5 show the percentages of individuals reporting experiences in research and service, respectively.

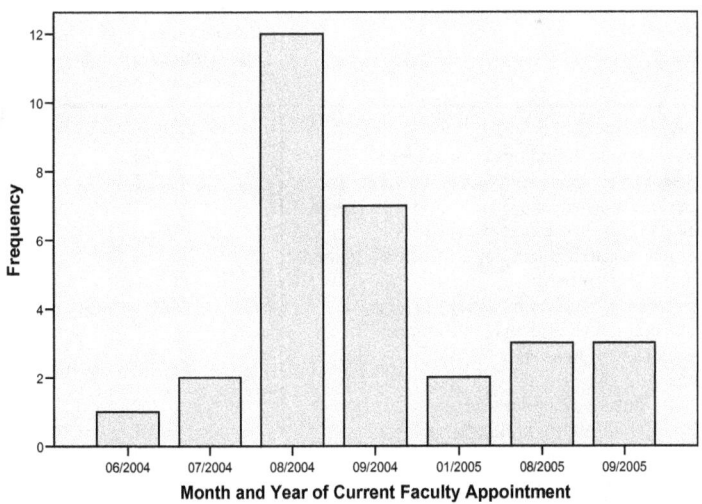

Figure 1. First-Year Faculty Date of Current Faculty Appointment

Table 3. Teaching Experiences Prior to Obtaining a Faculty Position

Experience	Percent of survey participants reporting this experience (N=30)
Graduate Teaching Assistantship	83.3
Teaching laboratories	80.0
Grading	76.7
Teaching lecture courses	60.0
Exam creation	60.0
Syllabus construction	50.0
Teaching discussion sections	50.0
Professional development courses/workshops	46.7
Developing and articulating a teaching philosophy	43.3
Course design	40.0
Curriculum development	33.3
Student advising	30.0
Creating a teaching portfolio	20.0
Secondary school teacher (7-12)	10.0
Other	
• M.Ed. in Science Education	3.3
• Outreach activities with elementary school children	3.3
• Teaching during Post-doc	3.3
• Field trip leader	3.3
• Tutoring	3.3
• Primary school teacher (K-6)	0.0

Listed from most commonly to least commonly reported. This Table represents the aggregate results of all 30 faculty in the study.

Table 4. Research Experiences Prior to Obtaining a Faculty Position

Experience	Percent of survey participants reporting this experience (N=30)
Conduct research	90.0
Publish research findings (co-author)	86.7
Present research at professional meetings	83.3
Research assistantship	76.7
Attend research seminars/workshops	73.3
Review research papers for professional journals	53.3
Submit grant proposals	40.0
Developing/Articulating a research agenda	40.0
Publish research findings (sole author)	26.7
Research apprenticeship	16.7
Other	
• Post doc position/training	6.7
• Grad student with a field project	3.3
• Master's thesis	3.3
• Training undergrads	3.3
• Worked on a grant with another author	3.3
• Grant reviewer/Analyses of data	3.3

Listed from most commonly to least commonly reported. This table represents the aggregate results of all 30 faculty in the study.

Survey respondents were also asked to rate their own level of preparation for the research, teaching and service requirements of their current faculty position (Table 6, first column). The mean perceived level of support reported by new the early-career science faculty in their current academic position is noted in the second column of Table 6.

To add additional context to the meanings of these perceptions of preparation and support, a one-way ANOVA was used to compare differences by discipline, gender, highest degree earned, citizenship and ethnicity. The impacts of the presence of post-doctoral experience, which academic title they

Table 5: Service Experiences Prior to Obtaining a Faculty Position

Experience	Percent of survey participants reporting this experience (N=30)
Member of disciplinary/professional society or association	66.7
Service on departmental committees	50.0
Service on institution-wide committees	40.0
Apply expertise to service in the community	23.3
Other	
• Member of student senate/graduate student committees	6.7
• Helped lead a department field trip	3.3
• Write about policy matters on campus	3.3
• Reviewer for journals	3.3

Listed from most commonly to least commonly reported. This table represents the aggregate results of all 30 faculty in the study.

Table 6. Self-Reported Level of Preparation and Level of Satisfaction With Support for Research, Teaching and Service in Current Faculty Position

	How prepared do you feel for _____ in your current position?	How satisfied are you with the support you are receiving for _____ in your current position?
RESEARCH	3.83 (1.002)	3.41 (1.040)
TEACHING	3.80 (0.847)	3.70 (0.794)
SERVICE	3.00 (1.069)	3.15 (1.027)

Variables are on a five-point Likert scale where 1 = the least and 5 = the most. Variables are reported as mean ± SD.

held, whether it was their first-faculty appointment and tenure status were also explored. There were no significant differences in preparation by discipline, highest degree earned or tenure status. Nor were there differences in perceived support for these same variables. There were not enough faculty in categories within title, citizenship and ethnicity to provide meaningful comparisons in these areas.

There were statistically significant differences when gender, post-doctoral experience and first faculty appointment were examined. Female science faculty reported feeling significantly less prepared for the research requirements of their positions than their male counterparts (3.38+/-1.193 vs. 4.19+/-0.655; $df = 1, 28$; $F = 5.309$; $p = 0.029$). Faculty reporting prior post-doctoral experience felt significantly less prepared for teaching than those that did not complete a post-doctoral position (3.44+/-0.699 vs. 4.21+/-0.814; $df = 1, 28$; $F = 7.742$, $p = 0.010$). Additionally, the faculty with post doctoral experience reported being more satisfied with the support they were receiving for research than the faculty without similar experience (3.88+/-0.957 vs. 2.73+/-0.647; $df = 1, 25$; $F = 11.971$, $p = 0.002$).

Compared to the seven participants that had held a prior position, the college science faculty in their first faculty position reported feeling significantly less prepared for teaching (3.61+/-0.839 vs. 4.43+/-0.535; $df = 1, 28$; $F = 5.875$; $p = 0.022$) and service (2.77+/-0.973 vs. 3.71+/-1.113; $df = 1, 27$; $F = 4.657$; $p = 0.040$) than their more experienced colleagues. The groups felt equally prepared for their research role ($p = 0.988$) and equally supported in their current position for research ($p = 0.519$).

When separated by institutional type, significant differences existed in preparation for teaching ($df = 3, 26$; $F = 3.249$; $p = 0.038$) and support for research ($df = 3, 23$; $F = 3.787$; $p = 0.024$). Tukey post-hoc tests revealed faculty at institutions categorized as Baccalaureate institutions reported significantly lower preparation for teaching than faculty from Associate's colleges (4.60+/-0.548 vs. 3.17+/-1.169, $p = 0.022$). In addition, faculty at Doctorate-granting institutions reported having greater support for their research than their counterparts at Associate's institutions (4.00+/-0.816 vs. 2.00+/-0.00, $p = 0.043$). All other support comparisons were similar across institution types.

Tables 7, 8 and 9 show the frequency counts for teaching, research and service experiences, respectively, separated by institution type. Most differences occurred in the category of teaching. The key findings are that new early-career science faculty working at Baccalaureate institutions (n=6) reported having no experience in teaching lecture courses, creating exams or designing syllabi prior to their faculty appointment. At least 57% (range 57-100%) of new the early-career faculty employed at all other institution types reported having this experience. No new faculty member in this study employed at a Doctorate-granting institution had developed and articulated a teaching philosophy, despite 56.5% of the faculty from other institution types having done so.

When reporting their research preparation, only 20% of new the early-career faculty at Associate's colleges reported having presented research at a

Table 7. Chi-Square Table of First Year Science Faculty Teaching Experiences Prior to Employment Separated by Institution Type of Current Position.

TEACHING EXPERIENCE		Doctorate n (%)	Master's n (%)	Baccalaureate n (%)	Associates n (%)	Total %	χ^2, df, p
Graduate Teaching Assistantship	NO	1 (3.3)	2 (6.7)	1 (3.3)	1 (3.3)	16.7	0.069, 3, 0.995
	YES	6 (20.0)	10 (33.3)	5 (16.7)	4 (13.3)	83.3	
Grading	NO	4 (13.3)	2 (16.7)	1 (3.3)	0 (0)	23.3	6.442, 3, 0.092
	YES	3 (10.0)	10 (33.3)	5 (16.7)	5 (16.7)	76.7	
Course Design	NO	4 (13.3)	7 (23.3)	5 (16.7)	2 (6.7)	60.0	2.332, 3, 0.526
	YES	3 (10.0)	5 (16.7)	1 (3.3)	3 (10.0)	40.0	
Teaching Laboratories	NO	2 (6.7)	3 (10.0)	0 (0.0)	1 (3.3)	20.0	2.009, 3, 0.571
	YES	5 (16.7)	9 (30.0)	6 (20.0)	4 (13.3)	80.0	
Student Advising	NO	5 (16.7)	7 (23.3)	6 (20.0)	3 (10.0)	70.0	3.594, 3, 0.309
	YES	2 (6.7)	5 (16.7)	0 (0.0)	2 (6.7)	30.0	
Teaching Lecture Courses	NO	2 (6.7)	4 (13.3)	6 (20.0)	0 (0.0)	40.0	12.937, 3, 0.005
	YES	5 (16.7)	8 (26.7)	0 (0.0)	5 (16.7)	60.0	
Curriculum Development	NO	6 (20.0)	7 (23.3)	6 (20.0)	1 (3.3)	66.7	9.418, 3, 0.240
	YES	1 (3.3)	5 (16.7)	0 (0.0)	4 (13.3)	33.3	
Creating a Teaching Portfolio	NO	7 (23.3)	9 (30.0)	6 (20.0)	2 (6.7)	80.0	8.438, 3, 0.038
	YES	0 (0.0)	3 (10.0)	0 (0)	3 (10.0)	20.0	

professional conference, versus 92% or more of the faculty at other institution types. There were no apparent differences in service-related background experiences by institution type in this population. The service experiences of this group were largely limited to membership in a professional organization.

Table 7 (cont.)

TEACHING EXPERIENCE		Doctorate n (%)	Master's n (%)	Baccalaureate n (%)	Associates n (%)	Total %	χ^2, df, p
Primary School Teacher	NO	7 (23.3)	12 (40.0)	6 (20.0)	5 (16.7)	100.0	0.000, 3, 1.000
	YES	0 (0.0)	0 (0.0)	0 (0.0)	0 (0.0)	0.0	
Secondary School Teacher	NO	7 (23.3)	9 (30.0)	6 (20.0)	5 (16.7)	90.0	5.00, 3, 0.172
	YES	0 (0.0)	3 (10.0)	0 (0.0)	0 (0.0)	10.0	
Exam Creation	NO	3 (10.0)	3 (10.0)	6 (20.0)	0 (0)	40.0	13.482, 3, 0.004
	YES	4 (13.3)	9 (30.0)	0 (0.0)	5 (16.7)	60.0	
Syllabus Construction	NO	4 (13.3)	5 (16.7)	6 (20.0)	0 (0.0)	50.0	11.476, 3, 0.009
	YES	3 (10.0)	7 (23.3)	0 (0.0)	5 (16.7)	50.0	
Teaching Discussion Sections	NO	5 (16.7)	6 (20.0)	3 (10.0)	1 (3.3)	50.0	3.086, 3, 0.379
	YES	2 (6.7)	6 (20.0)	3 (10.0)	4 (13.3)	50.0	
Developing and Articulating a Teaching Philosophy	NO	7 (23.3)	5 (16.7)	3 (10.0)	2 (6.7)	56.7	7.127, 3, 0.068
	YES	0 (0.0)	7 (23.3)	3 (10.0)	3 (10.0)	43.3	
Professional Development Workshops/Courses	NO	5 (16.7)	5 (16.7)	4 (13.3)	2 (6.7)	53.3	2.363, 3, 0.501
	YES	2 (6.7)	7 (23.3)	2 (6.7)	3 (10.0)	46.7	
Other	NO	6 (20.0)	10 (33.3)	4 (13.3)	5 (16.7)	83.3	2.229, 3, 0.526
	YES	1 (3.3)	2 (6.7)	2 (6.7)	0 (0.0)	16.7	

Order of experiences indicative of the order in which survey questions were asked.

Table 8. Chi-Square Table of First-Year Science Faculty Research Experiences Prior to Employment Separated by Institution Type of Current Position

RESEARCH EXPERIENCE		INSTITUTION TYPE				Total %	χ^2, df, p
		Doctorate n(%)	Master's n(%)	Baccalaureate n(%)	Associates n(%)		
Research Assistantship	NO	1 (3.3)	3 (10.0)	1 (3.3)	2 (6.7)	23.3	1.264, 3, 0.738
	YES	6 (20.0)	9 (30.0)	5 (16.7)	3 (10.0)	76.7	
Conduct Research	NO	0 (13.3)	0 (16.7)	1 (3.3)	2 (0)	10.0	7.407, 3, 0.060
	YES	7 (23.3)	12 (40.0)	5 (16.7)	3 (10.0)	76.7	
Publish Research Findings (Sole Author)	NO	3 (10.0)	10 (33.3)	4 (13.3)	5 (16.7)	73.3	5.893, 3, 0.117
	YES	4 (13.3)	2 (6.7)	2 (6.7)	0 (0.0)	26.7	
Publish Research Findings (Co-Author)	NO	1 (3.3)	1 (3.3)	0 (0.0)	2 (6.7)	13.3	4.265, 3, 0.234
	YES	6 (20.0)	11 (36.7)	6 (20.0)	3 (10.0)	86.7	
Research apprenticeship	NO	6 (20.0)	9 (30.0)	6 (20.0)	4 (13.3)	83.3	1.869, 3, 0.600
	YES	1 (3.3)	3 (10.0)	0 (0.0)	1 (3.3)	16.7	
Present research at professional meetings	NO	0 (0.0)	1 (3.3)	0 (0.0)	4 (13.3)	16.7	17.640, 3, 0.001
	YES	7 (23.3)	11 (36.7)	6 (20.0)	1 (3.3)	83.3	
Submit grant proposals	NO	3 (10.0)	6 (20.0)	5 (16.7)	4 (13.3)	60.0	3.552, 3, 0.314
	YES	4 (13.3)	6 (20.0)	1 (3.3)	1 (3.3)	40.0	
Review research papers for professional journals	NO	1 (3.3)	7 (23.3)	3 (10.0)	3 (10.0)	46.7	3.989, 3, 0.263
	YES	6 (20.0)	5 (16.7)	3 (10.0)	2 (6.7)	53.3	
Attend research seminars/workshops	NO	2 (6.7)	2 (6.7)	2 (6.7)	2 (3.3)	26.7	1.218, 3, 0.749
	YES	5 (16.7)	10 (33.3)	4 (13.3)	3 (10.0)	73.3	
Developing/Articulating a research Agenda	NO	4 (13.3)	8 (26.7)	2 (6.7)	4 (13.3)	60.0	2.857, 3, 0.414
	YES	3 (10.0)	4 (13.3)	4 (13.3)	1 (3.3)	40.0	
Other	NO	4 (13.3)	12 (40.0)	4 (13.3)	3 (10.0)	76.7	
	YES	1 (3.3)	0 (0.0)	0 (0.0)	0 (0.0)	3.3	

Order of experiences indicative of the order in which survey questions were asked.

Table 9. Chi-Square Table of First-Year Science Faculty Service Experiences Prior to Employment Separated by Institution Type of Current Position

SERVICE EXPERIENCE		INSTITUTION TYPE				Total %	χ^2, df, p
		Doctorate n (%)	Master's n (%)	Baccalaureate n (%)	Associates n (%)		
Member of disciplinary/professional society or association	NO	3 (10.0)	5 (16.7)	1 (3.3)	1 (3.3)	33.3	1.811, 3, 0.613
	YES	4 (13.3)	7 (23.3)	5 (16.7)	4 (13.3)	66.7	
Service on departmental committees	NO	3 (10.0)	8 (26.7)	2 (6.7)	2 (6.7)	50.0	2.343, 3, 0.504
	YES	4 (13.3)	4 (13.3)	4 (13.3)	3 (10.0)	50.0	
Service on institution-wide committees	NO	4 (13.8)	7 (24.1)	5 (17.2)	1 (3.4)	58.6	3.381, 3, 0.336**
	YES	3 (10.3)	5 (17.2)	1 (3.4)	3 (10.3)	41.4	
Apply expertise to service in the community	NO	5 (17.2)	11 (37.9)	3 (10.3)	3 (10.3)	75.9	3.905, 3, 0.272**
	YES	2 (6.9)	1 (3.4)	3 (10.3)	1 (3.4)1	24.1	
Other	NO	5 (17.2)	9 (31.1)	5 (17.2)	4 (13.8)	79.3	1.504, 3, 0.681**
	YES	2 (6.9)	3 (10.3)	1 (3.4)	0 (0.0)	16.7	

** N = 29 responses for these questions.
Order of experiences indicative of the order in which survey questions were asked.

Discussion

This study extends the current literature on college faculty to include a specific academic group: first-year, early-career college science faculty. It provides information from four science disciplines and sixteen different institutions, and represents the range of academic roles that new, early-career faculty will face in the sciences. Future faculty preparation in the sciences differs by institution and individual; thus, it remains difficult to generalize. The primary contribution of this study is an empirical inventory of the actual background experiences of thirty new, early-career science faculty in teaching, research and service.

The study participants earned degrees from 26 separate institutions, both domestic and international. Among research experiences prior to becoming a faculty member, conducting and presenting research, attending research seminars or workshops, publishing (co-authorship) and research apprenticeships were reported by 73.3% or more of the respondents. The only teaching experiences that the respondents reported as often were a graduate teaching assistantship (83%), teaching laboratories (80%) and grading (77%). There were no service experiences reported by more than 67% of the respondents.

There are multiple ways to interpret these findings. One is that doctoral preparation for future science faculty may be improving. One doctoral education study reported that 83% of science students held a teaching assistantship (TA) and that 28.5% of science students were prepared to teach a lecture class (Golde and Dore, 2001). The current study also documented that 83% of the early-career science faculty reported being a TA prior to becoming a professor. However, 60% of the of the first-year science faculty in this study reported they had taught lecture courses, a large increase from science contingent in the Golde and Dore (2001) study. Another relative improvement was the presence of teaching laboratories. Eighty percent of the early-career science faculty reported having taught laboratories, versus only 44.7% of the science students in Golde and Dore (2001). The results may indicate a positive direction especially in the percentage of potential faculty that are acquiring desired teaching-related experiences. The new, early-career faculty in this study listed teaching lecture courses as the most valuable preparation for teaching as a college faculty member. Boyer (1991) claimed that teaching lecture in the first few years as a faculty member without prior experience and pedagogical knowledge makes the students a teaching experiment for new faculty. He further writes that this is an unethical, yet common experience for many [future] faculty. This research indicates that preparation of faculty to teach in the sciences is improving. This research supports the continued development of graduate students and teaching assistants as potential future faculty members as set forth in the volume by Nyquist, Abbot, Wulff and Sprague (1991).

These results could also indicate a continuing lack of breadth in the preparation of college faculty in the sciences. Breadth is referred to here as the range of experiences that new faculty report. Based on the lack of a range of teaching and service-related experiences as reported by the faculty in this study, the focus in faculty preparation (via doctoral education) remains narrow, including mainly conducting and presenting research, co-authorship of research findings, teaching laboratory and lecture classes, and membership in a disciplinary association. Other roles that faculty members face, such as seeking funding, designing courses, advising students and service to the institution, are often not included in graduate education. Less than 50% of the respondents reported these and related experiences.

Even within the broad category of research, there may be too narrow a focus on conducting research and publishing. Only 40% of the faculty surveyed reported having submitted grant proposals and articulating a research agenda. The new, early-career faculty commented that there was "a lack of independence" in their research preparation. Others commented that the most important elements lacking from their preparation as professors were "preparation in grant writing," "submitting grant proposals" and "going [through] the full process of revise and resubmit." Walker, Golde, Jones, Bueschel and Hutchings (2008) reported that graduate education at the doctoral level is largely based on an apprentice-style model where graduate faculty are the masters and the students are the apprentices. It would certainly be easy make an argument that the ability to do these things on one's own as a college faculty member may be the most important skills to have honed in order to acheive success in academic research, especially at academic institutions that place a high value on the publications and grantsmanship of their faculty.

The specialization (or depth) of research conducted in science doctoral education may postpone (or even inhibit) the success of early-career science faculty. One faculty member remarked on the struggle to begin a research agenda in the new position due to the "lack of a model for [conducting research at an] undergraduate institution without resources" in their graduate training, indicating a lack of awareness of different institutional situations for faculty. Another example of the failure to consider other types of institutions in the training of future faculty was the new science professor who alluded to there being more to their faculty position than research when they gave the advice to "just do it [research], but don't think it will save you if you teach badly."

When faced with working at institutions that have teaching and service as equal or greater components of faculty life, new, early-career science faculty may be at a particular disadvantage. As one example of this disadvantage, the faculty employed at Baccalaureate colleges reported feeling significantly less prepared to teach than their counterparts at Associate's colleges ($p=0.22$). The impact of feeling less prepared to teach may have the greatest impact on faculty time management. Balancing time among the many responsibilities of being a faculty member creates a great deal of stress for freshman and junior faculty (Menges, 1999; Boice, 1992; Sorcinelli, 1988). The faculty in this study, especially those at Baccalaureate colleges, will most likely personify that research. They will have to dedicate a larger percentage of their time to teaching, having limited experience in designing syllabi or exams or teaching lecture courses. Moody (2006) reports that faculty with little or no experience in teaching will spend nearly all of their time preparing lectures. In addition, survey respondents commented that they were unaware of the additional time and effort required to participate in departmental and institutional service work in their new positions.

The sciences may still be promoting faculty as scientists at the expense of being science educators. One faculty commented, "I was trained to be a researcher, not a teacher, while I was in graduate school." When asked what important element was lacking in their teaching preparation for their current faculty position, 21 of the 30 faculty in this study reported that interacting with students, assessing student learning or preparing and giving lectures was omitted from their experiences. One could certainly make an argument that these are critical experiences that faculty should have. Also, when teaching begins to account for faculty time away from research, as is often the case in new and early-career faculty, many faculty revert to using lecture as the primary (and often sole) method of instruction (Moody, 2006). This means that often the introductory and lower level courses are left unchanged (National Research Council, 2003). Faculty without any or with little teaching experience may be more likely to do this (Moody, 2006; Boice, 1992).

Graduate preparation of science faculty may be improving in the number that experience delivering instruction (through lectures and laboratories), but new, early-career faculty in the sciences remain under-prepared to face their role as college science faculty, due to the lack of a range of experiences in all areas of faculty life. The small range of academic experiences reported by the faculty in this study, if coupled with the traditional pitfalls of new faculty in the academy (e.g., isolation, unclear expectations, lack of knowledge of different institutional types, issues of time and stress management), could have a long-lasting and damaging impact on the future of college-level science instruction.

This research does not yet tease out the entire influence of demographic variables (gender, ethnic background, institution type, etc.) or the impact of being hired at different types of academic institutions. Preliminary separation of gender effects showed that females felt less prepared for their research role than their male counterparts. This finding supports the work of previous research documenting less support for females in the sciences (National Research Council, 2006) This is problematic as proportionately more women in the sciences seek academic positions than men (National Research Council,

2001). If this issue is not successfully addressed, the gender gap in the sciences will continue to widen over time.

This study provides an empirical inventory of experiences of early-career science faculty. The fact that the faculty who responded to this survey were from employed at multiple institutional types, ranging from community colleges to research institutions, and the small sample size of this study only allows for general conclusions. In addition, the sciences are often compressed and the main areas (in this case, Biology, Chemistry, Earth Science and Physics) combined as a whole. Future research that addresses these factors, separates the disciplines (and even subdisicplines) and that can recruit enough participation in all groups can strengthen the impact of this data and provide a platform from which to design and implement more specific and effective future faculty preparation programs for the graduate students in the sciences. In addition, without the context of interviews to clarify some of the additional questions that the responses raise, this research offers only a snapshot of the experiences of newly-hired early-career faculty science faculty. Futhermore, this research does not clarify where the experiences of these faculty members were obtained; whether it was in graduate school or a different setting. These important questions would add different levels of applicability to and enhance this study. With that in mind, the differences in variables by gender (research preparation) and the type of institution (teaching preparation) that appear in this small study indicate that continued study on this topic is warranted.

Nyquist and Woodford (2000) interviewed faculty and administrators across institution type and reported that the faculty they hire are unaware of institutional differences and their effects on faculty life, new faculty are not prepared to teach in an unsupervised setting and new faculty have little or no experience in working collaboratively or across disciplines. Despite a majority of the early-career science faculty in this study reporting a teaching assistantship (83%) as an experience they had, this study did not ask how that experience was mentored, what exactly the person did in their assistantship, or the level of independence that they had. This leaves no real way for the assessing how early-career faculty will be able to cope with the responsibilities of being faculty members at the institutions that hire them.

There remains a need for programs like Preparing Future Faculty that address the range of responsibilities that early-career college science faculty face at different institution types. Improvements are still needed in publishing research, seeking and receiving funding, teaching and learning, and service roles. While these efforts are often best based in academic departments, some departments may not themselves be prepared to offer complete programs. The training of doctoral students in the sciences may be able to address the issue of improving the ability of first-year, early-career science faculty members to be independent teachers, researchers and active academic citizens, if and only if, this training continues to add additional types of experiences to the traditional apprenticeship-style initiation of new faculty. Academic departments could include doctoral students in decision making processes such as curriculum design and advising students in order to allow them to gain a better understanding of how institutions function. Institutions could make better efforts to include doctoral students on committees outside of their departments. A science education course or set of courses based on college instruction/adult learning, if required for prospective college faculty, could provide this background and address learning and curricular standards of science teaching. Continuing future faculty programming in the sciences may act as a catalyst for progress.

These improvements, however, need to also happen at the institutions that hire new faculty. Improving new faculty orientation programs to address the gaps in preparation may facilitate improved teaching and learning for students while also allowing faculty to be aware of where they need to enhance their experiences (or where to get assistance). In addition, a greater presence of post-doctoral teaching opportunities, under supervision of a current faculty member may provide settings for gathering additional experiences before starting faculty positions. Departments exploring how to offer successful mentoring programs on their campuses and encouraging and funding professional development for teaching in the sciences would add to the improvements once a faculty member begins their careers on campus.

There may also be programs that can be sponsored by professional organizations. One example, the Mathematical Association of America offers Project NExT (New Experiences in Teaching), combines components of PFF, mentoring and education in "addressing all aspects of an academic career: improving the teaching and learning of mathematics, engaging in research and scholarship, and participating in professional activities. It also provides the participants with a network of peers and mentors as they assume these responsibilities" (Project NExT website, http://archives.math.utk.edu/projnext/). Improving the background experiences so that early-career faculty are better prepared for a range of academic positions can likely lessen the stress and increase the job satisfaction they will undoubtedly face. This, in turn, has the potential to improve the teaching and research profiles of beginning college science faculty. Future research that can document the impact of these additions may provide the strongest evidence for successful preparation of future science faculty.

References

Adams, K. (2002). *What colleges and universities want in new faculty*. Washington, DC: Association of American Colleges and Universities.

Astin, A.W., Korn, W. S., & Dey, E. L. (1991). *The American college teacher: National norms for 1989-90 HERI faculty survey*. Los Angeles: Higher Education Research Institute, Graduate School of Education, University of California, Los Angeles.

Boice, R. (1991). Quick starters: New faculty who succeed. In M. Theall & J. Franlink (Eds.), *New directions for teaching and learning: No. 48. Effective practices for improving teaching* (pp. 111-121). San Francisco: Jossey-Bass.

Boice, R. (1992). *The new faculty member: Supporting and fostering professional development.* San Francisco: Jossey-Bass.

The Carnegie Foundation for the Advancement of Teaching. (2006). *Classification descriptions.* Retrieved January 15, 2008, from http://www.carnegiefoundation.org/classifications/index.asp?key=785

Cataldi, E.F., Bradburn, E.M., and Fahimi, M. (2005). *2004 National Study of Postsecondary Faculty (NSOPF:04): Background Characteristics, Work Activities and Compensation of Instructional Faculty and Staff: Fall 2003.* Washington, DC: National Center for Education Statistics (NCES 2006-176).

Committee on Graduate Education. (1998). *Report and recommendations.* Washington, DC: Association of American Universities.

Committee on Science, Engineering and Public Policy. (1995). *Reshaping the education of scientists and engineers.* Washington, DC: National Academy Press.

Committee on Undergraduate Science Education. (1997). *Science teaching reconsidered: A handbook.* Washington, DC: National Academy Press.

Council of Graduate Schools. *PFF Web.* www.preparing-faculty.org

DeNeef, A.L. (2002). *The preparing future faculty program: What difference does it make?* Washington, DC: Association of American Colleges and Universities.

Feibelman. P.J. (1993). *A Ph.D. is not enough: A guide to survival in science.* New York: Addison-Wesley.

Fink, L.D. (1983). First year on the faculty: Getting there. *Journal of Geography in Higher Education,* 7(1): 45-56.

Fink, L.D. (Ed.) (1984a). *New directions for teaching and learning: No. 17. The first year of college teaching.* San Francisco: Jossey-Bass.

Fink, L.D. (1984b). First year on the faculty: Being there. *Journal of Geography in Higher Education,* 8(1): 11-25.

Gaff, J.G. (2002). The disconnect between graduate education and the reality of faculty work: A Review of recent research. *Liberal Education,* 88(3), 6-13.

Golde, C.M., & Dore, T.M. (2001). *At cross-purposes: What the experiences of today's graduate students reveal about doctoral education.* Philadelphia: The Pew Charitable Trusts.

Goldsmith, S.S., Haviland, D., Dailey, K. & Wiley, A. (2004). *Preparing Future Faculty Initiative: Final Evaluation Report.* San Fransisco, CA: WestEd.

Mathematical Association of America. (n.d.). *Project NExT.* Retrieved January 30, 2008, from http://archives.math.utk.edu/projnext/

Menges, R.J. (1996). Experiences of newly hired faculty. In L. Richlin (Ed.), *To improve the academy: Vol. 15. Resources for faculty, instructional, and organizational development* (pp. 169-182). Stillwater, OK: New Forums Press.

Menges, R.J. (1999). Dilemmas of newly hired faculty. In R. J. Menges & Associates (Eds.), *Faculty in new jobs: A guide to settling in, becoming established, and building institutional support* (pp. 19-38). San Francisco: Jossey-Bass.

Menges, R.J. & Associates. (1999). *Faculty in new jobs: A guide to settling in, becoming established, and building institutional support.* San Francisco: Jossey-Bass.

Moody, J. (2006). Visualizing yourself as a successful college teacher, writer and colleague: Pointers for college and university faculty. In J. Moody (Ed.), *Demystifying the profession: Helping junior faculty succeed.* San Diego, CA: JoAnn Moody.

National Research Council. (2006). *To recruit and advance: Women students and faculty in science and engineering.* Washington, DC: The National Academies Press.

National Research Council. (2003). *Improving undergraduate instruction in science, technology, engineering, and mathematics: Report of a workshop.* Washington, DC: The National Academies Press.

National Research Council. (1999). *Transforming Undergraduate ducation in Science, Mathematics, Engineering, and Technology.* Washington, DC: The National Academies Press.

National Science Board. (2000). *Science & engineering indicators – 2000* (National Science Board Report NSB-00-1). Arlington, VA: National Science Foundation.

Advisory Committee to the Directorate for Education and Human Resources. (1996). *Shaping the future: New expectations for undergraduate education in sciences, mathematics, engineering and technology* (NSF Report 96-139). Arlington, VA: National Science Foundation.

Nerad, M., Aanerud, R., & Cerney, J. (2004). So you want to become a professor! Lessons from the PhDs-ten years later study. In A. Austin & D. Wulff (Eds.), *Paths to the professoriate: Strategies for enriching the preparation of future faculty* (pp. 137–158). San Francisco: Jossey Bass.

Nerad, M. & Cerney, J. (2002). Postdoctoral appointments and employment patterns of science and engineering doctoral recipients ten-plus years after PhD completion. *Communicator, 35*(7), 1-2, 10-11.

Nyquist, J.D., Abbott, R.D., Wulff, D.H., & Sprague, J. (Eds.) (1991). *Preparing the professoriate of tomorrow to teach: Selected readings in TA training.* Dubuque, IA: Kendall/Hunt.

Nyquist, J. & Wulff, D.H. (2000). *Recommendations from national studies on doctoral education.* Retrieved Feburary 15, 2008 from University of Washington, Center for Instructional Development and Research Web site: http://www.grad.washington.edu/envision/project_resources/national_recommend.html

Nyquist, J., Woodford, B.J., & Rogers, D.L. (2004). Re-envisioning the Ph.D.: A challenge for the twenty-first century. In A. Austin & D. Wulff (Eds.), *Paths to the professoriate: Strategies for enriching the preparation of future faculty* (pp. 194-216). San Francisco: Jossey-Bass.

Pruitt-Logan, A.S, Gaff, J.G., & Jentoft, J.E. (2002). *Preparing future faculty in the sciences and mathematics: A guide for change.* Washington, DC: Association of American Colleges and Universities.

Rice, R.E., Sorcinelli, M.D. &, Austin, A.E. (2000). *Education Working Paper Series: Inquiry No. 7. Heeding new voices: Academic careers for a new generation.* Washington, DC: American Association for Higher Education.

Reis, R. M. (1997). *Tomorrow's professor: Preparing for academic careers in science and engineering.* New York. IEEE Press.

Sorcinelli, M.D. (1988). Satisfactions and concerns of new university teachers. In J.G. Kurfiss (Ed.), *To improve the academy: Vol. 7. Resources for faculty, instructional, and organizational development* (pp. 121-133). Stillwater, OK: New Forums Press.

Sorcinelli, M.D. (2000). Principles of good practice: Supporting early-career faculty. In R.E. Rice, M.D. Sorcinelli, & A.E. Austin (Eds.), *Education Working Paper Series: Inquiry No. 7. Heeding new voices: Academic careers for a new generation* (pp. 27-38). Washington, DC: American Association for Higher.

Sorcinelli, M.D. (1992). New and junior faculty stress: Research and responses. In M.D. Sorcinelli, & A.E. Austin (Eds.), *Developing new and junior faculty: No. 50. New directions for teaching and learning.* (pp. 27-37). San Francisco: Jossey-Bass.

Schwartz, A.T., Archer, R.A., El Ashmawy, A.K., Lavalee, D.K., & Eikey, R. (2003). *And gladly teach: A resource book for chemists considering academic careers.* Washington, DC: American Chemical Society.

Tierney, W.G., & Bensimon, E.M. (1996). *Promotion and tenure: Community and socialization in academe.* Albany: State University of New York Press.

Turner, J.L., & Boice, R.. (1987). Starting at the beginning: Concerns and needs of new faculty. In J. Kurfiss, L. Hilsen, L. Mortensen, & E. Wadsworth (Eds.), *To improve the academy: Vol. 6. Resources for faculty, instructional, and organizational development* (pp. 41-55). Stillwater, OK: New Forums Press.

Walker, G.E., Golde, C.M., Jones, L., Bueschel, A.C., & Hutchings, P. (2008). *The Formation of scholars: Rethinking doctoral education for the twenty-first century.* (pp. 89-119). San Francisco: Jossey-Bass.

Whitt, E.J. (1991). Hit the ground running: Experiences of new faculty in a school of education. *The Review of Higher Education, 14,* 177-197.

Wulff, D.H., & Austin, A.E. (2004). *Paths to the professoriate: Strategies for enriching the preparation of future faculty.* San Francisco: Jossey-Bass.

Kenneth S. Sagendorf is the Deputy Director for Faculty Development in the Center for Educational Excellence and an assistant professor at the United States Air Force Academy. He has been involved in graduate education and future faculty preparation for the last 10 years.

www.ingramcontent.com/pod-product-compliance
Lightning Source LLC
Chambersburg PA
CBHW072131160426
43197CB00012B/2064